NAZARBAYEV AND THE
MAKING OF KAZAKHSTAN

Nazarbayev and the Making of Kazakhstan

JONATHAN AITKEN

continuum
LONDON • NEW YORK

CONTINUUM
The Tower Building, 11 York Road, London SE1 7NX
15 East 26th Street, New York, NY 10010

www.continuumbooks.com

First published 2009

British Library Cataloguing-in-Publication Data
A catalogue record for this book is available from the British Library.

ISBN: 978-1-44115-381-4

Typeset in Adobe Minion by Tony Lansbury, Tonbridge, Kent.
Printed and bound in Great Britain by the MPG Books Group

To Elizabeth

With my love and gratitude for her encouragement and for her acceptance of my many absences from home on visits to Kazakhstan.

Contents

Acknowledgements

I gratefully acknowledge the assistance given to me by the numerous individuals from Kazakhstan, or with special knowledge of Kazakhstan, who gave me interviews, help, hospitality and guidance during the writing of this book. Most of their names are recorded in the *Source Notes*. Some people preferred to talk off the record under conditions of anonymity, and I am grateful for their help also.

My special thanks go to Sir Richard Evans, not only for his wise counsel and interviews about the President and the country he has come to know so well, but also for inviting me to travel with him on his aircraft for several journeys to and around Kazakhstan.

I am grateful to the Foreign Ministry of Kazakhstan for providing me with in-country hotel accommodation in Astana and Almaty, and to the Akim of Atyrau for hospitality and hotel accommodation in his city.

I particularly thank Erlan Idrissov, former Foreign Minister of Kazakhstan, former Ambassador in London and currently Ambassador in Washington DC. I am immensely grateful to him for many interviews and for his frequent encouragement and inspiration.

Most of the typing of the book was carried out by Prue Fox, with occasional help from Helen Kirkpatrick, Rosemary Gooding and Susanna Jenners. To all of them, especially Prue Fox, my warmest thanks.

Finally, I thank my publishers at Continuum, particularly Robin Baird-Smith, Ben Hayes and Nick Evans.

Lastly, my love and gratitude to my wife Elizabeth, who put up with my many absences from home on long trips to Kazakhstan, and the flood of documents, tape transcriptions, books and research papers which were the consequence of two years work on this biography.

JONATHAN AITKEN
London, April 2009

ix

Prologue – Understanding the Journey

Kazakhstan is colossal in size, complicated in its history, colourful in its culture and has a more compelling narrative as a modern nation state than most outsiders know. Much of that narrative revolves around the country's first President, Nursultan Nazarbayev, but his life can only be understood in the context of the land where he was born, raised and became a leader.

Geographically, Kazakhstan is greater than Western Europe. Its northern border with Russia is longer than that of Canada with the United States. Five times bigger than Texas, it is the ninth largest country in the world, beginning on the shores of the Caspian sea where Asia meets Europe and ending on the edge of Western China. From snow-clad mountains a little lower than Everest to grassland steppes larger than the American Mid-West, this is an extraordinary land mass of such space and soul that it transcends people, politics and the passing phases of time.

Until 1991, Kazakhstan was not a country. It had no legal frontiers with any of its regional neighbours, some of whom claimed territorial rights over its borders and resources. The history of such disputes was discouraging. For centuries the nomadic tribes of Kazakhstan had been plundered and conquered by foreign invaders. The most ruthless of these colonial masters were the 20th century leaders of the Soviet Union. Under Stalin, over two million Kazakhs died from starvation, epidemics and execution. Another million were driven off their lands and into exile or servitude under the yoke of Communism. These departures were matched by an inflow of ill-treated new arrivals. During World War II, Stalin ordered the deportation into Kazakhstan of half a million people. Most were from the Northern Caucasus and the Volga German areas, but they included Moscow intellectuals and political dissidents.

In the years of Nikita Khrushchev's rule, one and a half million more Soviet deportees were forcibly moved into collective farms in Kazakhstan. As a result, the Kazakh people became a minority in their own homeland. In later years vast areas of their traditional grazing grounds in the north-east were

1

contaminated by secret nuclear tests. The Kremlin's military leaders ordered over 450 thermonuclear explosions in the region around Semipalatinsk, with contemptuous disregard for the health consequences to the local population. Other Soviet experiments such as the draining of the Aral Sea and the Virgin lands scheme caused massive environmental damage. Yet, despite their mistreatment, the Kazakhs had an ancestral instinct for survival. They knew how to weather all storms.

Surviving meant learning to live by Moscow's rules. So the philosophical nomads became obedient communists while upholding their traditions as proud nationalists. No one played these ambivalent roles more skilfully than Nursultan Nazarbayev.

His journey began in a shepherd's yurt on the mountain meadows of the steppes. He grew up in a poverty-stricken nomad family which had been scarred by Stalin's terrors yet were shrewd enough to secure a good Russian education for their son. Nazarbayev's first job was as a blast-furnace worker in a steel plant which trained him as a metallurgist. His early career as a young Communist Party official ran through the eras of Nikita Khrushchev, Mikhail Suslov, Leonid Brezhnev and Yuri Andropov. At the age of 44, Nazarbayev was appointed Prime Minister of the Soviet Republic of Kazakhstan by the ailing Konstantin Chernenko. The next Soviet leader, Mikhail Gorbachev, saw Nazarbayev as a kindred spirit in the reforms of *perestroika* and *glasnost*, eventually offering to appoint him Prime Minister of the Soviet Union. Nazarbayev turned the offer down. By that time, the Soviet Union was in chaos and he had an eye for the future.

As one of the leading figures in the Soviet hierarchy after Gorbachev and Yeltsin, Nazarbayev knew that the end of communist domination was coming. Although he played a vital role in supporting Boris Yeltsin's stand against the Moscow coup plotters in August 1991, those days were the harbingers of political extinction for Gorbachev and for the Soviet Union, which broke up five months later. Without a drop of blood being shed in his own country during these upheavals, Nazarbayev emerged from the wreckage as President of the new nation state of Kazakhstan.

In the years immediately after independence, Nazarbayev had to wrestle with extraordinary crises. They included hyperinflation, the collapse of the currency, food shortages and the emigration of two million people, most of them skilled workers and managers. On the strategic front, his greatest challenge was the discovery that he had inherited ownership of the world's fourth largest arsenal of nuclear weapons. Rogue states were after them. Rejecting their offers, Nazarbayev opted for disarmament. He had delicate diplomatic dealings with Washington, took new initiatives with Beijing, and hung on through a roller-coaster ride of turbulent relations with Moscow. He steered through the worst of the turbulence by relying on direct negotiations with his old friend President Yeltsin, whose cooperation was vital on many issues, particularly oil rights in the Caspian.

What kept Nazarbayev going through the darkest days of Kazakhstan's dramas was a combination of a steelworker's stamina and a reformer's vision. He never faltered in his ancestral man of the steppes belief that his people would yet again weather the storms. But, as a modern man of politics, he had difficulty in convincing older Kazakhstanis to accept free-market forces. His meeting in 1991 with Margaret Thatcher, when he was still the Communist Party leader in Kazakhstan, was pivotal in persuading Nazarbayev to embrace economic freedom and privatisation. He immersed himself in the study of these concepts, reaching out to a new generation of advisers and ministers to implement them. For a while, the results of his policies were chaotic, and many mistakes were made. But Nazarbayev persevered with his reforming agenda, and by the turn of the century Kazakhstan had become a largely free-market economy, growing at an annual rate of over 10 percent. This growth was dented by the Asian stockmarket crash of 1998 and devastated by the global economic crisis of 2008–2009. But by then Kazakhstan had built up over $50 billion of reserves, mainly from surplus oil revenues, in a national fund which Nazarbayev used in late 2008 with other resources to inject over $25 billion into banks, construction companies, pension funds and infrastructure projects. With this bailout from the public finances, and with the underlying strength of the oil and gas sectors of the economy, Kazakhstan today looks better placed than any other country in its region to weather the world recession.

Fifteen years earlier the outlook was far more pessimistic. In the early 1990s, the consensus of international opinion was that Kazakhstan could not survive as a nation state, nor would Nazarbayev last as its leader. Today both the President and the country seem to be secure. Nazarbayev's leadership skills are internationally recognised as successful and the long-term economic future looks bright. Even so there are international media criticisms about the governance of Kazakhstan.

The judiciary is not independent. The press is less than free. Recent elections have not reached the standards of a full and fair democratic process. There is widespread corruption at many levels of Kazakhstani society. The President's inner circle of friends and family members have sometimes been tarnished by allegations concerning oil revenues deposited in Swiss bank accounts, commissions paid on government contracts, violations of human rights and even the murder of a leading opposition politician. Nazarbayev has managed to stay aloof from these scandals. However, at times his reputation has been indirectly damaged by his association with old cronies and former relatives whose misbehaviour has caused them to be exiled as black sheep.

When these subjects are covered in later chapters it will be seen that Nazarbayev has not disregarded the complaints of his critics. In particular he has been responsive to pressure coming from the OSCE (Organisation for Security and Cooperation in Europe) which Kazakhstan will chair from 2010. On progress towards religious freedom, press freedom, human rights and fair elections, Kazakhstan has done more than Russia, China and other states of the region put together. So it is fair to say that Nazarbayev is slowly travelling on the road from autocracy to democracy even though he has some distance to go. His argument, examined in later chapters, is that because there was no experience whatsoever of democratic politics or market economics in Kazakhstan history, the newly independent nation should not move too quickly in developing a programme of electoral reform. "The economy first, political restructuring next", says Nazarbayev, adding that "Democracy in Kazakhstan is not the start of its journey but rather its destination". Some international commentators have been critical of this approach, but domestic public opinion seems broadly supportive of the President's pace of progress on the roadmap towards democracy.

No road in Kazakhstan is short. But in the two decades since Nazarbayev became the country's President, important milestones have been passed. This is the most economically successful nation to emerge from the collapse of the Soviet republics, rich beyond computer projections in oil, gas, and other natural resources. Its constitution has created a stable system of government. It maintains good, if subliminally anxious, relations with Moscow, Beijing and Washington. Its 15.5 million population contains a growing middle class, increasingly prosperous and sophisticated thanks to the rising generation of educated young people. Their progress is symbolised by the brash new capital of Astana whose futuristic skyscrapers give it the image of being the most exotic and multi-ethnic seat of government in the 21st century world. These features of contemporary Kazakhstan are so little known that millions of international moviegoers actually believed that Borat might be real!

Few of Kazakhstan's achievements would have been made without Nursultan Nazarbayev. His story has never before been told in the West, even though it is one of the most colourful and influential odysseys in modern times. But his journey can only be understood by starting in the heart of the steppes, the land from which he came.

1

Ancestry and Childhood

The journey began at a shepherd's hut in Ushkonyr, a remote, primitive yet magnificent grassland plateau on the steppes of the Alatau Mountains in Central Asia. It would be difficult to imagine a more symbolic birthplace for the nomad's son who was destined to become the first President of the newly independent nation of Kazakhstan.

To this day Ushkonyr can be identified with one part of the country's heritage on account of its scenic beauty, wide open spaces, snow-capped mountains, rock escarpments, streams, rivers, wild horses and huge flocks of sheep and cattle. An even more important part of the heritage is the character of the tribal families, handed down from the ancestors of whom they are so fiercely proud, for they tamed this vast wilderness.

Sometimes the land was conquered by their own nomadic spirit. At other times in their history the Kazakhs were themselves conquered and subjugated by oppressive foreign rulers. During one of these periods of oppression, when the country was called the Soviet Republic of Kazakhstan, a baby was born on 6th July 1940, named Nursultan Nazarbayev. His arrival into the world could scarcely have been a more obscure event. Yet to those familiar with the traditions and superstitions of the Shaprashti tribesmen from the area, the birth of this child seemed connected to promising portents of destiny and mysticism.

The destiny came from the warriors and tribal leaders that formed the hereditary chain of ancestors in the baby's lineage. The mysticism came from the answered prayers that had been offered nine months earlier by Nursultan's childless parents at the shrine of a local saint.

Ancestors are important to Kazakhs. In nomadic times they signified essential lines of demarcation between blood relatives and strangers, friend and foe, land owner and land predator. To this day, it is still expected that the son of an established Kazakh family should know the names and histories of his male antecedents for the previous seven generations. So before he was five years old the young Nursultan was taught to revere the patriarchal

5

figures in his ancestral heritage. The most famous of these was his great-great-great-great grandfather, Karasay Batyr (1703–1753), a legendary warrior who had protected his homeland from Jungar invaders in the 18th century. A more recent ancestor was the grandfather whose surname was taken by his modern descendants. He was Nazarbai, the builder and owner of a watermill in his village. He grew so prosperous as a result of selling water that around 1900 he became the local judge. He was elevated to this position after a secret ballot held among an electorate of 58 tribal elders, 30 of whom voted for him.* The seal of authority for Nazarbai's judgeship, which he held until his death in the 1930s, survives in an Astana museum.

The family mentor who liked relating the tale of the judge's narrow election victory was his widow Mirzabala Nazarbai. She was a doting if not domineering grandmother to her grandson, so much so that in modern terminology she might be called a control freak. One manifestation of her dominance within the family was that she insisted on taking possession of the infant Nursultan immediately after he was born, reluctantly handing him back to his mother only for breast feeding. Another feature of Mirzabala's controlling nature was that when Nursultan started to make his first steps as a toddler, she knitted a sack for his lower body to stop him walking away from her. "My grandmother's fear was that I would be struck by an evil eye", recalled Nazarbayev; "so, in order to protect me she kept me beside her in this sack all day long, pretending to our neighbours that I could not walk."

The third and perhaps most bizarre of Grandmother Mirzabala's efforts to be the pivotal figure in her grandson's life was that she made him address her as "mother". This seemed strange to little Nursultan who has recalled:

My grandmother was a very authoritative person. She liked running things and as the oldest member of the family, we had a duty to respect her wishes. She often told me "I'm your mother". And she said "Your mother is not your mother, she is your sister-in-law. Your father is not your father, he is your elder brother." So out of obedience to my grandmother I went along with this, and for the first five years of my life I called my real mother "sister-in-law" and my father I called "elder brother", even though my father was not at all happy about it.

Nursultan's father, Abish, was by nature a conciliator but he could also be a stronger character than this anecdote suggests. In an earlier family drama he had defied Grandmother Mirzabala and many of his other relatives when they urged him to divorce his wife Aljan on the grounds that she was barren, having failed to produce any children in the first six years of their marriage. Although it was a stigma in a rural Kazakh community for a couple to be

---

* Telling the story of his grandfather's election in an interview for this biography in 2007, President Nursultan Nazarbayev joked: "It shows how democratic we were over a hundred years ago! Who says we don't know about democracy in Kazakhstan!"

childless, Abish loved Aljan and refused to divorce her. Instead, they made a pilgrimage together to the shrine of a local saint, Ata Raimbek. In accordance with the superstitions about Raimbek's miraculous powers, a sheep and a goat were sacrificed to the saint. Then Aljan and Abish walked round the shrine seven times holding a rope between them and praying to God for children. During the night of these prayerful perambulations, Aljan had a dream in which she was being followed by a blind dog which threatened to attack her. Suddenly, a woman in white appeared and shooed away the dog. The following morning the curator of the Raimbek shrine was asked to interpret Aljan's dream. He said: "An evil spirit has been following you but the woman in white has banished it forever. Now God will give you children."

Nine months later, on 6th July 1940, Aljan gave birth to her first child, Nursultan. It was the height of summer and almost the entire population of Chemolgan, the village where the Nazarbai family lived, had decamped to the *jailau* or upland grazing grounds of Ushkonyr.

The name Ushkonyr means three brown hills, a description that has to be magnified to the Kazakh scale of these pastures nestling in the foothills of the Alatau mountain range whose snow-tipped peaks, between 3,000 and 7,900 metres high, sparkle like an elongated diamond necklace that stretches across the 1,000 miles of border territory running from eastern Kazakhstan into western China. Since time immemorial the nomadic tribesmen of the region had regarded the *jailau* of Ushkonyr as fertile grasslands for feeding their flocks. In the summer of 1940, over half a million sheep and cattle were grazing at Ushkonyr but they were no longer owned by the nomads. They were the property of a Soviet collective farm administered by Communist Party officials based in the neighbouring town of Kaskelen, some 20 miles downhill from the upland pastures.

The agricultural workers of the collective were mainly shepherds and herdsmen. They and their families spent their summers around Ushkonyr living in *yurts*, the traditional peasant huts of rural Kazakhstan which in outward appearance look like a mixture of an Inuit igloo and a Native American tepee. During the first week of July 1940, in the Nazarbai *yurt* on the *jailau* of Ushkonyr, Abish's wife Aljan began her labour pains.

There is uncertainty as to the precise birthplace of the baby who 51 years later was to become the first President of the Independent Republic of Kazakhstan. When this author visited Ushkonyr and the surrounding district in 2007, there emerged a considerable conflict of evidence among local witnesses about the location and circumstances of Nursultan Nazarbayev's arrival into the world.

Some senior residents of the area were sure that the future president was born in a *yurt* on the hills of Ushkonyr. One of these witnesses pointed to a grassy knoll situated between an escarpment of rocks and a mountain stream, declaring confidently: "I know that Nazarbayev's birthplace was right there." Other contemporaries recalled reports of Aljan suffering from such agonising labour pains that the local midwife had to move the expectant mother by donkey cart nine miles downhill to the village of Chemolgan. Another variation of the story was that the birth complications became so problematic that Aljan had to be moved again to the small township of Kaskelen. There, aided by the area's only supply of hot running water and medical equipment, a senior midwife safely delivered the baby.

Wherever the birth actually took place, Abish Nazarbayev was miles away from it tending his sheep and cattle in the wide open spaces of Ushkonyr. When he eventually came down from the hills, he was given the news that he was the father of a baby boy by an old lady from Chemolgan, Madame Togaibayeva. Abish was so carried away with joy that he promptly presented Togaibayeva with one of his family's most precious possessions, a Singer sewing machine, quoting an old Kazakh proverb: "The one who brings good news deserves a good reward."

Although old Kazakh sayings, traditions and superstitions played an important part in the early years of Nursultan Nazarbayev, his childhood was moulded by a mixture of influences both ancient and modern. On the ancient side, he was brought up in the nomadic culture of reverence for ancestors, proximity to nature, and bonding with the extended family of relatives who were his tribal kinsmen. On the modern side, he was exposed to the new multi-ethnicity of races and religions that had been imported by the Soviets into 20th century Kazakhstan. He was also a beneficiary of a new emphasis on education which had never before been part of his family's lifestyle.

Chemolgan, a village on the banks of the Kaskelenka River 25 miles east of the city of Almaty, was in the 1940s a mixed community of some 900 inhabitants. Only 200 of them were native Kazakhs. The rest were a disparate collection of multi-national settlers who had been displaced or driven from their homes as a result of the Bolshevik revolution of 1917. These new arrivals, many of them victims of Stalin's purges, included Ukrainians, Poles, Chechens, Armenians, Mishetyin Turks, Kurds, Balkars, Germans and ethnic Russians.

Relations between these incoming groups and the Kazakh villagers were harmonious. This may have been something to do with the Kazakh tradition of friendliness and hospitality towards visitors. Or it may have been based on the shared imperatives of survival, as rural life for every Chemolgan household of that period was hard under the iron but usually incompetent hand of Soviet collectivisation.

Chemolgan derives its name from the Kazakh word *chem* or candle. As there was no electricity in the area, the literal translation "village of candle-light" was an appropriate description for this community which was a centre for housing the local labourers of the Soviet collective farm. In the early 1940s most of these labourers were women because the able-bodied men had been drafted into the army for the war against Hitler's Germany. However, Nursultan's father Abish stayed at home because he had a withered arm damaged in a fire some years earlier. "What I remember most about my father during my childhood was that he did not stop working from dawn to dark", recalls Nursultan Nazarbayev. "I don't think he ever stood still. I think that is part of his legacy to me – a determination to work hard, to persevere in times of adversity and to accomplish his mission."

Abish's principal mission was to feed his family, which soon expanded to four young children, Nursultan, Satipaldi, Anipa and Bolat. Wages for labourers in the collective farm were inadequate, so survival depended on what could be grown or raised on the plot of private land allocated to each household. The Nazarbayevs were permitted to own one quarter of a hectare (0.6 of an acre) on which they kept 5 sheep, 20 chickens, a horse and a cow. The cow, which had to be milked by Aljan at 4 am every morning, was the most vital source of nutrition, providing a daily supply of butter, milk and Kurt – a regional Kazakh cheese. This livestock, together with the fruits and vegetables grown on the plot, provided enough food to keep the family well nourished. It was a considerable achievement due to Abish's talents as a gardener combined with his skills as a multi-lingual bargainer and trader. "My father could grow anything", recalled his youngest son Bolat. "Our land regularly produced two crops a year of potatoes and corn. His pride and joy were his apple trees which again produced an exceptional yield because he was so good at grafting and pruning. The surplus fruit and vegetables he sold off to our neighbours, trading with them in their own languages. Besides Kazakh, my father spoke fluent Russian, Turkish and Balkar. He also learned to communicate in other tongues because there were so many ethnic groups exiled to our area by Stalin's cruelty."

As a child, Nursultan absorbed from his father a facility for languages and a tolerance for other cultures. When he was five years old there were two important changes in his life. His grandmother died and he started preparing for school. The death of grandmother Mirzabala had the effect of introducing more normal child–parent relationships into the family. Nursultan became close to his mother Aljan, whom he describes as having "the strongest influence on me, always showing me the very special love of a mother for a son. I can't put this into words; she just showed her love in the most powerful of ways. She was very romantic by nature and she caught my imagination as a child by her storytelling and beautiful singing."

Nursultan's imagination was also caught by his first steps in education at the village school in Chemolgan. It had 70 pupils split up into three classes. Two of these classes were taught in the Russian language and one class was taught in Kazakh. Only seven children (6 boys and 1 girl) attended the Kazakh class, among them Nursultan who usually came top of it. One of his classmates was Esimbay Saduakas, who recalls:

We were well taught in our small class at Chemolgan and our teachers were very dedicated. Nursultan was a clever boy who worked hard and didn't seem to be as mischievous as the rest of us. His best subject was maths, where a strict old teacher Mr Karasayev was very rigid with us in lessons. Nursultan was also the best at reading aloud.

Reading aloud did not stop at the schoolroom door for young Nursultan. Although his parents were both illiterate, they took immense pride in their eldest son's educational progress. After discovering from his schoolteachers that the boy was a good reader, Abish started to invite the neighbours in to hear the legends of Kazakh history and literature, read aloud by 10-year-old Nursultan. He himself recalls these evenings with mixed feelings:

My father was so enthusiastic that on many evenings he called several friends to our house to listen to me reading. The light of a kerosene lamp was all we had at that time, so at the end of a long day at school and then after helping with the feeding of the animals my eyes grew tired. Sometimes I fell asleep with my face falling into the book. So I tried to avoid these reading evenings. But my father got upset with me and made me keep on reading aloud to all these old people.

Despite his resistance to these public sessions, Nursultan's enjoyment of private reading increased. By the time he was 12 years old, he was something of a bookworm. He read almost everything on the shelves of his school's small library. If he knew that one of his relatives was travelling to Almaty for shopping, he would ask if they could buy a book for him. Usually these were Kazakh classics by authors such as Abai, but as Nursultan's Russian improved he began reading authors such as Tolstoy, Chekhov and Pushkin. Later on in his schooldays he devoured Russian translations of European authors, particularly enjoying the novels of Honoré de Balzac, Victor Hugo and Jules Verne. Sometimes these literary interests seemed obsessive to other members of the Nazarbayev family. His younger brother Bolat remembers a scene in which their mother began shouting at the teenage Nursultan: "You are reading too much. Your brain will boil. Get out into the fresh air!" The maternal order was obeyed – but only briefly. A few minutes later Nursultan stealthily climbed back into the house through a window and returned to his books.

As this anecdote suggests, there were occasional tensions in Nursultan's life between farm work and homework. He sometimes incurred his parent's anger if he became so immersed in his reading that he forgot to water the vegetables or failed to move the cow to a new piece of pasture. Yet despite the trouble he got into from these lapses, the boy understood that his family's greatest wish was that he should benefit from the new educational opportunities that previous generations of Kazakhs had missed. "My father was always telling me 'go and study, go and study', so I did", he has recalled.

The happiest times of Nursultan's early years were the summer vacations he spent in the high grazing country around Ushkonyr. "I always loved the mountains, walking in them with my father, helping him to cut grass with a scythe, and enjoying the wild nature up there", he says. To this day the Alatau range around Ushkonyr is populated by many more wolves, mountain goats, deer, occasional bears and snow leopards than human beings. Keeping such predators away from the collective farm's sheep and cattle was an important part of Abish's job as a herdsman. Nursultan remembers many idyllic moments of their father–son relationship when they were out in the wilderness together, watching over the flocks at night, sitting round a campfire singing songs to the music of a *dombra* – a traditional Kazakh lyre which the young boy learned to play.

Sometimes Abish and Nursultan climbed above the snow line of the mountains on hunting trips. The highest peak in the area became an object of fascination for the boy after his father told him that the panoramic view from its summit included Lake Balkash. This was an exaggeration for the lake lies some 150 miles west of Ushkonyr and can not be seen by the naked eye. However, Nursultan was determined to conquer the peak, so on a glorious summer's day in the early 1950s he made an ascent of it on his own. "This was one of the most spectacular moments of my childhood", he remembers. "When I reached the top it seemed as if I was flying on the wings of an aeroplane. I stood there on the roof of the world. As I gazed into the distance across the great plains and valleys of the steppes below me I was actually looking towards the site of Astana – the future capital of our country."

The leader who later founded Astana as the seat of government of independent Kazakhstan may be forgiven if his youthful memories of this view from the mountain top have grown in the telling over the last half century. Yet the anecdote offers a revealing glimpse of the forces of nature and scenic beauty that helped to shape the childhood of the future president. It may also offer an insight into the competitive and even visionary streaks that were developing in the character of the young Nursultan Nazarbayev.

At his school in Chemolgan, Nursultan's competitive streak was bringing him to prominence. His report card for the sixth grade shows that he consistently received a score of 5 (the highest mark in the Soviet educational system, equivalent to an A*) in all his subjects, which were: Kazakh language and literature; Russian language and literature; History; Maths; Geometry; Algebra; Physics; Biology; Art; English and Music. "He was the brightest boy in our school, no question about it", recalls his classmate Esimbay Saduakas.

He was always asking questions of the teachers and he really tried hard at his homework too. I remember how he used to rehearse the answers to the questions we had been set. One day, I came unexpectedly into his house and found him practising his answers in front of a mirror. "What are you doing, Nursultan?", I asked him. "Are you trying to become a movie star or something?" "No", he replied. "I am just saying my homework over and over again because I want to be able to answer the teacher's questions clearly and confidently."

By the time he was 10 years old, Nursultan's confidence was growing as other boys deferred to him in and out of the classroom. He was the only one of his contemporaries trusted to drive a donkey cart to a nearby village where on certain days deliciously moist black bread was on sale at a baker's shop. This bakery was so popular that its queuing customers were rationed. They were only allowed to buy two slices of bread each time they came to the counter. As a small boy from another village, Nursultan was unfairly treated by the local shoppers. Often he was pushed to the back of the queue by aggressive housewives, impatient for their bread. He overcame this problem by bringing an escort group of friends with him in the donkey cart. These young Chemolgans were organised by Nursultan into a team who protected each other and had the persistence to keep going round in the queue all day long until they had each made several purchases of the two slices of bread quota.

On the homeward journey from one of these expeditions to the bread shop Nursultan experienced what he calls "the most frightening episode of my childhood". It was late in the evening and one of the boys in the donkey cart became afraid of the dark. Another boy decided to play a trick to raise the fear levels. This boy ran ahead and hid in a cemetery beside the road back to Chemolgan. As the donkey cart passed by the cemetery, a figure wrapped in a white blanket arose from one of the graves wailing and shrieking in an impersonation of a ghost. The startled donkey reared up and bolted. The boy on whom the trick was being played had a similar reaction, for he leapt out of the cart and ran off into the night screaming with terror. Ten-year-old Nursultan had to get the donkey under control and start a search for the boy, who had vanished. "When we found him he was unconscious", he has recalled. "We could not bring him round, and I was afraid he was going to die. Even when he did regain consciousness he could not speak. For many years afterwards this poor boy had a bad stammer. It was a dramatic evening for everyone."

There were not many dramas in the tranquil life of Chemolgan during the upbringing of Nursultan Nazarbayev. One historic event he remembers came in 1953 when loudspeakers were installed in the centre of the village so that Communist Party officials could announce the death of Stalin. A more enduring development was the connection of electricity to Chemolgan in 1954. This was a great leap forward in the quality of life for all the local families.

The Nazarbayevs had no home of their own in Nursultan's early childhood. They moved around, like true nomads, from borrowed yurt to borrowed house. But in about 1945, Abish built a two-bedroom house for his expanding family on the edge of the village. In one corner of it stood a table where Nursultan sat every evening, doing his homework. "His mother used to bring him his meals to this table so he could continue at his studies without a break", recalled his cousin and contemporary, Mrs Narjamal Ibirayqizi, the niece of Aljan. "We all knew from his earliest years that Nursultan was exceptionally hard working. His mother used to say that he was 'one in a thousand'."

This maternal perception of Nursultan's uniqueness was enhanced by a childhood dream of her son when he was 13. According to family accounts of it, Nursultan dreamt that he was made to climb one of the highest peaks in Ushkonyr, Mount Alakeldi, carrying a heavy sack of salt on his back. When he finally struggled to the summit, he looked down to the bottom of the hill he had climbed and, far away in the distance, he saw his school classmates gazing up at him. Aljan's interpretation of this dream was to tell her son that he would make greater achievements than any of them.

In 1956, Nursultan and his contemporaries were faced with a difficult decision when Chemolgan School announced that it could no longer continue to teach the small group of seven Kazakh pupils in their native language. The members of the class were offered a choice. Either they could stay in the village school and be given their lessons only in Russian, or they could move five miles away to a larger school in Kaskelen where they would continue to be taught in Kazakh.

Abish and Aljan Nazarbayev decided that their eldest son should stay in Chemolgan. Nursultan had other ideas. He argued against his parents until he eventually persuaded them to let him be transferred to Kaskelen School. His advocacy was so persuasive that the parents of the other six Kazakh pupils followed suit. This early display of leadership was not rooted in fears of linguistic inadequacy. For the teenage Nazarbayev already spoke and read fluent Russian which, as he well knew, was the lingua franca of the Communist Party and therefore an essential ingredient in any ambitious young man's quest for advancement. What motivated the boy more in his choice of school was his deep-seated feeling of identity with his Kazakh roots and heritage.

From his parents and their circle of friends, the young Nazarbayev absorbed a colourful understanding of Kazakhstan from ancient times. In the traditional Kazakh story telling ways of oral history, the earliest legends he was taught included the first stirrings of the distinctive nomadic civilisation that that had its roots in the Sak, Usun, Hun, Kanglys, Oguz and Kipchak peoples, who roamed across the steppes between the 5th century BCE and the 13th century CE. One tale that caught his childhood imagination was the story of how Queen Tomiris of the Saks led her people to victory against the invading Persian army of King Cyrus. At the end of the decisive battle, the Queen cut off the King of Persia's head and dumped it into a sack full of blood with the cry "You craved for blood – now quench your thirst!"

Other bloodthirsty invaders, among them Attila the Hun in the 4th century and Genghis Khan in the 13th, fared better in their attempts to conquer the nomads. Like every Kazakh schoolboy, Nazarbayev was taught that all Kazakh khans or kings were direct descendants of Genghis Khan's eldest son. He also learned the details of the khans' constant wars over three centuries against Junghar attackers from China, followed by the struggles against the Russian Imperial forces of the Tsars. These epics, rarely mentioned in Soviet classrooms but told over and over again round the family fireplace, left their mark on the young Nazarbayev. He grew up to be a proud Kazakh. He knew from history that his people could be subjugated but they would never be subservient. They might be conquered and crushed, but they remained courageous and capable. In that spirit of suppressed yet strong nationalism, he accepted what he was offered from the Soviet school system. This was one of the few aspects of Communism which worked. It certainly provided Nazarbayev with a good education.

In September 1957, Nursultan Nazarbayev enrolled at Kaskelen School. He was accompanied by his mother, who took one look at the boarding facilities for out of town pupils and decided they were not good enough for her son. So she located some distant relatives in the town and arranged for Nursultan to lodge with them in the hope that he would be better fed and supervised at their home.

First impressions of the new boy Nazarbayev on the teachers at Kaskelen School were favourable. He was interviewed at the end of his first week by the deputy headmaster, Mr Seitkhan Issayev, who assessed him as able, intelligent, and unusually talented: "I could see at once that he was the smartest boy in the tenth grade" recalled Issayev. "I taught him ancient Greek history and modern European history. He had an unusual thirst for knowledge, asking me clever questions and often taking books away after class to read in the evenings. As often as not, these books went wider than the curriculum. He wanted to learn more than the syllabus offered."

Soviet secondary education in the 1950s set high standards. By any measurement, Nursultan Nazarbayev was well read and well taught. He formed a taste for French literature but a distaste for Shakespeare, which he later blamed on poor Russian translations. He showed such aptitude at maths and physics that his schoolmates predicted that he would become a scientist. Away from his schoolbooks he was a noted rifle shot and horseman. He had a good singing voice and became a competent player of the accordion and the *dombra*. "Nursultan was good company, gregarious by nature", said his classmate Kydyrgali Baybek. "Like his father, he was a conciliator rather than a confronter. If he did not like someone he would not quarrel with him openly, and only gradually allowed his feelings of dislike to become clear."

Perhaps these behaviour patterns were an early indication of the young Nazarbayev's future political skills. They were complemented by some signs that he might one day be good at diplomacy too. For the mixture of pupils at Kaskelen was so multi-ethnic that Nursultan grew up in a cosmopolitan atmosphere. He contributed to the harmony of it by becoming a useful solver of problems and settler of quarrels, getting noticed by the teachers for his willingness to sit down and mediate between protagonists rather than to encourage playground fights, the usual method for solving schoolboy disputes. He was trusted as a mediator because he seemed genuinely interested in the other cultures around him.

An example of this interest was shown when a surprising letter arrived at the school in 1957 from a Chinese student in Beijing, asking if anyone would like to become his pen friend. This seemed such an extraordinary request from an unknown correspondent in an unknown country (as China was, even to its neighbours, in the 1950s) that the letter was at first treated with considerable suspicion. Eventually, after checking with the regional headquarters of the Communist Party, the Headmaster pinned up a translation of the letter on the notice board, asking if anyone would like to reply to it. Nursultan Nazarbayev was the only one of Kaskelen School's 250 pupils to take up this offer, starting what became an exchange of several letters with his Beijing penfriend. When asked why he was bothering to do this, he told the deputy headmaster: "Because I am interested in learning about China."

Nursultan's intellectual curiosity gave him wider horizons then his contemporaries. He was also blessed with deeper family roots than were usual in the rootless local community of newly arrived immigrants. For although he had been raised in hardscrabble poverty, he took immense pride in his Kazakh ancestry. He felt secure in his home environment, honouring his parents Abish and Aljan with a love that was warmly reciprocated. So as he came towards the end of his schooldays in the summer of 1958, 18-year-old Nursultan was a well-rounded young man with academic abilities that he knew were good enough to win him a place at one of the Soviet Union's best universities. "In my last months before graduating from high school I had more or less decided to become a scientist specialising in chemistry", he has recalled. "That was partly because I was good at science and partly because I had been impressed by the speeches of the new Soviet leader, Nikita Krushchev, who often made broadcasts about the importance of chemistry in raising the productivity of agriculture. So that is what I planned to study at a top university in Moscow."

These plans turned out differently. For all his ambition, industry and talent, Nursultan Nazarbayev did not in the end go to Moscow or to university. Instead he stayed at home, earning his living in his local region by the strength of his body rather than by the thoughts of his brain. This was a deliberate choice. He took it because he had read a book from his school library which so inspired him that it changed his life. The title of the book was *How the Steel Was Forged*.

2

Student and Steelworker

The book *How the Steel Was Forged* was an important influence in the life of Nursultan Nazarbayev. However, it was only one factor in the decision-making process that made him alter the course of his projected career away from being a university scientist towards becoming a manual steelworker. The other elements in this change of plan were a loving concern for his over-burdened parents; an inspirational conversation with a Ukrainian geologist; a local newspaper advertisement; and an intuitive sense of vocation, perhaps even of destiny, which so often throughout his life was to call him to make unexpected choices.

The book was pure Soviet propaganda but with a well-written and exciting narrative. Its author, Nikolai Ostrovsky, told the story of a young Komsomol or Communist Youth League member who was working in a steel making plant. He and his team of fellow steelmakers were given an assignment of great national importance. Their task was to build a railway line of extra-strength steel through difficult terrain within a tight timetable. The obstacles in the way of achieving this objective became horrendously difficult. They included steel production delays, sickness, terrible weather, landslides along the route of the line and an increasingly unattainable completion date. Yet by superhuman endeavours of body and mind, in the end the hero of the book led his fellow workers to victory and the accomplishment of their mission on time. "This book was a great inspiration to me," recalled Nazarbayev. "It was not really about steel, it was about the human spirit. Its message was that by belief, commitment, and an eagerness to serve, a good team of men can achieve an almost impossible mission."

Nazarbayev's personal sense of mission as he approached his 18th birthday was tempered by worry about his parents. He had an exceptionally good relationship with them. He loved their high spirits, their sense of humour, their warmth of heart, and the wild streak of creative Kazakh romanticism that ran through their lives. Although they were illiterate they had other talents. Aljan composed beautiful songs which she sang to her own accompaniment

17

on the *dombra*. She also told her children stories of nomadic legends in the Kazakh tribal tradition, some of them lionising the family's most famous ancestor, the 18th century war lord Karasay Batyr.

Abish was a quieter character but out on the steppes with his eldest son he displayed an occasional gift for poetry. Orally he could compose his own verses, often in praise of the glory of nature, sometimes in loving adoration of Aljan, and occasionally for the entertainment of his son. Abish enjoyed creating witty rhyming caricatures about village personalities. Nursultan was amused by these satirical poems. But when he learned them by heart and recited them to his schoolmates, they caused trouble. Angry parents who had been the subject of these parodies came round to complain to Abish: "How dare your son make up such rude poems about me?"

Abish must have enjoyed seeing off these complainants, but he did not have much time in his life for humour. For he was a man crushed by the pressures of rural poverty. The painful accident that had crippled his right arm combined with the incessant demands of his double workload at the collective farm and on the family's small plot of land took their toll. By the time he had reached his early fifties he was not a fit man. "I was worried about the health of my father and mother", recalled Nursultan Nazarbayev. "They both worked far too hard. I did not like the idea of going off to Moscow for three or four years and leaving them to cope with all their burdens."

At the time of his graduation from high school when these concerns were much on his mind, Nazarbayev had an important conversation with a geologist. He was the son of a Ukrainian family in the village. One summer this young man came back to visit his parents wearing the black uniform and insignia of a geologist of the Soviet Union. His official attire gave him status in the eyes of the boys of Chemolgan who gathered round him in the evenings to listen to him describing his work. "I can remember him pointing to an iron water pipe and telling us 'I am the man responsible for it, because I found the iron ore from which it is made'", recalled Nazarbayev.

I was fascinated by him and by his great pride in being in the team of professionals who find the treasures of the earth. Then he told us about the technology that turned his iron ore discoveries into steel. He described in detail the process of how you melt the ore in a blast furnace until it becomes molten metal and is eventually shaped into a steel pipe. As I listened to him night after night I said to myself "one day I too will be a geologist".

The problem about becoming a geologist for Nazarbayev was that it would mean spending most of the next three years studying in Moscow. Having graduated from Kaskelen School with the highest honours, this was the route he was expected to take. But his nagging worries about his father's health made him pause to give equally serious consideration to the option of staying in Kazakhstan. When weighing up these choices in the summer of 1958, Nazarbayev saw an advertisement in a local paper offering jobs for steel-workers. The advertisement announced that a giant new steel plant was being built in Termirtau, a town only 300 miles from Chemolgan in the province of Karaganda. It would be one of the biggest steel plants in the world, producing over 3 million tonnes of steel a year. Training courses at the Temirtau Technical School were offered to Young Communist League members who were willing to study metallurgy in preparation for their jobs in the steelworks. The advertisement added "A metallurgist has a noble and proud profession. It is a job for real men who will earn the highest wages."

Nazarbayev was immediately attracted by this advertisement. Becoming a metallurgist instead of a geologist seemed only a small variation of his professional ambitions. He was attracted by the vision of an internationally important steelworks and by the promise of "the highest wages". So within days of reading about the Temirtau steel plant he applied for a job there by presenting himself at the nearest recruiting office, the Communist Youth League or Komsomol headquarters in Stalin Avenue, Almaty. The Komsomol manager on duty was Sabit Zhadanov. "I remember the young Nazarbayev well from that June day in 1958 when I first set eyes on him", recalls Zhadanov.

He was dressed in the simple rural clothes of a boy from the villages – loose cotton trousers, open-neck shirt and sandals. I interviewed him and discovered that he had just graduated from his school with excellent results. So I said to him that a young man with his abilities should go to university in Moscow and train there to be a diplomat or an administrator. But he was very stubborn. He quoted one of the mottos of Komsomol which was: "If you are a member of Komsomol you will be the first to face the challenges of the front line and the last to take the bonuses and privileges of the easy life." I could see he was determined to be a steelworker at Temirtau and so I enrolled him for one of the first jobs there.

Temirtau had been presented in the advertisement as a thriving centre of steelworking but when the 18-year-old Nazarbayev arrived there with his enrolment papers in September 1958 not a single bar of steel was being produced because the building of the plant had not begun. All that existed was a small town surrounded by a vast construction site in a chaos of cranes, trucks, tractors, bulldozers, piles of metal, girders, timber and tents for the workers. However, one major obstacle to progress was that no roads existed. So before he could study metallurgy or make steel, Nazarbayev was required to become a building labourer. His first job was to mix the concrete for the approach roads to the non-existent steelworks whose sole feature was one magnificently tall but non-operational chimney.

After his early weeks as a concrete mixer Nazarbayev and around 300 of his fellow workers with secondary education qualifications were sent away from Temirtau to Dneprodzerhinsk in the Ukraine to be trained in steel-making. Seventy-one of these trainees were Kazakhs. "We were all 18-year-old village boys like Nazarbayev", recalls Maksut Narikbayev.

None of us had ever been away from our homes so when we assembled together at Almaty railway station it was an historic journey for us. It took us five days to reach Moscow. When we changed trains there I remember how some Russians pointed at us saying "Look at those Chinese!", which of course we were not, but the taunts made us feel very alien and uncomfortable. The journey from Moscow to Dneprodzerhinsk took another two days. When we arrived there we were told we were very honoured to be given our training in one of the greatest steel plants in the Soviet Union. Then we were split up into three groups as welders, bridge crane operators and steelmakers. Nazarbayev was put into the steelmakers' group which was to be trained to work in the blast furnace. Because he could speak good Russian he was immediately chosen to be the leader of his group.

Nazarbayev's leadership skills became apparent in a number of episodes during his 20 months in Dneprodzerhinsk. The first involved the visit of a celebrated Kazakh singer Bibigul Tulegenova. She and her programme of national folk songs had huge emotional appeal to the small number of Kazakhs in the city. But as she was unknown to most Ukrainians her concert seemed likely to fill no more that a handful of seats in Dneprodzerhinsk's 1,000-seat auditorium. Determined to drum up support for Kazakhstan's most famous musical artiste, Nazarbayev took on the task of promoting Tulegenova's big night. It was a challenge that combined the organisational, musical, nationalistic and political elements in his character. Mobilising his fellow students as word of mouth advertisers and ticket distributors he eventually succeeded in packing the concert hall to standing-room only capacity. At the end of the performance it was Nazarbayev who came up on stage to present the diva with a huge bouquet of flowers (paid for by a whip-round he had organised) and to deliver a moving speech of appreciation in honour of Bibigul Tulegenova. "We were amazed how well he had done and how passionately he spoke", said his fellow student Kabidulla Sarekenov. "From that time on a lot of us looked up to him."

Nazarbayev's speaking ability was tested to the full a few months later in the very different surroundings of a police station when he narrowly prevented the entire group of Kazakh trainees from being sent home in disgrace. The episode took place on 31st December 1959. The Kazakh boys were seeing in the New Year in a restaurant when one of them, Jumash, started a fight with the bandleader. His supporters fought back. In the ensuing punch-up the Kazakhs were outnumbered and had to run away. They were detained by the Ukrainian authorities who held them at police headquarters overnight and told them that they were all going to be deported back home.

The deportations were cancelled after Nazarbayev delivered what might be called his first political speech. "I will always remember how Nazarbayev addressed the authorities in that police station", recalled one of the detainees, Maksut Narikbayev.

He began by holding up his hands and saying, "Just as the fingers on our hands are all different we are all different". Then he argued that we did not all deserve punishment. He made Jumash apologise publicly to the bandleader and asked the Ukrainians not to press charges against him. Gradually he won everyone, even the bandleader, round to taking a less serious view of the incident. In the end nobody was sent home. It was quite a triumph for Nazarbayev and we all thanked him afterwards.

The triumph was acknowledged by senior Ukrainian officials as well as junior Kazakh students. The most important figure present in the police station that night was a Communist Party leader, Dimitri Pogorelov. He was evidently impressed by the "we are all different" speech and its comparison with fingers on human hands. "Nazarbayev, you are really smart", said Pogorelov. "If you go on being so smart you will end up becoming the Head of Kazakhstan's government in 25 years time." This was a joke at the time, but 30 years later the prediction came true when in 1989 Nursultan Nazarbayev was appointed First Party Secretary of the Soviet Republic of Kazakhstan.

Back in 1959, the Communist Party could be paranoiac about its foreign students in Dneprodzerhinsk. This was demonstrated by a second episode, again involving Nazarbayev, of young Kazakhs getting rounded up in the middle of the night at a police station. This time the cause was panic on the part of the authorities about the possible consequences of an incident at the United Nations headquarters in New York. The panic was started by a fiery speech to the UN General Assembly from the Soviet leader Nikita Khrushchev. His peroration culminated in unscripted shouts of "We will bury you!" as he took off one of his shoes and hammered it on the podium. Inside the UN, the cosmopolitan audience of world leaders were underwhelmed by these histrionics. The tone of their reactions was reflected in the amused cynicism of the British Prime Minister, Harold Macmillan, who asked during the shoe-banging: "Could we please have an official translation of this?" However, 5,000 miles away in Dneprodzerhinsk, the Communist Party leaders hastening to the live broadcast from the UN took fright, fearing that Khrushchev's belligerence might provoke World War III. In this alarmist mood their first reaction was to intern all foreigners who they thought might be less than loyal when it came to defending Dneprodzerhinsk against attack from the West. This was the reason why in the small hours of the morning on 9th September 1959 Nursultan Nazarbayev and his fellow Kazakh metallurgy students were hauled out of their beds and taken away to a central police station.

The overreaction of the Dneprodzerhinsk party officials to Khrushchev's speech looks absurd in hindsight when recorded in cold print over 50 years later. Yet at the height of the cold war these tensions were real to the Soviet authorities and terrifying to the Kazakh students.

We had no idea what was happening, recalled Maksut Narikbayev, but I do remember that the one who kept a cool head in the police station was Nazarbayev. We all asked him "What is happening? Why are they doing this to us?" We were really frightened. But Nazarbayev kept telling us to keep calm, and eventually he was the one who found out from a policeman that we were there because of Khrushchev's speech even though we knew nothing about it. It was Nazarbayev who assured the big bosses that we Kazakhs were loyal citizens of the Soviet Union. After that we were all released and went back to our normal routine.

The routines at the Dneprodzerhinsk training institute were strict. For six days a week the students spent five hours in the classroom studying the theory of metallurgy, followed by five hours on the shop floor of the steelworks learning the practical work of steelmaking. This left little time for sports or other recreations but Nazarbayev managed to be a regular attendee at night wrestling classes. Although smaller in build and shorter in height at 5ft 9 inches than many of his fellow wrestlers, Nazarbayev won most of his bouts. One day the instructor told him to take on the local Ukrainian champion of his age group, Nicolay Litoshko. At first sight it looked an unequal match, for the Ukrainian was a taller and heavier and more experienced fighter – at least in his own opinion. "I remember saying to the instructor 'why do you want me to wrestle with this slim little boy?'", recalled Litoshko. "But I soon found out because the boy was very good. He overpowered me and threw me on my back. When I had lost the fight after several tough rounds I had a lot of respect for my opponent. 'Are you Chinese?' I asked him and he replied 'No, I'm from Kazakhstan.'"

It was not an unusual occurrence for Nazarbayev and other Kazakhs to be mistaken for Chinese in the old Soviet Union. To the experienced observer there are distinctive features in the Kazakhs which make them quite different in appearance from Chinese people, even though there are some oriental characteristics common to both nationalities. However, for most of the 20th century Kazakhstan did not exist as a separate nation so the young Kazakhs studying in the city of Dneprodzerhinsk became accustomed to racial misidentifications. Nazarbayev had to endure two of them on the day he won his wrestling match with his Ukrainian opponent. After their bout had finished the two young fighters had a vodka together. "When I discovered he had a long bus ride ahead of him to get back to his training institute dormitory, I invited him to come and stay the night at my parents' home", recalled Nicolay Litoshko. "As soon as my mother set eyes on Nazarbayev she said to him 'you poor young Korean, you look hungry. Let me cook you a good meal'."

Madame Yakaterina Litoshko cooked many good meals for Nursultan Nazarbayev who became almost an adopted son to her during his 18 months in Dneprodzerhinsk. He often slept over on Saturday nights in the Litoshko home where Madame Yakaterina ironed his shirts and darned his trousers. Nursultan's friendship with Nicolay Litoshko became strong. "What struck me most about the young Nazarbayev was his competitiveness, and his energy", recalled Litoshko.

He would try anything and he wanted to win at everything. He hated losing at wrestling – or at other sports. I remember one day I took him rowing. It was his first time on the river so naturally he was no good at it and he got into difficulties in handling the oars. But he would not give up, and he kept on trying to compete. When he got out of the boat, blood was pouring from his hands where he had cut himself.

Bloodshed of a more serious nature was troubling Nursultan Nazarbayev when in August 1959 reports trickled out of Temirtau about riots and their brutal suppression by Soviet troops. It emerged that a large number of brick-layers, concrete layers and building labourers had assembled on a square in the centre of the steel-plant site to protest about their working conditions. Their grievances included food shortages, inadequate winter clothing, and contaminated drinking water. The management refused to talk to the pro-testors who then took the law into their own hands by looting the food shops. On the night of this looting Soviet troops were brought into Temirtau. In the ensuing clashes many of the workers – rumoured to be over 100 – were shot dead. At the time, the news of the Temirtau riots was ruthlessly suppressed. However, they were serious enough to be reported in the US media and to bring the future Soviet leader, Leonid Brezhnev, to the city on an emergency visit. As these events reached the ears of Nursultan Nazarbayev and his fel-low Kazakh students in Dneprodzerhinsk, they were alarmed. For they were scheduled, at the end of their course, to go back to Temirtau to open up the new steel plant in the same conditions for workers.

In this worried state of mind, Nazarbayev completed his course at the Dneprodzerhinsk Training Institute. With his close friend Kabidulla Sarekenov, he made the long journey by train from the Ukraine to Kazakhstan eventu-ally arriving on the No 107 bus from Karaganda station to Temirtau at 4 pm on 1st May 1960. The city was closed down for the May Day celebrations. When the two young men turned up at the address they had been given for their dormitory, they found only an empty building. So they dossed down for the night in its cellar and reported for duty the following morning at the office of the steel plant's blast furnace. The reception they received was discouraging. "Guys, you aren't supposed to be here yet", said the manager. "The blast furnace is still under construction. We don't have jobs for you, or any money to pay you." Some of the other returning trainees from Dneprodzerhinsk were so upset that they went back to the collective farms in their villages. But Nazarbayev and Sarekenov were given 50 roubles each as an advance on their future wages and temporarily billeted at a medical isolation centre nine miles outside Temirtau. From there they moved into adjacent bunk beds in their workers' dormitory, a five-storey building three miles from the steel plant. Throughout the months of May and June, Nazarbayev returned to his earlier occupation as a concrete mixer until the blast furnace was completed on 28th June 1960. After that date he was enrolled as a full employee and steelmaker.

The steelworks opened on 2nd July 1960. It was a showpiece plant, the only one of its kind in Central Asia. The Soviet leadership marked the event with parades, rallies and speeches. The firing up of the blast furnace was the centrepiece of the inauguration ceremonies and the first shifts were manned by hand-picked workers, among them 20-year-old Nursultan Nazarbayev.

Nazarbayev's job as the first batch of hot iron was smelted at Termirtau was junior blast furnace attendant. He was one of seven in this category on his shift. Apart from his training at Dneprodzerhinsk, his main qualification for joining this élite group of blast-furnace workers was that he was young and strong. "It was a tough life because the temperature in the blast furnace area was over 40 degrees Centigrade", he has recalled.

I wore heavy protective clothing and I sweated so much during my eight hour shift that I had to take frequent drinks of specially prepared water to keep my body fluids at the right level of salt. As I struggled with the heavy tools guiding the flow of the molten metal as it came out of the furnace tap, I realised that I was personally experiencing the same hardship and agony that I had read about in that book *How the Steel Was Forged*.

Nazarbayev must have been good at his job because within 12 months of the opening of the plant he had been promoted from junior blast furnace attendant to senior blast furnace attendant and then to deputy gas man and senior gas man. This was a meteoric rise in the hierarchy of steelworkers and it was accompanied by several good pay rises. By the time he reached his 21st birthday in July 1961, Nazarbayev was earning 400 roubles a month. This was such a high wage for a young man that he could afford to live well. To his surprise the Temirtau shops were exceptionally well stocked. "The food stores had red and black caviar, sturgeon, and good quality cognac and wine", he has recalled. "The clothes shops were full of imported items – a rare luxury in those days." It was not difficult to identify the reasons why the shelves in the subsidised stores patronised by steel-plant employees were well stocked. The Soviet authorities had been so alarmed by the riots in the city two years earlier that they had made exceptional efforts to keep the Temirtau workers happy in order to prevent outbreaks of further unrest.

Even after spending his money freely in the shops, Nazarbayev could afford to send 200 roubles a month home to his parents. Although they appreciated this filial generosity, his father Abish did not approve of how his son earned his wages. In 1961, Abish made the journey from Chemolgan to Temirtau and watched Nursultan in action on the night shift. As it happened, there was a bad accident that particular night resulting in the death of one of the blast-furnacemen. Nursultan was involved in the grisly task of clearing up the mess. His father, who had watched the whole ordeal in the boiling heat, tried to persuade his son to quit his job: "Why are you torturing yourself?", asked Abish "I have seen a lot in my life but I have never experienced such hell. Give it up."

Far from giving up the world of steelmaking, Nursultan Nazarbayev was increasing his commitment to it. He undertook a programme of further studies on the science of metallurgy by attending evening classes at the Karaganda Polytechnical Institute. This was located seven miles from the Temirtau plant, so when Nazarbayev finished his 8-hour day shift at the blast furnace he had to travel to the Institute for another four hours of education on subjects such as the theory of metallurgical processes; the physics and chemistry of metallurgy; the resistance of materials; and the history of steelmaking. He often came home exhausted from such a long day's physical and mental labour.

"Home" for Nazarbayev was an unheated hostel dormitory in central Temirtau.

Our living conditions seemed particularly intolerable [he has recalled]. We lived four to a small room. We kept warm by sleeping in twos on iron bunk beds covered with mattresses. There was no place to hang our clothes out to dry. We left our canvas work clothes out in the frost because it was easier to put them on when they were frozen than when they were wet and heavy.

These conditions were harsh but Nazarbayev and his dormitory mates were too tired to complain about them.

At the end of each day we were totally worn out, he recalls. I would just crash into my bunk and sleep and sleep. When we were woken up at 5:30 the next morning to get ready for the day shift, I often found that my body had not recovered from the previous day's work.

Recovery came in the 48-hour rest period that blast-furnace workers were allowed after four successive days or nights of intense shift work. After coming off their fourth shift it was the custom for each team of workers to head for a local café where the group leader would order two or three bottles of vodka and a dish of chicken pieces. Then they would sleep off the vodka and their accumulated tiredness, spending the rest of the break in various forms of recreation.

Nazarbayev relaxed in the same way as the rest of us, recalled his contemporary, Vladimir Kolbasa. Sometimes we would go fishing for pike in the local reservoir. Sometimes we would do sports. All of us made regular walks around a hill in the middle of Temirtau which we nicknamed "the mount of love" because that was where we met our girlfriends.

Spare time, like work time, was dreary and monotonous for the steel plant employees of Temirtau. But unlike most of his fellow workers, Nazarbayev had three escape routes from the dull routines of his job. The first was his love of reading. The second was his habit of visiting his family. The third was his talent for organisation.

Thanks to the good education he had received from his teachers at the schools of Chemolgan and Kaskeven, Nazarbayev had a hinterland of intellectual and literary interest which he explored through reading. "I often saw him with his nose in a book or newspaper", said his friend Arguen Junasov, "and he enjoyed telling us all about what he had read in little summaries which he gave us during smoke breaks."

Another contemporary, Toktarkhan Iskakov, recalls those smoke breaks for a different aspect of the future president's character.

Nazarbayev was always full of curiosity. He never stopped asking questions during our smoking time. What did we think of such and such a movie? Had we read this or that article in the newspaper? He was always on the move in his mind. I thought he was smart and active.

It was true that the young Nazarbayev travelled in his mind on voyages of discovery. He was not a deep philosophical thinker, but he read as widely as his arduous life as a steelworker would allow him. The official Communist Party newspaper did not provide him with an open window on the world, but he studied its reports carefully and respectfully. Russian novels gave him greater enjoyment, but his highest literary pleasures came from reading the legends of Kazakh folklore told in narrative form.

The regime of uniformity and conformity in a Soviet steel plant never diluted Nazarbayev's romantic spirit of Kazakh nationalism even though he kept it well hidden. He refreshed the roots of that spirit by making visits back home to Chemolgan which was 10 hours' travelling time from Temirtau. He had a deep sense of loyalty to his parents and to his extended family. Among his many relatives he was well respected, not least because none of them earned anything like as much as his 400 roubles a month salary. However, some of the villagers in Chemolgan thought he looked tired and strained from the exertions of his job when he came home on visits. His cousin Abilda Medenov remembers questioning Nursultan anxiously about his loss of weight and receiving the defiant reply: "Yes, my job is so hard that it is making me lose weight. But I shall persevere with it, and persevere so hard that I will one day be recognised as the best steelmaker in the plant."

Perseverance was a key ingredient in the developing character of the young Nazarbayev. He needed physical perseverance to meet the demands of four successive day shifts on the blast furnace shop floor from 7 am to 3 pm, followed by four successive night shifts from 11 pm to 7 am, with a 48-hour break period in between. He also needed mental perseverance to concentrate on his technical studies at the Karaganda Polytechnic Institute for an additional four hours immediately after coming off his night or day shifts at the plant. This was his standard routine throughout the years 1960–1963. He found it hard going but he stuck with it, he said:

because I was full of ambition. In the short term my job was boring. Its only satisfaction was when you were told after a certain number of shifts that you had melted 100,000 tons of steel from the iron ore. But in the longer term I wanted to be a well-qualified metallurgist, which is why I persisted with my studies and passed the exams at the Institute. Also I wanted to be recognised as a good steelworker.

Recognition was coming Nazarbayev's way for another reason. His contemporaries noticed that he was a good organiser. During the 48-hour break period between shifts, he was the administrative figure who fixed the arrangements for fishing expeditions, drinking parties, or amateur singing evenings.

He liked to run things, said his friend Kuanish Omashev, and he ran them well. He was particularly noticed for organising the weddings of fellow workers in our shop. He had an eye for detail and he could do everything from making sure the drink did not run out to being the toastmaster.

It was not just a private set of friends who observed Nazarbayev's organisational abilities. The Communist Party machine was always on the lookout for talent, especially as the Temirtau community expanded. In 1960, when the plant opened, there had been less than 2,000 men on the payroll but within three years there were over 30,000, divided into some 40 "shops" or groups of workers. These shops were made up of 800–1,000 men but only about 100 of them in each shop were elected to party membership. Nursultan Nazarbayev was keen to join this élite. "I was an ambitious young man and party membership was the route to advancement", he recalls. "If I had thought it would have helped my ambition in those days to be a Buddhist I would have become a Buddhist. But as it was, I became a member of the Communist Party – and a good one."

3

Young Communist, Young Husband, Young Rebel

Communism was not in Nursultan Nazarbayev's blood or background. His heritage was rooted in the sturdy independence of Kazakh nomads. His values came from his father who had a small property owner's respect for private land and a small farmer's resentment at the state collective agricultural system. However, outside the four walls of his home, Communism was the only ideology on offer throughout Nazarbayev's education and early employment. He had to go along with it in order to get ahead in life. So a combination of realism and ambition soon turned him into a committed communist.

In his village school years at Chemolgan Nazarbayev was a Pioneer – Communism's equivalent of a boy scout. When he moved on to Kaskelen School as a teenager he was invited to join Komsomol, the young communist league. Membership of Komsomol was not an exclusive distinction, for it extended to 80 of the 120 pupils at the school. However, Nazarbayev quickly caught the eye of his contemporaries as a potential leader, for in 1957 he was elected as the school secretary of the League. "He was a very responsible Komsomol secretary", recalled the deputy headmaster of Kaskelen School, Seitkhan Issayev. "He was good at organising school welfare programs and social outings. He had a lot of energy, so he was exceptionally active."

Communist activity was matched by communist indoctrination. In his school classes, Nazarbayev was taught the basics of Marxist-Leninist theory. He learned about Soviet leaders past and present. He was made to recite the Communist manifesto until word perfect. There is no evidence that any intellectual or political doubts ever entered Nazarbayev's head during this period of his life. He simply swallowed the ideology hook, line and sinker, so much so that he made ostentatious efforts to demonstrate his party loyalty. One of the earliest public photographs of Nazarbayev was taken when he was 17 years old, carrying a red flag at a May Day parade on 1st May 1958. His expression in the photograph conveys enthusiasm for both the cause and the celebration of it.

Becoming a member of Komsomol was easy, for the youth league threw its net wide and accepted most applicants. Becoming an adult member of the Communist Party was more difficult. The process of party membership involved recommendation, investigation, selection, probation and confirmation. How the young Nazarbayev navigated his way through these difficult waters, and then nearly lost his party membership soon afterwards is an interesting story.

In his early months as a blast-furnace attendant at the Temirtau steel plant Nazarbayev was noticed for his hard work. "That was an important first step in my career because it was often said that only the best workers could become party members", he recalled. However, it was his photogenic appearance rather than his industrial competence that propelled him to recognition by senior party officials. They were interested in good propaganda as a tool for recruiting workers from all over the Soviet Union to Karaganda Magnitka, the official title for the Temirtau steelworks in Karaganda province. The name was a play on words designed to compare the plant to Magnitka Gorsk, the largest steel complex in Russia. As Moscow's planners had decided to employ 40,000 people at Karaganda Magnitka there was some validity in the comparison. But attracting such a huge workforce to one of the most isolated wildernesses of rural Kazakhstan was a major problem. This was how Nazarbayev's photograph became important.

In September 1960, three months after the opening of the steelworks, *Kazakhstanskaya Pravda*, the official newspaper of Soviet Union Kazakhstan, published an attractive picture of the 20-year-old Nursultan Nazarbayev. He was wearing the protective clothing of a blast-furnace attendant with wide-brimmed felt hat tilted backwards at a slightly rakish angle. Beneath the hat his handsome profile, broad smile, sparkling eyes and gleaming teeth were more reminiscent of a model in a Madison Avenue advertising campaign than of a steelworker sweating in the heat of a molten iron ore furnace. The portrait must have been taken in a carefully posed photo-shoot. For similar pictures of Nazarbayev gazing winsomely towards the steel-plant chimney appeared in newspapers throughout the Soviet Union, accompanied by captions suggesting that Karaganda Magnitka was a great place to work. "That photograph made me famous", recalled its subject.

One effect of the fame was that soon after the publication of the photograph Nazarbayev was elected secretary of the Komsomol group of young workers at the steel plant. In this role he made his mark in two episodes which his contemporaries well remember.

A popular Communist slogan in the 1950s was: "What the Party wants, Komsomol does." In that spirit the Karaganda party committee instructed

Komsomol to carry out a clean-up campaign in Temirtau under a national voluntary work directive known as the *Subbota* or *Subbotnik* scheme. The idea behind it, originally conceived by Lenin, was that all good members of the youth league should spend part of their Saturdays or Subbotas in unpaid work for the good of the community. As Temirtau was a fast-expanding city there was no shortage of worthy community projects such as sweeping the streets, clearing the construction rubble, or sweeping up leaves in the park. However, there was a distinct shortage of volunteers for these tedious tasks as most young workers preferred to spend their Saturdays relaxing or playing sports.

I'll always remember how Nazarbayev managed to persuade us to work in the *Subbota* scheme which he was leading [recalled one contemporary steelworker, Kuanish Omashev]. It was an environmental scheme for a hilly part of the city. It was a barren, empty area in those days so the city council issued an order, passed down to Komsomol, for trees to be planted all around it. Now at the end of our working week we were tired blast-furnacemen and we didn't want to spend our days off planting trees for no wages. But Nazarbayev made fiery speeches at Komsomol meetings urging us to support this *Subbota* scheme, speaking with strong arguments and good humour. So we followed his lead and went tree planting with him on many Saturdays.

Temirtau's "Mount of Friendship" is now an elegant city-centre park lined by tall trees, so Nazarbayev's Subbota scheme 45 years earlier evidently served the community well. His exhortations urging his fellow workers to support the scheme with their voluntary labour are interesting because they are one of the earliest examples of his skills as an orator. "Fiery speeches" laced with humour were later to become Nazarbayev's stock in trade as a politician, but he may never have had to persuade a more difficult audience than those tired young blast-furnacemen who were so reluctant to give up their Saturdays to tree planting.

Two other features of Nazarbayev's youthful efforts at leadership in Komsomol were that he could be critical of mediocrity and enterprising in taking unorthodox initiatives of his own. Both characteristics were displayed in an episode involving summer construction work by a *Stroi-otriad* or student labour team. In the summer of 1963, he as a student of the Karaganda Polytechnical Institute was sent off to Balyktkulsky, a rural village near Karaganda, with orders to put up a number of agricultural buildings for the local collective farm. This was a typical assignment for a Stroi-otriad, which was essentially a team of cheap labour drawn from students and young workers. The Stroi-otriad leader from this particular project was an Estonian, Alexsandr Willelm, who was ineffective at his job, not least because he had failed to assemble the right types and quantities of construction materials.

The result was that the Stroi-otriad team wasted most of their time sitting around doing nothing.

Nazarbayev became so impatient with this situation that he was openly critical of Alexsandr Willelm and organised a coup against him. A Komsomol meeting was convened at which resolutions were passed removing Willelm and electing Nazarbayev as his replacement.

Immediately after being elected as our new leader, Nazarbayev disappeared [recalled a fellow member of this Stroi-otriad team, Tokhtarkhan Iskakov]. None of us knew where he had gone. But he reappeared a day or two later with a big consignment of new construction equipment which enabled us to get the job done. As a team we were very happy, the buildings went up on time, and we even got good student wages.

From these two examples of the Subbota tree planting scheme and the Stroi-otriad construction project it is easy to see why Nazarbayev was building up a reputation inside and outside the youth league as an effective Komsomol leader. He was learning how to work the system and how to motivate his contemporaries. He was also becoming a good speaker and an operator who delivered results. These qualities impressed the rank and file Communist Party membership as well as some senior officials. One of these was the secretary of the Karaganda regional council, Bayken Ashimov, who later became Prime Minister of the republic. "I was touring the Temirtau steelworks on an official visit in 1960 when I met the young blast furnacemen who were on their shift", he has recalled. "One of them stood out as a visibly good communicator, full of drive and energy. This young man was Nazarbayev. He impressed me, and many others."

In 1961 these favourable impressions led to an approach being made to Nazarbayev, asking if he would like to be a candidate for party membership. This suggestion came from his shift leader.

He talked to me one day and tried to persuade me about the advantages of joining the party [recalls Nazarbayev]. He said things like, "you have a fine career ahead of you, but to succeed in this career you need to be a member". Actually I did not need any persuasion. I wanted to join the party because it was the only way ahead for someone with ambition.

Nazarbayev was told that the blast-furnace shop of party members had voted for him to become a candidate but that he would have to go through a one-year probationary period.

It was explained to me that I would be observed and tested in that year [he has recalled]. If in that time I showed myself to be a good young worker who did not get into any trouble with the police, didn't drink too much, never skipped my duties, and didn't get into trouble with girls, then I could expect that at a meeting one year after I became a candidate the comrades would elect me to full party membership.

The communist system preferred colourless uniformity to colourful in-dividuality when it came to choosing future party members. Nazarbayev has said that his year on probation "was not easy". His room-mate in the single a workers' dormitory at Temirtau, Kabidulla Sarekenov, has revealed one aspect of the difficulties which was that Nazarbayev kept falling in and out of love.

Nursultan in those days was what we called a "walker" or a ladies man [recalls Sarekenov]. That was partly because he was good-looking as that famous *Pravda* photograph showed. But he himself was romantic. Two of the great loves of his life were a beautiful Ukranian gymnast, Ludmilla Kerenish Kalnysh, and an even more beautiful tall Russian waitress who worked in the canteen. Her name was Orlova and their relationship was so serious that we used to joke about how Nursultan would one day become Count Orlov. But there were many others. Women threw themselves at him.

The passions of Nazarbayev's private life in his early twenties evidently did not reach the ears of the party membership scrutiny committee. Although this body was watching out for any weaknesses in a candidate's personal behaviour, he passed all the required tests. In July 1962, soon after his 22nd birthday and the ending of his year on probation, Nursultan Nazarbayev was elected to full membership of the Communist Party.

Becoming a fully fledged Communist brought a few privileges, such as better career advancement. However, the real change was that obligations and duties increased. Nazarbayev was required to take on additional respon-sibilities as a Komsomol leader, to attend numerous committee meetings as a youth representative of the party, and to fulfil a large number of speaking engagements. One of his biggest audiences was at the 10th annual conven-tion of the Kazakhstan Komsomol. Over a thousand delegates assembled in the Opera House of Almaty, among them a young woman Komsomol member, Manura Akhmetova, who was later to have a successful political career of her own.

This was the first time I had ever met Nazarbayev and I was completely bowled over by him [she has recalled]. He was handsome, charismatic, and his speech woke everyone up because he was not afraid to be critical of the inadequate conditions for workers at the Karaganda steel plant – poor housing, inadequate transport, too few hospitals and so on. He made a big impact.

Waking delegates out of their torpor at large party gatherings with con-troversial criticism was to become a lifelong trademark of Nazarbayev's speechmaking. But in these early days the criticisms were muted and the reactions favourable. As a result of his growing effectiveness as a speaker, Nazarbayev was elected as a Komsomol delegate to an international youth and student festival held in Helsinki. It was a prestigious event attended by representatives from over 100 nations from 5 continents. For Nazarbayev it was exciting to make his first trip outside the Soviet Union and to meet his contemporaries from Western countries including the United States.

The Helsinki festival consisted of plenary sessions on the main floor of the conference hall and smaller workshops, seminars and debates in other locations. Nazarbayev, who was accommodated on a Soviet cruise liner with other Komsomol delegates, was an eager participant in these activities. One of the events which attracted considerable media attention was a debate between American and Soviet speakers on the merits of Communism versus capitalism. Nazarbayev had been carefully coached by senior party members for his part in the debate and was well prepared with statistics and serious arguments on the merits of the Soviet Union. However, as so often happens in student debates, the protagonists started to descend to the level of personal knockabout. The two American speakers from New York's Columbia University, Peter Horn and Karen Lagodo, attacked Nazarbayev on the grounds that he was too polished a debater to be a genuine steelworker. "You've probably been sent to this festival because your father is some bigshot communist official", asserted Lagodo.

"I have no such father. I am an ordinary worker in the blast furnace of a steelworks. Just look at my hands!", retorted Nazarbayev, thrusting his calloused fingers and rough palms towards his opponent as he noted the contrast with her smooth skin and manicured nails. This theatrical gesture worked wonders as Karen Lagodo was compelled to inspect Nazarbayev's hands and to admit that they were so hard and bruised that their owner must be a genuine manual labourer. The local and international press reported these exchanges colourfully, much to Nazarbayev's advantage. The publicity raised his profile at the festival, whose organisers arranged for him to be photographed in Helsinki's Senate Square alongside the Soviet Union's superstar delegate, the world's first cosmonaut, Yuri Gagarin.

Returning from Helsinki, Nazarbayev was given a warm welcome by Kazakhstan's Komsomol organisers, who sent him round the country on a speaking tour. Interesting though he found this new level of political activity, he had a higher priority on his mind. For when he had been seen off on his outward journey to Helsinki by his room-mate Kabidulla Sarekenov, Nazarbayev had confided to him while standing on the platform of Almaty station: "When I get back from Helsinki, I think I'm going to marry Sara."

* * *

Sara was Sara Kunakayeva, a beautiful daughter of Alpys Kunakayev, a Karaganda merchant trading in consumer goods. Sara's mother had died when she was only five years old. This bereavement caused the family to fall on hard times. As a result, Sara left school at 12 to work in an electrical shop, eventually qualifying as an electrician. In that role she got a job at the Karaganda steelworks. She was provided with accommodation in a women's dormitory in Temirtau, which was located just 100 metres from the men's dormitory where Nazarbayev was living.

There was not much in the way of recreation or entertainment for the workers of Karaganda so a popular way of spending Saturday nights was to go dancing. The most notable feature of these evenings was that the men far outnumbered the women, so Sara was never short of partners on the dance floor. Nazarbayev was one of several young steelworkers who noticed her striking beauty, but he hesitated to approach her.

In those days I had been brought up to believe that it was not right to walk over to a lady you did not know and ask her to dance. It was considered too forward [he has recalled]. But then I saw that other men were inviting Sara to dance, so I decided to go ahead and do the same. I remember that she was wearing an elegant black skirt and a white blouse. She looked really good.

Although Sara accepted Nazarbayev's invitation to dance, the attraction between them, at least on sartorial grounds, was not mutual. According to the couple's daughter, Dariga Nazarbayev, her mother was initially unimpressed by her father.

My mother saw him as rather a provincial village boy. She did not think much of his dress sense. The fashion at the time was for men to wear slim cut trousers and shirts, but my father was wearing wide flapping trousers and a thick turtleneck sweater. However, my mother did notice that underneath his sweater my father had strong, broad shoulders.

After their first dance, Nursultan was smitten by Sara and persuaded her to let him walk her back to the women's dormitory. But she seemed uninterested in further encounters. Indeed, she had so many admirers that Nazarbayev's broad shoulders may have been useful in protecting himself from being knocked down in the rush. Some of her suitors were jealous and aggressive in keeping a potential rival at bay. One of them even threatened to push Nazarbayev into the flames of the blast furnace if he did not stop trying to see Sara. It was probably a threat of hot air rather than of cold-blooded murder, but the combination of Sara keeping her distance and her suitors warning him off made Nazarbayev deploy more subtle tactics.

In love as in war, time spent in reconnaissance is rarely wasted. Nazarbayev took the trouble to study Sara's routine. He discovered that she was a member of the Temirtau choir. Further researches showed that she was in the habit of attending choir practice once a week and that immediately after the choir practice her routine took her on to dancing lessons. At these lessons, unlike the Saturday night dances, Sara was not surrounded by a throng of ardent dancing partners.

In his pursuit of Sara, Nazarbayev decided to become a member of the Temirtau choir. He asked his friend Kabidulla Sarekenov to join him in this enterprise. "Enrol in a choir! What on earth has got into you?", was his room-mate's astonished reply. When it became clear that Nazarbayev's sudden enthusiasm for choral music was about Sara rather than singing, Sarekenov tried to talk him out of the plan. "But he convinced me in the end. He can usually persuade anyone to do anything if he tries hard enough."

The choir's new recruits were both tenors. They stood in the back row while the sopranos – among them Sara – were at the front. From his vantage point Nazarbayev could only glimpse the back of Sara's head. Even on this limited basis it was love at first sight. For years afterwards, Nazarbayev joked to friends; "I loved her for her back view. I fell even more in love when I could see her face from the front."

After choir practice Nazarbayev promptly signed up for dancing classes. With no competition from other partners he was soon doing waltzes and quicksteps with Sara. She began responding to his advances. Later, she was to tell her daughter Dariga: "I liked his way of talking, his drive and his ambition. I began to realise that he was a man with a powerful force inside him, a man I could trust."

Before these feelings of mutual trust could develop into a relationship, there was a difficult obstacle to be overcome. Nazarbayev was already engaged to be married. However, it was an unusual engagement because his fiancée was a young woman to whom he had never proposed and for whom he had formed a deep dislike.

Betrothal rather than engagement would be the more appropriate word to describe Nazarbayev's relationship with his first fiancée because the decision that they should marry had been made by their parents. Nursultan was only five years old when the decision was taken. In the autumn of 1945 he had been visiting, with his father Abish, the home of the Isanovich family, who were neighbours in Chemolgan. The Isanoviches were in a festive mood, celebrating the arrival of the latest member of their family, a newborn baby daughter whom they named Astai. The naming ceremony developed into a betrothal ceremony as both sets of parents formally agreed that their two offspring should be married. Although Astai was in her cradle and Nursultan was a toddler, their betrothal was a binding obligation in accordance with the customs of the Kazakhs.

Nursultan seems to have been the only one of the six family members involved in the betrothal who had 20th century doubts about the validity of this 14th century practice. His anxieties surfaced when he went to school.

Even in first grade I was teased by my classmates who would taunt me with shouts of "here comes the bridegroom" [he has recalled]. I was terribly embarrassed. As the teasing went on I started to hate the sight of this little girl. I avoided her. Whenever I caught sight of her in my childhood I would run away.

Running away, or even going away to Temirtau to become a steelworker, did not mean that Nursultan Nazarbayev's obligation to marry Astai had ended. This was the firm view of Nursultan's mother, Aljan, who was strongly in favour of this village equivalent of a dynastic alliance. She kept inviting the teenage fiancée Astai to the Nazarbayev home, welcoming her warmly and declaring "Our house will one day be your house". This traditional saying meant that the marriage was imminent. It could hardly have been further from the mind of the bridegroom, whose thoughts on this subject were increasingly turning in the quite different direction of Sara Kunakayeva.

In the summer of 1962, Nazarbayev made a visit back home to his family in Chemolgan when on vacation from the Karaganda steelworks. His mother insisted that she and her eldest son should call on Astai's family, who were mourning the recent death of their husband and father. On entering the house Nursultan was re-introduced to Astai who was now a young woman of 17 – an appropriate age to be married in that community. "I was so much against her that I refused to look her in the face", recalled Nazarbayev. "In fact I immediately tried to leave the room. But she ran after me, grabbed me by the hand and said 'why are you running away?'"

For the first time in their lives, Astai and Nursultan had a conversation about their childhood betrothal. Astai said that on his deathbed her father had reminded her that she had been promised in marriage to the son of Abish. The only way that promise could be annulled was by Nursultan himself formally agreeing to end the betrothal and setting Astai free.

So you must say right now – you will marry me? Or you will set me free? [demanded Astai. It is not clear which answer was the one the young lady was hoping for when she issued this ultimatum. Nursultan did not hesitate.] I set you free to marry another man [he replied, recalling afterwards] I said those words with great relief, because from then on I was free to concentrate on Sara.

*   *   *

Concentrating on Sara was not plain sailing. Aljan was furious at the ending of the betrothal. Her anger complicated her relations with her son in the short term and with her future daughter-in-law in the long term. Nazarbayev himself, having extricated himself from one engagement did not find it as easy as he had hoped to find happiness in another one. For Sara remained elusive, still courted and fêted by other admirers. Nazarbayev was disappointed by her apparent lack of responsiveness to him. He did not enjoy being one of a crowd of suitors. So as a romantic reminder of his early dances with Sara, he sent her a photograph of himself. It was a studio portrait for which the 21-year-old Nazarbayev posed in the unaccustomed attire of a tuxedo and black bow tie. On the back of it he wrote in thick black ink with his fountain pen: *As a Memory to Save – Nursultan 1962.*

It is not known whether this inscription or the undoubtedly handsome picture (which survives in the Presidential archives) stirred Sara's heart. But what did bring her into a deeper relationship with Nazarbayev was an encounter far removed from a photographic studio, a choir practice or a Saturday evening dance. It was the scene of a serious industrial accident on the shop floor of the steelworks.

In the early summer of 1962, while doing night-shift duty at the blast furnace, Nazarbayev had been present at a molten metal overflow crisis when a red-hot channel of liquid iron ore burst its banks and flooded across the shop floor, injuring some of the workers. There were strict procedures for such accidents. The rule was that the men of the shift when the incident took place had to remain on duty for as long as was needed to clear up the mess and get the production line restarted. Nazarbayev toiled around the clock to remove the spilt metal and scrub down the shop floor. After more than 24 hours of cleaning-up operations, he was covered in soot with his eyes and teeth the only part of his features not blacked out by a thick coating of grime. At this moment of maximum exhaustion, a woman worker approached him to ask if there was anything she could do to help. It was Sara. She was on duty that night in the electrical substation. Recognising Nursultan from his build, she came to him to express her concern for what had happened in the accident. Her sympathetic conversation was a turning point in their relationship. While the flames of the blast furnace were damped down, the fires of love ignited. Some weeks later Nazarbayev proposed to Sara with the words "Marry me, and I will show you the world". She accepted. Neither of them could have dreamed how well this romantic promise would be fulfilled.

At the time of their engagement the young couple's world consisted of the steelworks, the Communist Party and the city of Temirtau. Within those limits Nursultan Nazarbayev and Sara Kunakayeva tied the knot in what one of the guests called "a typical Komsomol wedding". This meant that every detail was organised, supervised and paid for by the youth league out of its official budget.

The marriage took place on 25th August 1962. It consisted of a short civil ceremony followed by a party in a local restaurant. About 60 guests attended, most of them steelworkers and party officials plus relatives from the bride and groom's families. The youngest person present was Nazarbayev's 10-year-old brother Bolat, who remembers the occasion as "a really exciting and happy evening with lots of music, dancing and singing", culminating in many choruses of an old Kazakh folk song "Ainam Koz". Three significant wedding gifts were presented to the couple. The first was a double bed that had been paid for by contributions from Nazarbayev's fellow blast-furnace workers. The second was an envelope from Abish and Aljan containing all the money Nursultan had been sending them at the rate of 200 roubles a month since becoming a steelworker four years earlier. They had not spent a single cent or kopek of it on their own needs, but had carefully saved it to give their eldest son and his bride a good start in life. The third and most important wedding present was from Komsomol – the keys to a brand-new apartment in downtown Temirtau.

The ceremony in which those keys were handed over at the wedding was fulsome, but the gift turned out to be a disappointment. For when the bride and groom went to the address of the apartment they found only a construction site. The 80 apartments in the still-to-be erected block would take nearly a year of building work before anyone could move into them.

Deflated by the discovery that they had no matrimonial home, Nursultan and Sara went to live with a friend who had a tiny one-bedroom apartment which he shared with his wife, two small children and his grandmother. The bride and groom had to spend their wedding night in the same room as the grandmother, an experience Nazarbayev has described as "unforgettable". He also did not forget his first experience of learning that the Communist Party had a habit of promising far more than it could deliver.

*   *   *

Nazarbayev was not disenchanted with the Communist Party but nor was he enamoured of it. He was pleased to be a party member; he continued to do his share of duty as a Komsomol leader; and he became more and more in demand as a public speaker. The growing burden of these activities, which included being a delegate to the republican and national congresses of the Young Communist League, sometimes created pressures on his family life. His close friend, Kabidulla Sarekenov, remembers an incident when the newly married Mrs Sara Nazarbayeva became upset with her husband for taking on too heavy a schedule of speechmaking:

I saw Nursultan one evening when he was rather pleased with himself because of all the applause an audience had given him after one of his speeches [recalled Sarekenov]. So I asked him what he had been talking about and he replied rather proudly "my experiences at the Helsinki conference". I joked back at him "So what's new about that" because I was aware that he had given that speech over and over again many, many times. To my surprise, Nursultan became upset with me when I told him he was doing too much. He insisted that I should walk back with him to his home, and on the way he went on arguing that he was not overdoing his speechmaking. However, he lost that argument when we reached his home because Sara was there outside, standing on the doorstep in a purple dressing gown with her arms folded. She was furious with him for coming back so late after making yet another speech.

Although he was behaving like an obsessive young politician, Nazarbayev insisted he was not thinking of becoming one. "I loved my job as a steel-worker and had no thoughts of giving it up", he recalled. At the age of 26 he had seven years of seniority in the industry, having been promoted through three grades of blast-furnace attendant and two grades of gasman. By 1967 he was the senior gasman on his shift. He had accumulated many benefits and a pay grade of over 500 roubles a month. He had finished his studies at the Karaganda Polytechnic Institute and achieved the full qualifications of a Metallurgist Engineer. So his future at the steelworks looked bright until he was unexpectedly summoned to the Communist Party headquarters and offered the official position of First Secretary of Komsomol for the City of Temirtau.

The offer of this appointment to a salaried position of considerable influence in the hierarchy of the party might have been expected to appeal to Nazarbayev as the first step on the ladder of a political career. But he turned it down. His reasons for this refusal were purely pragmatic. He was earning high wages and had a young family to support. He enjoyed his job. He had no interest in leaving it for full time political work as a party apparatchik. He did not want to take the two-thirds cut in salary that the Komsomol post required, nor did he wish to lose his accumulated seniority benefits as a steel-worker.

Although these were Nazarbayev's private thoughts on the new job that was being offered to him, he did not express them publicly when he appeared in front of the Temirtau city party committee. "I did not say anything about salary or seniority", he has recalled. "After all, a party member was supposed to care about 'higher interests'."

Because he felt it inappropriate to explain his real interests, Nazarbayev's refusal of the Komsomol position made him appear stubborn if not arrogant. His attitude put him on an immediate collision course with Lazar Katkov, the formidable secretary of the city party committee. "Don't fool around with Comrade Katkov", advised Nazarbayev's friends when they heard of his defiance. Despite such warnings, he remained in a defiant mood, even after coming before the committee for a second time and receiving a fierce lecture from Katkov on the imperatives of obedience to party discipline. By this time Nazarbayev was regarded as a rebel who must be brought into line. He was summoned for a third interview, in front of the full membership of the committee. Nazarbayev now came up with a plausible, if less than candid explanation for his conduct.

Please understand that I am worried about the shortage of qualified metallurgists at the steel-works [he said]. I was sent away to study in order to obtain the full professional qualifications of a steelworker. I am needed at the plant, but you could find lots of other people qualified to take on this political position at Komsomol.

This argument cut no ice with Lazar Katkov who condemned Nazarbayev for his disobedience and declared: "Either you will agree to serve or you will be expelled from the party." This was such a serious threat that Nazarbayev almost gave way. But in the end he stood firm, saying afterwards, "Somehow I had an uncontrollable desire to resist such strong pressure. So I simply said that I would think it over carefully."

Some members of the committee were thinking it over carefully too, particularly the director of the steelworks who may have had some sympathy for the argument about the shortage of qualified metallurgists. He advocated a more lenient approach. Others supported him in his view that expulsion was too extreme a punishment. So in the end, another appointee was given the Komsomol position and Nazarbayev was sentenced to receive an official reprimand. But the wording of it was left to Lazar Katkov who delivered it in harsh language. Nazarbayev was condemned "for refusing ... for political immaturity ... for demonstrating indifference". The statement concluded "This strong reprimand is to be placed in his record to serve as an example to others."

Nazarbayev was so incensed by the severity of his reprimand that he decided to dispute the umpire's decision. As soon as he left the room in which his sentence had been delivered he jumped into his car and drove to the headquarters of the regional Party Committee in Karaganda province. The officials of this regional party body were superior in rank to the officials of the Temirtau city Party committee.

This was where I got lucky [Nazarbayev has recalled], because it just so happened that the regional party boss, Nikolai Semenov, personally hated the city party boss, Lazar Katkov. So when Semenov listened to my appeal he became angry and started shouting things like "Why is this happening? When we are having so much trouble recruiting good metallurgists why are we kicking one out and putting him in a political job. The Temirtau city committee are wrong!"

A few days later the regional party committee overruled the city committee's decision. Nazarbayev's reprimand was expunged from the record.

and Lazar Katkov was officially criticised for the wrong approach to selecting personnel. He was furious, shouting at Nazarbayev "One day I'll get you for this". It was a threat which was never carried out because three months later Katkov was moved to an obscure administrative position in the Dzhambul region.

Although this victory of the young rebel over the domineering city official must have seemed sweet to Nazarbayev at the time, it did not last. For less than a year later Katkov's replacement as city party secretary, Nikolai Davydov, called Nazarbayev into his office: "I know all about you and your difficulties with Katkov", said Davydov, "but I would still like to ask you to work with the city party committee in an official position as second secretary of the committee in charge of the heavy industry department. You will be dealing with your plant so you will not be leaving the steel industry."

Nazarbayev was far from pleased by this request and would have liked to reject it for the same reasons that had caused him to turn down the original appointment. Two factors changed his mind. The first was that Davydov had asked him to take the heavy industry job for only one year. The second was that Nazarbayev's friends advised him "Don't tempt fate with another rebellion".

These combined considerations made Nazarbayev accept the new appointment. He took it on believing that he would be allowed to return to his old job in the steelworks within 12 months. This was a vain hope, for promotions to posts he could not possibly refuse soon came his way. By 1968, Nazarbayev's days as a young rebel were over. His career as a full-time official of the Communist Party had begun.

4

Climbing the Party Ladder

Nazarbayev's new job as second secretary of the Temirtau city party committee in charge of industry and capital construction meant a reduction in his pay but an increase in his responsibilities. Instead of receiving 500 roubles a month as a senior gasman in the blast furnace he was paid 150 roubles a month as a party official. However, he spent more time than ever at the steelworks. "I did not sit in the office pushing a pencil. I spent day and night at the construction sites of the steel plant supervising the political activities", he has recalled.

These activities were wide-ranging, for in the 1960s nothing happened in Temirtau's industry without the political approval of the party. Nazarbayev's 18-hour working day could involve big decisions such as signing off the steel plant manager's plans for building extensions to the factory floor. But it could also bring him into face-to-face contact with human problems and minor incidents. "Every day I met with dozens of people who came to me around the clock with the most diverse and sometimes unexpected situations", he has recollected. "A foreman might be threatening to take a crew off the job if the supply of concrete wasn't more regular, or a worker's wife might want us to influence her alcoholic husband to stop drinking." The energy Nazarbayev showed in dealing with such a wide scope of issues impressed his bosses. They soon moved him up to the position he had originally refused to accept – First Secretary of Komsomol. This had become an important promotion because of the demographics of Temirtau. A 1963 census had reported it was the city with the highest birth rate in the Soviet Union. It was also the industrial centre with the highest influx of young workers. As a result of these population factors, the youth league that Nazarbayev took charge of had over 30,000 members. They were divided into three main groups: high-school pupils, students and steelworkers. In the schools he supervised the ideological teaching of Marxist-Leninist doctrine and provided programmes for the Pioneers – the party's equivalent of boy scouts and girl guides. In the institutes and colleges he was continuously exhorting the students to work harder. At the steel plant he urged the young employees to produce more and better-quality steel. In this cheerleader role Nazarbayev encountered many of the problems that were to prove endemic causes of the later economic failure of the Soviet Union. Lack of motivation, indiscipline, absenteeism, alcoholism and low productivity were high among the negative characteristics of the 1960s generation in the Soviet republics. Temirtau reflected the local manifestations of Communism's malaise and had special problems of its own. Because there was so little for young people to do in the city there was often a breakdown of order in the streets, particularly at weekends. Nazarbayev had some success in controlling the vandals by confronting them with vigilantes led by Komsomol officials wearing red arm bands.

A greater problem in the Temirtau community was its high turnover of residents. The steel-plant workforce had grown to 40,000, but a third of its employees left their jobs within six months and returned home. This continuous churning was caused by workers voting with their feet against the conditions in the city. Nazarbayev was well aware of the popular discontent but powerless to persuade the ruling powers in Moscow to respond to it.

I don't remember any conversation from top visiting officials about the living conditions of the steelworkers or the builders [he has recalled]. No such conversations ever occurred because no one at the top thought about the ordinary people, about their housing, hospitals, childcare, food or consumer goods. Yet these problems grew like a snowball rolling down a hill.

The snowball effect caused many delays to the construction programme. It also disrupted production at the steelworks. As the Party leader, Nazarbayev was not responsible for these stoppages. But two quick promotions brought him into the front line of decision-makers. In 1970 he was appointed deputy to the First Secretary of the Temirtau party committee, Nikolai Davydov, and in 1972 he was put in charge of steel production as secretary of the party committee of the Karaganda steel plant.

As Nazarbayev took over his new responsibilities, the Karaganda steelworks were sinking into what he called "a state of near anarchy". The high turnover of departing workers was only one of a multitude of problems which included chaotic management, a desperate shortage of trained engineers, an appalling accident record, confusing changes in shifts, long breaks in steel production, and severe cuts in staff wages under Moscow's unworkable policy edict: "Less pay – more output".

In the early months after his appointment Nazarbayev took a great deal of personal criticism for the poor production figures and low morale at the steelworks. So did the director of the plant, Oleg Tishchenko. But Nazarbayev, who was developing the skills of a shrewd politician, made two moves that eventually improved both his personal position and the future of the Karaganda Magnitka or steel complex.

Nazarbayev's first move was to rally the Communist Party members on the shop floor. There were approximately 3,000 of them out of a total labour force of 40,000, but Nazarbayev worked tirelessly to turn the card-carrying members into a team of leaders who would encourage their workmates towards better discipline and commitment.

Right after I became secretary of the party committee I think I made the right decision by relying completely on the rank and file party members on the shop floor [he has recalled]. I saw over and over again how 5 or 10 per cent of the real dedicated party members in a team could unite the others and get things moving. It was only with their help that we were able to keep the collective from falling apart.

Although it was no small achievement to improve morale in a way that prevented further anarchy at the steel plant, nevertheless the production figures were sinking into a quagmire of decline both in output and in quality. Nazarbayev soon realised that the problems could not be solved at local level. If Karaganda Magnitka was ever to succeed, decisions of restructuring and re-allocation of resources would have to be made in Moscow. So far in the history of the Temirtau steel plant, Moscow's decision-makers had turned a deaf ear to its problems. To ensure that these problems were now heard, Nazarbayev embarked on a high-risk strategy. He became a whistleblower to the press.

There was only one newspaper that counted in the Soviet Union – *Pravda*. Although its editorial columns were carefully controlled, nevertheless its news pages sometimes reported stories which could make embarrassing reading for the party hierarchy. One such well-sourced article appeared on 8th June 1973 under the headline "The Truth About the Factory". It was the result of a journalistic collaboration between Nazarbayev and a *Pravda* writer, Mikhail Poltoranin, who had been taking an interest in the problems of Karaganda Magnitka. After several meetings with Poltoranin, Nazarbayev wrote the article himself and agreed to let it be published under his own name. The result was a devastating and detailed critique of all the design faults, construction failures and technical problems that were the root causes of the production collapse at the steelworks. In addition, Nazarbayev explained the reasons why the workforce was so unstable, highlighting the poor housing, schools, hospitals, utilities, transport and other necessities for the employees and their families in Temirtau.

The impact of Nazarbayev's article was explosive. He was sharply criticised by his fellow Party officials in Temirtau, and in the Party hierarchy across Kazakhstan who accused him of washing dirty linen in public. But the rank and file party members at the steel plant supported him and his article. Indeed, they were the primary sources of what *Pravda* had published, for Nazarbayev had been listening carefully to their complaints. "Because I was a fellow steelworker they opened up to me", he has recalled. "Many of them told me why don't you do something? 'Why don't you tell the big shots what's wrong here. We elected you to do that'."

The big shots in the Kremlin read Nazarbayev's criticisms in *Pravda* and took action. Within weeks, a state Commission of Inquiry was set up into Karaganda Magnitka. It consisted of 50 party officials and steel experts from Moscow headed by Vladimir Dolgikh, a senior secretary of the Communist Party Central Committee. When the commission assembled in Temirtau for the opening of the enquiry Nazarbayev was called as the first witness. The opening question put to him by Dolgikh was: "Explain why you have written all this in the newspaper."

Startled by the severe tone of Dolgikh's first question, Nazarbayev said to himself "Oh well, that's it! My party career is now over. I will go back to the shop floor and continue my life as an engineer." This pessimism was unjustified. For Dolgikh knew a great deal about steelmaking, having had a long career in the industry as Director of the Norilsk Metallurgical plant before his appointment to the central committee in Moscow. As Nazarbayev continued his evidence, the attitude of Dolgikh and other members of the commission changed from hostility to sympathy. During the next four days Nazarbayev took the key figures of the commission on a tour of the shop floors in the plant and of the many construction sites where there were problems. He also escorted Dolgikh and his fellow commissioners around Temirtau showing them what Nazarbayev called 'the catastrophic housing conditions for our workers' as well as pointing out the conspicuous absence of all other community facilities. The commission evidently agreed with the case that had been presented to them. For a few months later they published their report entitled: *About the efforts of the party committee of the Karaganda steel plant to strengthen discipline and create a stable collective.* The broad thrust of this report was that it praised the local work of the party committee headed by Nazarbayev and blamed the failures of the steel plant on mistakes made at the centre in terms of bad planning, lack of investment and errors of judgement. This was a most unexpected outcome. It was unusual, to say the least, for a Moscow appointed commission to blame Moscow's decision makers for industrial failures in another Soviet Republic.

The next development in the Karaganda Magnitka saga was that the Central Committee of the Communist Party decided to hold hearings on the commission of inquiry's report. These hearings were to be chaired by the legendary Mikhail Suslov, who had been one of the most formidable Soviet leaders ever since his promotion to the Presidium by Stalin in the 1940s. By 1972, Suslov was the chief ideologist and senior member of the Politubro, exercising immense influence over the whole range of political, military and industrial decision-making. How this 70-year-old "grey eminence" at the levers of power in the Kremlin came to inter-react with 32-year-old Nursultan Nazarbayev, a political neophyte from Kazakhstan, is a fascinating story.

Nazarbayev travelled to Moscow in December 1972 to attend the Central Committee's hearings on the performance of Karaganda Magnitka. He was accompanied by a 20-strong delegation of party officials from Kazakhstan. But as they checked into their hotel on the eve of the hearings Nazarbayev was startled to receive a message telling him that Comrade Suslov wanted to see him immediately. As he was escorted to the Politburo chief's office. Nazarbayev became agitated. "What the hell is going on?", he asked himself. "Suslov is a god in the Soviet Union – high up in the skies. What on earth does he want to see me for?"

While he was sitting in Suslov's waiting room, the awestruck Nazarbayev spotted a pair of cheap rubber galoshes at the base of the coat stand. The sight of these commonplace items of footwear, used particularly by the older generation in the harsh Russian winters, made him revise his assessment of his host. He began to realise that the owner of these grandfatherly galoshes might not be an exalted deity but an ordinary human being who walked to his office on his own two feet. "From that moment I resolved to talk frankly to Comrade Suslov as man to man", recalled Nazarbayev.

The dialogue between the old Kremlin statesman and the young Karaganda Magnitka party secretary opened on a surreal note of ignorance. As soon as they were alone together Suslov walked his guest to a giant wall map of the Soviet Union.

"Show me where this Temirtau place is and tell me about it", he began.

"It's flat. There was nothing there before the steel mill", replied Nazarbayev as he pointed to the location on the map.

"Any trees, any greenery?"

"No. It's too flat and the climate is too harsh."

"What is the weather like there?"

"In winter it is minus 30 degrees. In summer it is over 40 degrees."

"And you decided to build a steel plant in such a place?"

"That decision had nothing to do with me", said Nazarbayev.

After establishing the basic facts of Temirtau's climate and geography, Suslov began grilling his visitor with detailed questions. He was shocked by many of the answers, particularly by Nazarbayev's description of the poor conditions for the steelworkers and the lack of security at the plant. "When building materials are delivered to the plant to make repairs they are stolen before the repairs can be carried out, because there is no fencing and no secure area at the steelworks", explained the younger man, emphasising that unless new basic investment in infrastructure was provided, Karaganda Magnitka would continue to perform badly. After over an hour of these revelations, Mikhail Suslov was convinced.

"What are you planning to say at the hearing tomorrow?", he asked.

"Here are my speaking notes", replied Nazarbayev. "I've been told that I've got just ten minutes."

Suslov skimmed through the text of the prepared speech. "I suppose you were told to say this by the members of the regional committee." When Nazarbayev nodded the senior member of the Politburo gave him a clear order.

"Don't say all this rubbish. Give the true facts exactly as you have given them to me in answer to my questions."

"But if I do that I will be in trouble afterwards", replied Nazarbayev.

"Don't worry. You will be safe. I will protect you", said Mikhail Suslov.

Encouraged by his protector's promise, Nazarbayev threw caution to the winds when he addressed the Central Committee. Instead of the defensive remarks in his prepared text he delivered a fiery denunciation of the failures by Moscow's leading bureaucracies in relation to Karaganda Magnitka.

The atmosphere became electric [recalled Nazarbayev]. Nobody except Suslov had expected to hear such critical evidence. All the big bosses woke up as they listened to me, this unknown young man from God-knows-where, telling them that the ministry of coal had failed to deliver the right coke to heat the furnaces; that the ministry of construction had put up poorly made structures in the wrong place; that the ministry of housing had built inadequate worker's accommodation five kilometres from the steel plant; and that the Ministry of Metallurgy and Heavy Engineering had completely failed in many ways that I explained in detail.

More detail, corroborating Nazarbayev's attack, was provided by evidence from the director of the steel plant. Suslov then invited questions to the various officials and ministers who had been criticised. They floundered badly, unable to provide convincing answers. Eventually Suslov became furious. "You have misused the money of the Soviet Union", he told the Minister of Metallurgy. "You have turned a major government project into an organisation of wheelers and dealers", was his condemnation of the Minister of Construction. Other senior officials were subjected to similar outbursts of Suslov's withering scorn for the lack of housing and other facilities in Temirtau. At the end of the day's hearing, Suslov declared "A special resolution will now be prepared by the Committee asking the USSR Council of Ministers to improve the living conditions and recreational facilities for the steelworkers of Karaganda." His parting shot was to appoint Nazarbayev as a member of the drafting committee for this special resolution.

Although he was the youngest member of the committee, Nazarbayev was the most influential voice on it. The resolution, swiftly approved by the USSR Council of Ministers, ordered an annual building programme that included 80,000 square metres of housing, two childcare centres, three schools and a sports complex. In addition, there were special development projects such as a new hospital, a palace of culture, a training institute in metallurgy, a 15,000-seat stadium, a 50-metre swimming pool, and a holiday resort for the steelworkers. Nazarbayev was then given the job of making sure the decree was implemented on the ground. This was no small task in an era of labour shortages and equipment bottlenecks but within four years the entire programme had been accomplished.

Our main achievement was to provide housing for everyone who was on the waiting list, for we built well over 100,000 new apartments [recalled Nazarbayev]. We also provided a much better quality of life for families living in the city. The end result was that the turnover of workers leaving the steel plant within a year fell from 33 per cent to 9 per cent.

A more stable workforce at Karaganda Magnitka became a more productive workforce. Within the same four-year period as the improvements in the housing and social facilities, productivity at the steel plant increased by 60 per cent. These results were achieved by two forces. The first was the political backing of the Council of Ministers in Moscow, which provided new investment of over 300 million roubles to fund the new infrastructure at Temirtau and the steelworks. The second force was the personal contribution of Nursultan Nazarbayev, which deserves careful analysis for the light it throws on his emerging character and reputation as a politician.

There were four component parts in the story of how Karaganda Magnitka was transformed by Nazarbayev – his boldness, his skills as a communicator, his perseverance as an implementer and his personal ambition.

Nazarbayev had an impulsive streak in him. His initiative to brief a *Pravda* journalist on the problems of the steel plant was an extraordinary move by a Communist Party official in the early 1970s. He could easily have lost his job or at least been disciplined for this uncomradely whistle-blowing. It was even bolder of him to write and sign the offending article in his own name. For his openness meant that he was unable to back the politician's time-honoured defence mechanisms in circumstances when a leak causes embarrassment. He could not blame the journalist nor allege misquotation.

He had put his own head on the block. Why did he take such a risk? "Because I was angry, frustrated and upset". was his reply, "and I always thought of myself as a metallurgist and steelworker. My heart was with my fellow steel-workers who were working so hard only to be let down by the system. That was why I fought."

Fighting the system was a mission close to impossible inside the Moscow bureaucracy. Nazarbayev was lucky to obtain both the patronage and the protection of Mikhail Suslov. Yet the younger man made his own luck by one-to-one communication with the senior members of the Politburo. That was in turn built on the foundations of earlier good communication with the men on the shop floor and with the men from Moscow who had come to Temirtau as members of the commission of inquiry set up after the *Pravda* article. Looking at the episode in the round, it is clear that Nazarbayev by the age of 32 had acquired the political skills of good listening, effective speaking, and seizing his opportunities.

The implementation of the Council of Ministers' decree required further displays of these skills with perseverance and unorthodoxy. The latter quality soon came into play when it became evident that what had been approved in Moscow could not be delivered in Temirtau. This was mainly because there were too many construction sites and too few construction workers. "To get more construction workers, I decided to claim that the 1,500 agri-cultural workers sent by Moscow to help on the farms at harvest time were needed all the year round. But as soon as the harvest was over I reassigned them to construction projects", said Nazarbayev. "That extra labour force enabled us to get the jobs done on time."

Personal ambition was another vital ingredient in Nazarbayev's chem-istry. Winning the bureaucratic in-fighting with Suslov's help had been a good start, but Nazarbayev was well aware that his new patron could be a hard taskmaster. So delivering the construction programme was essential if the goodwill of Moscow was to be retained. Nazarbayev's motives for driving himself and the Temirtau labour force so hard were therefore a mixture of public good and private ambition.

The mixture worked. Four years after his first meeting with Suslov Nazarbayev was again summoned to see the senior Politburo chief in his Moscow office. "Do you remember the day you first came here?", asked Suslov. After receiving the inevitable answer he continued "Well, we did not forget you. I have called Kunayev myself. You will soon be promoted."

Dinmukhamed Kunayev was the First Secretary of the Kazakhstan Communist Party. The post made him the most powerful politician in the republic. He was also a high-ranking figure in the Soviet Union, having been a member of the Politburo for over 10 years, thanks to his friendship with Leonid Brezhnev. Kunayev's opinion of Nazarbayev was to go through many changes in the next 10 years, with phases that ranged from admiration to antipathy. Although their relationship was to become of great political importance in the history of the Soviet Union, in 1976 the two men were worlds apart and hardly knew each other. So Suslov's recommendation was a key ingredient in Kunayev's decision to appoint Nazarbayev to the position of secretary of the Karaganda regional party committee in charge of industry.

This appointment was an important step upwards on the party ladder for the 35-year-old Nazarbayev. It meant that he was rising in status from a local to a regional official with responsibilities ranging far beyond the Temirtau steelworks. He was now taking charge of a wider portfolio of mines, factories, chemical plants and construction projects across the province. Yet however gratifying to his ambition this public achievement may have seemed, Nazarbayev was anxious about a nagging private worry. "My experiences at Karaganda Magnitka had awoken me to the realisation that the whole Soviet Union was a great big fake in its inability to manage industrial projects profitably" was his secret conclusion from his dealings with the Moscow bureaucracy. It was not a happy state of mind for a Communist Party official just appointed to take charge of industry in one of the most important regions in a Soviet Republic.

*   *   *

Nazarbayev's upward promotion, together with his inward thoughts about the unworkability of the Soviet industrial system, faced him with a dilemma. "I had to make a serious choice about how I would live and work from then on", he has recalled. In essence this choice was about whether to join the insiders' club of committee party officials, or whether to keep his distance as an outsider from this self-perpetuating élite. Two factors made him choose the outsiders' role. One was his pessimistic diagnosis of the sickness that was beginning to paralyse the Soviet Union's economic and industrial policy. The other was his strong sense of identification with the grassroots membership of the Communist Party – the ordinary workers.

Nazarbayev had been genuinely shocked by his experiences with party officials over the problems at Karaganda Magnitka. The fact that he, with the backing of Mikhail Suslov, had been able to fix many of those problems had not blinded him to the deep fault lines that ran through the entire communist system of mismanaging industry.

I began to understand that there was a circle of non-responsibility staffed by party officials who would solemnly accept reports that were untrue about situations that did not exist based on facts and figures that were false [says Nazarbayev]. The Karaganda steel plant was a typical example of this. It had actually been planned to operate at a loss. Until I talked to *Pravda* and then Suslov, the hierarchy of officials were pretending that it was a profitable state enterprise. As I struggled for the next four years to turn it around, it dawned on me that Karaganda Magnitka was only one example of a culture of loss-making industries subsidised by the state. So even back in the mid-1970s I saw that one day the money would run out in state budgets all across the Soviet Union.

Because he could not bear the pretending and misreporting of so many of his fellow officials in the party's corridors of power, Nazarbayev kept himself apart from them and instead made considerable efforts to stay close to the workers on the shop floor. He did not always get a friendly reception from them now that he had become one of their "big bosses" in his capacity as regional party secretary for industry. Early on in his new job he was shouted at in the street by one of his old friends from the steelworks: "What are you doing with a white shirt on riding in a car driven by a chauffeur? Come on, get over to the blast furnace and see the problems we're facing." To his credit, Nazarbayev did go immediately to the floor of the blast furnace where the 70° Celsius temperature soon soaked his suit and shirt in sweat. The problem, a leakage in the molten steel channels, was solved within three days after a special meeting of the party committee allocated funds for the repairs.

This incident taught Nazarbayev a lesson that stood him in good stead when handling the most difficult part of his portfolio – the mining industry. He recognised that he had to earn the trust of the workforce. This was particularly difficult with the coal miners of Karaganda who operated the province's 26 underground pits. These men were something of a breed apart; sullenly resentful about their working conditions and the criticism they received from the party for failing to meet their production targets.

Nazarbayev's approach to the miners was collegiate rather than critical. He listened carefully to their complaints. He visited every one of their pits experiencing at first hand the dangerous problems of high methane levels, unsafe structures at the coal face, and tunnel collapses. On one of his underground tours, there was a rock fall in a shaft just a few metres from where he was standing. On this occasion no one was hurt but the roar of the rubble was a sharp reminder of the poor safety record in Karaganda's mines. It was matched above ground by the poor housing conditions for the miners, and a complete absence of social and welfare facilities in mining communities.

Nazarbayev soon realised that he was encountering a rerun of the failures that had bedevilled the steel industry of the province. Those common failures were poor centralised planning, inadequate investment, unsafe infrastructure and a callous, if not contemptuous, disregard by party officials of the need to provide the workers with decent living conditions.

For the second time in his career Nazarbayev brought about a showdown with Moscow over workers' problems in Karaganda. He sent a powerful report on the mines to the Central Committee of the Communist Party of the Soviet Union, following it up with intense lobbying. The result was that in June 1976, one year after Nazarbayev had become industry secretary of the regional party committee, the USSR Council of Ministers issued a decree requiring an improvement in the living and working conditions of the miners of Karaganda. The men at the coal face were grateful to Nazarbayev, who used the funds allocated by Moscow to build a huge number of new apartments for them close to the pits, to provide better community services and to make many improvements in their underground working conditions. In a further wave of reforms at the coal mines by Nazarbayev and the general director of mining, Nicolai Drizhd, several new pits were built and a huge new open-cast mine, the Burlinsky, was created in northern Karaganda. As a consequence of all these initiatives coal production stopped falling and by 1978 was showing a 40 per cent increase.

Coal and steel were only two of the industries in Karaganda province for which Nazarbayev was responsible as regional party secretary, but the results he achieved in them enhanced his reputation with the party hierarchy. However, the feeling of respect was not mutual.

Industrial progress was a vicious circle because each breakthrough cost us tremendous effort [Nazarbayev had recalled]. It was increasingly clear that this vicious circle was caused by the hideously deformed economic system that had practically turned its back on the people's needs.

These views, expressed now with the wisdom of hindsight, were kept to himself by Nazarbayev throughout the 1970s. In those days he was an ambitious young politician who had to work with the system, however much he might secretly despise its deformities. So he stayed quiet, toiled hard and earned his reward. In 1979, he received another promotion which changed him from a regional to a national figure. At the age of 38 he was elevated to the secretariat of the Kazakh Communist Party as the Party Secretary responsible for industry and economy, so becoming a member of the national cabinet and principal governing body of the Soviet Republic of Kazakhstan.

*   *   *

Nazarbayev's promotion to the secretariat of the Kazakh Communist Party in 1979 was initially an unsettling experience. He and his family did not enjoy their move to the republic's capital, Almaty.* Still less did they enjoy

* Almaty was formerly known as Alma-Ata. The name was changed in 1992. To avoid confusion the modern name is used throughout this book.

the rivalries and jealousies of Almaty society that surfaced in various forms in the early years after his appointment.

Nazarbayev had always been an unashamedly provincial figure. After his youth in a rural village, he had spent the next 20 years of his adulthood in the far from fashionable city of Temirtau. He and Sara lived there in a modest apartment. His circle of friends and relatives were mostly manual workers. Apart from the occasional visit to Moscow, he rarely travelled outside the Karaganda region. He still managed to do a fair amount of reading, principally newspapers and novels, but his horizons were limited. Away from the workaholic demands of his job, Nazarbayev's focus was on his home, his happy marriage to Sara, and the upbringing of their three daughters, Dariga (born 1963), Dinara (born 1967) and Aliya (born 1980). The simplicity of their family lifestyle left them unprepared for the complexities of their move into the official residence automatically assigned to a senior Communist Party politician in Almaty.

Almaty has for centuries thought of itself as a cosmopolitan city. Its location as a trading centre on the ancient silk route has given it the aura of an international meeting point of races, cultures and commercial enterprises. Under Soviet rule, Kazakhs were second if not third-class citizens in Almaty. They were an oppressed minority, sneered at by the ethnic Russians for their nomadic backgrounds. The *nomenklatura* or elitists of the Communist Party bureaucracy shared this low opinion of the native people of Kazakhstan. They did not change their opinion overnight just because a young Kazakh politician from Temirtau had risen with unusual speed to the rank of national cabinet minister.

The first signs of resentment about the meteoric rise of Nazarbayev came in the form of social snubs and slights. "As a family we were quite hurt by the treatment we received", recalls Dariga Nazarbayev. "When the party bosses called on us in our new home in Almaty, their wives would make unkind remarks about our cheap silverware and our dresses. We felt we were being ostracised by their circle."

Another curious manifestation of this ostracism was a trickle of anonymous letters that arrived at party headquarters criticising Nazarbayev's appointment and his conduct. The suspected authors were probably senior party officials who disliked the new secretary's unorthodoxy and informality. However, these were the very qualities that appealed to junior members of the administration in Almaty, particularly those who were Kazakhs. Among them was a young deputy minister in the department of culture, Kanat Saudabayev, who understood the tensions the new secretary's arrival created:

When Nazarbayev came to Almaty in 1979 he was like a breath of fresh air. Most senior officials behaved in the rigid and buttoned-up Moscow tradition of not interacting with lower ranking officials below their status. He was quite different. He shook up all the rules by doing things that party leaders had never done before, such as being the life and soul at social gatherings, playing the *dombra* at them, singing folk songs and being full of warmth and friendship to younger people. On Saturdays, he would come to the office in casual clothes. He also enjoyed sports. At that time people who were of his rank were not supposed to do things like play tennis. He took lessons in it and became very good at the game, but some of the Moscow people disapproved of that because tennis was thought to be a part of the Western way of life.

However unsettling it might have been for the old Muscovite hands in the Almaty administration, Nazarbayev's style was acceptable to his political leader, Dinmukhamed Kunayev, the First Secretary of the Kazakh Communist Party. Kunayev was himself a Kazakh, a man of two cultures who was completely at home in the Russian language and in the politics of the Kremlin. Nazarbayev was also fluent in both languages and his skills in Kremlinology were improving fast. But there was an important difference of outlook between the two outstanding Kazakh political leaders of their respective generations. While Kunayev was Moscow's man first and a Kazakh second, Nazarbayev was privately sceptical of the Moscow bureaucracy and openly proud of his Kazakh roots and culture. As Kanat Saudabayev saw it: "Nazarbayev was often going to Kazakh plays, reciting Kazakh poems and quoting Kazakh authors. This was almost unthinkable of a party official of his rank in the early 1980s, so he became a much-admired figure to the rising generation of Kazakh people."

The most important figure in the older generation of Kazakh people, Dinmukhamed Kunayev, also became a Nazarbayev admirer. The two men had barely known each other at the time of Nazarbayev's appointment to the Party Committee of the republic, but they soon established a personal rapport which became so warm that within a few months it was being compared to a father–son relationship. Perhaps the older man instinctively sensed that the time had arrived for him to be thinking about a Kazakh successor to himself in the post of First Secretary. Indeed, Kunayev voiced this thought in an unexpected comment to a group of senior party and government officials when explaining to them why he had given his new protégé the key responsibility for the industrial and economic development of the Republic. Speaking to an informal gathering of members of the national secretariat in 1981, Kunayev told them with less than tactful candour "None of you will be the next leader of the Soviet Republic of Kazakhstan. Don't be offended when I say this! Only Nursultan Nazarbayev has a good chance of being my successor as he is young enough and talented enough."

One of the ministers who heard Kunayev giving Nazarbayev this surprise endorsement was Sultan Dzhiyenbaev. "Some of our colleagues did not like it", he has recalled. "They became jealous of Nazarbayev. Personally, I was not jealous of him, perhaps because I was 20 years older. In my case, I was impressed by him and we soon established a good relationship."

There were other significant figures in the party hierarchy of Soviet controlled Kazakhstan who formed a favourable impression of Nazarbayev. One of them was Ibragim Yedilbayev, the deputy minister for non-ferrous metals. In 1979–1980, he toured over 30 mines and industrial plants with his new boss. "I liked Nazarbayev right from the start because he had so much energy", recalled Yedilbayev.

He called me into his office a month after his appointment and said that he wanted to go on a tour of the largest mines and metallurgical industries in all the provinces of Kazakhstan. When we went on this tour he amazed me by the intensity of his questions to the managers and workers. He was never a ceremonial visitor, he was always gathering information, taking detailed notes, and then afterwards sending out instructions which he followed up later to see if they had been carried out. He was a real hands-on party leader. In the mines and factories he visited there was always a lot of respect for him because he was a qualified metallurgist who had worked in the toughest part of the steel industry.

Although Nazarbayev was good on detail, he was even better at strategic thinking. He was keenly interested in the future long-term prospects for every mine or industrial plant he visited. Geology, reserves, capacity and marketing plans were always high on his agenda.

I could understand the way his mind worked as he began to form a strategy. It was to diversify away from the extractive industries towards the development of a manufacturing base [recalled Yedilbayev]. Despite all the difficulties in getting decisions from Moscow allowing us to do this, Nazarbayev managed to take some important initiatives. I will always remember the decisions he took at the Dzheskazgan copper mine in 1980. He himself came up with the idea of building a factory next to the mine to make copper wire. It was successful right from the start, and demonstrated that we had tremendous potential for developing a secondary manufacturing base for our minerals.

Nazarbayev was increasingly troubled by Moscow's practice of treating Kazakhstan as if it was one big quarry for the benefit of the rest of the Soviet Union. The republic was rich in deposits of zinc, copper, chrome, coal, lead, titanium, uranium, phosphorus and many other valuable minerals across the entire periodic spectrum. However, more than 90 per cent of the output was exported to other parts of the Soviet empire with no visible quid pro quo for Kazakhstan.

Our manufactured exports to other republics were a mere 12–15 per cent of finished products. The rest were raw materials [Nazarbayev has recalled]. I made great efforts to change this balance towards industry but I did not have many tangible results. The problem was that we needed new investment in the manufacturing industry, but we were not allowed to spend one rouble without permission from the central government. If we got anything at all it was only due to our persistence.

Networking in Moscow with charm, cunning and persistence became second nature to Nazarbayev as he struggled to win development projects for his republic. Who you knew in the corridors of power was far more important than the merits of the project being proposed. An amusing yet disturbing example of this unwritten law of the Kremlin jungle was provided by the story of how Nazarbayev won a diesel factory for northern Kazakhstan in 1982.

Soon after he became the Party Secretary responsible for industry in the Kazakh Republic, Nazarbayev discovered that the USSR's Council of Ministers were planning to build a huge diesel engine plant at Yelabuga in southern Russia. Nazarbayev wanted its location changed to Kustanai in northern Kazakhstan, a remote town which needed an influx of male workers because it had a large surplus of single young women employed in a textile factory. Bypassing the usual bureaucratic channels, Nazarbayev made an appointment to see the key Kremlin decision-maker, A. P. Kirilenko, a senior figure in the Politburo who was the de facto deputy to President Leonid Brezhnev. Kirilenko was typical member of the Soviet leadership's gerontocracy at that period. He was in his late 70s. His health was frail, his consumption of vodka was prodigious, and his faculties were in decline – so much so that he did not have the slightest idea who his visitor from Kazakhstan was. Despite or perhaps because of this ignorance he greeted Nazarbayev with the bear hugs and cheek kisses normally reserved for an intimate friend. After this enthusiastic welcome, Kirilenko's concentration wandered. He dozed off and paid little attention to Nazarbayev's presentation of the case for bringing industry to Kustanai. However, at the end of this strange conversation Kirilenko came to life and asked: "So what is it you want?"

"I want the diesel plant to be built in Kazakhstan."

"Who should I call about this?", demanded the Politburo chief.

"Call Polyakov, the minister for the auto industry", replied Nazarbayev.

Kirilenko fumbled in his desk until he found his Kremlin telephone directory. He handed it over to his visitor with the request: "Identify his number and dial it for me!"

When Minister Polyakov came on the line he heard: "This is Kirilenko. I am sending Comrade Nazarbayev to you. Do whatever he asks you."

A few minutes later Nazarbayev was presenting his case in the Minister's office. Polyakov seemed bemused, asking several times, "How did you get the support of Comrade Kirilenko?" Whatever his reservations about the decision-making process, the Minister for the automobile industry was not going to dispute an instruction from the second highest figure in the Politburo. Before the appointment was over the order to locate the Soviet Union diesel factory in Northern Kazakhstan had been signed. Nazarbayev had achieved a great strategic success for the industry of his republic. The jobs created by the project also brought romantic benefits for the ladies of Kustanai, who were delighted by the arrival of 5,000 new male workers in their city. It had been a strange route to these achievements but that was the way business was often done in the closing years of the Brezhnev era.

Leonid Brezhnev, General Secretary and President of the Soviet Union, 1964–1982, did not impress Nazarbayev. The ageing statesman made a disastrous state visit to Kazakhstan in 1980 to attend the celebrations marking the 60th anniversary of the republic. Accompanied by the entire Politburo, Brezhnev arrived at a reception for over 1,000 guests in the Government Reception House in Almaty. It was immediately obvious that the Soviet President was capable of neither coherent speech nor independent mobility. He had a vacant, expressionless gaze in his eyes. He could utter only monosyllabic grunts. He walked with great difficulty, supported by two large medical attendants on either side of him. It was not clear whether he even recognised his host and close friend, Dinmukhamed Kunayev, who had been appointed by Brezhnev to be First Secretary and leader of Kazakhstan for the past 20 years.

As the guests took their seats, Kunayev rose to propose a toast to the Soviet President. After Brezhnev's numerous official titles and positions had been declaimed, glasses were raised in his honour. But when the moment came for him to respond, Brezhnev struggled to his feet and without saying a single word tottered towards the exit. Everyone on the top table, including Nazarbayev, felt obliged to follow the leader as he abruptly departed from the Reception House, leaving the amazed anniversary guests behind him. As he was helped into his limousine and driven away, it became apparent that Brezhnev had completely forgotten where he was or why he had come there. "What can you feel for such a man other than pity?", was Nazarbayev's comment on this embarrassing spectacle.

The embarrassment of the ailing, ageing Soviet gerontocracy was to get even worse. Brezhnev's decline into impotent incapacity continued for the next two years until he died in 1982. His successor, Yuri Andropov, was terminally ill with cancer when he took over the reins of power and lasted for only 15 months. The next General Secretary, Konstantin Chernenko, suffered from such acute emphysema that he was barely able to carry out his official functions before he too passed away in March 1985. In Washington DC, President Ronald Reagan made the mordant comment "I keep making dates to meet the Soviet leaders, but they keep dying on me."

These deaths and terminal illnesses paralysed decision-making across the Soviet Union and deepened the gloom of economic and political stagnation. Yet one rejuvenating decision was taken in the Soviet Republic of Kazakhstan when the veteran Prime Minister, Bayken Ashimov, retired at the age of 68 after 20 years in his post. His obvious successor in terms of ability and reputation was Nazarbayev. At that time he enjoyed the wholehearted backing of the Soviet Union's most powerful appointee in Kazakhstan, First Secretary Dinmukhamed Kunayev, who recommended his nomination to the Politburo in Moscow. So in March 1984, Nursultan Nazarbayev, at the age of 44, was poised to become the youngest Prime Minister of any republic in the Soviet Union.

5

A Frustrated Prime Minister 1984–1986

Before Nazarbayev could take up his duties as Prime Minister, protocol required him to have an audience in Moscow with the General Secretary of the Communist Party of the Soviet Union, Konstantin Chernenko. Because the Soviet leader was in poor health, the appointment was difficult to arrange and devastating in the bad impressions created when it eventually did take place.

On his first visit to Moscow as Prime Minister-designate, Nazarbayev had to remain in his hotel room for three days waiting for the summons to Chernenko's office. Eventually the call came through with the unexpected message: "The General Secretary cannot see you now. He is ill. Go back home."

After returning to Kazakhstan for a week, Nazarbayev was recalled to Moscow where he was again required to stay cooped up in his hotel room for three days. On the third day he received the order: "Keep waiting. The General Secretary is not in Moscow. He is probably resting in his country residence." The following day Nazarbayev was told to go back to Almaty, as Chernenko was unavailable.

At his third attempt to have his appointment confirmed, Nazarbayev was escorted to the General Secretary's office by a senior Politburo member, Yegor Ligachev. Chernenko was unable to rise to greet his guest. His face was expressionless, his eyes were vacant and his skin had the grey pallor of terminal illness. As he stretched out his arm for a limp handshake, the movement seemed to give him breathing difficulties for he wheezed in uncomfortable gaspings, apparently unable to speak. Ligachev took charge of the meeting, introducing Nazarbayev with a summary of his career ending with the reminder that he would be the youngest Prime Minister in any of the Soviet republics. After Ligachev had finished this lengthy monologue, Chernenko finally made his only contribution to the proceedings, croaking out the question "How old is he?"

"He is coming up to 44. He will be the youngest Prime Minister", repeated Ligachev.

Chernenko then attempted to rise from his chair and walk towards Nazarbayev. But the General Secretary's emphysema was too severe for such an effort. His knees buckled and he collapsed in breathlessness. He was narrowly saved from crashing to the floor by a sturdy young medical attendant who caught his arm and helped him back to his chair. The meeting was over. "It left a terrible impression", recalled Nazarbayev.

Before his departure from Moscow another high-level meeting took place that made a favourable impact on Nazarbayev. This was his appointment with Mikhail Gorbachev, a new member of the Politburo who in the eyes of many Kremlin insiders was emerging as the likely successor to Chernenko. The two men, whose destinies were to become closely entwined in the final years of the Soviet Union, had met before. But this was the first time they felt able to have a wide-ranging conversation of profound political intimacy. Although the two words which came to be closely associated with Gorbachev – *perestroika* (reconstruction) and *glasnost* (openness) – were not mentioned, nevertheless both men found themselves kindred spirits tuned to the wavelength of reform. "I liked Nazarbayev very much", recalled Gorbachev. "He had an energetic and attractive personality. He was open to new ideas. He was smart. He was not an intellectual but he was street smart. We quickly established a good rapport."

Before the end of their meeting in January 1984, this rapport had become strong enough for Gorbachev to ask his guest a strange question: "What do you think, do you have a backbone?"

At first Nazarbayev did not understand the meaning of these words, but Gorbachev amplified them with the comment: "Difficult times lie ahead. There will be an assault, a fight. It won't be easy."

As he took office as Prime Minister of the Soviet Republic of Kazakhstan, Nazarbayev realised that the first fight on his hands was against inertia. His elderly predecessor, Bayken Ashimov, had survived in his job for two decades by supporting the status quo, suppressing uncomfortable facts, agreeing with Moscow and doing everything to please his political boss, Dinmukhamed Kunayev. Conformity to this pattern was expected of the new Prime Minister by Kunayev who regarded the Kazakhstan Council of Ministers as a sub-department of the Communist Party's central committee. Under this colonial style of government it had become the custom of the republic's Prime Minister to ensure that directives handed down from Moscow were rubber stamped in Almaty. Nazarbayev was determined to challenge this subservience which he believed was greatly to Kazakhstan's disadvantage. So as early as his second cabinet meeting he jettisoned the usual bland procedures. Deference was replaced by debate as he insisted on discussing and questioning the instructions from the Kremlin. Often he added to them, changed them, and issued new instructions of his own, together with a timetable for their implementation by his fellow ministers. As one of them said afterwards, "We realised that we were not going to be able to fool this man. We knew we would have to work a great deal harder to carry out his orders."

Nazarbayev set a fast pace with his own standards of hard work. Having previously held the industry portfolio, he knew that area of government well. But now he was chairing the Council of Ministers he needed to bring himself up to speed on all the departmental issues of the day, particularly agriculture, transport, welfare, housing and economic affairs.

Agriculture was a vital sector in Kazakhstan because its vast areas of cultivated land (approximately 150 million acres) played such a crucial role in the annual "battle for bread". This was the phrase that the Moscow propaganda machine used to describe the recurring problem of feeding the 250 million people of the Soviet Union. To brief himself on the republic's problems of failing harvests and disappointing livestock production, Nazarbayev appointed two specialists to advise him. One was an agricultural scientist, the other was a practical farmer. Because of the demands of the Prime Minister's schedule, these two experts meet their boss at 9 pm every evening to give him a daily tutorial on all aspects of agriculture. One young prime ministerial aide who attended these tutorials was Nurtai Abikayev.

As Mr Nazarbayev's assistant, I was amazed by how hard he worked night after night to master the subject. His curiosity was almost limitless [recalled Abikayev]. He would not be afraid to ask really detailed questions such as "how many seeds do you have to plant in each square metre of land and at what depth, in order to produce a good harvest at the target level?"

Moscow's targets for Kazakhstan's agriculture, and the republic's officially announced production figures in meeting them, were fanciful inventions. Nazarbayev soon unearthed the true facts and decided he must set the record straight in order to have realistic targets determined by the republic's true agricultural potential. However, he found himself obstructed at every turn by senior officials, some of them close to First Secretary Kunayev.

Livestock production was one area that particularly troubled Nazarbayev as his investigations progressed. In the Semipalatinsk region he discovered that there were 330,000 fewer head of livestock than the official figures had stated. "What are you planning to do about this?", he asked the regional leader, Sagidulla Kubashev, who had reported the missing cattle to his Prime Minister.

"What can I do when, up there, they told me not to make much noise about it?", replied Kubashev, pointing his finger towards the ceiling. "Besides, they have offered to restore the right number of livestock."

"Up there" meant the circle of officials around First Secretary Kunayev who exercised the ultimate administrative and political power in the Republic of Kazakhstan. The more Nazarbayev investigated the livestock situation, the more abuses he discovered. Sometimes he found blatant scams like the imaginary herd of horses near Kzyl-Orda. Their herdsmen were getting paid, but their 30,000 equestrian charges had mysteriously vanished. A more common fraud was the habit of skimming large numbers of livestock away from the state herds and off to private farms, some of them owned by government officials. The discrepancies in the livestock production figures caused by these corrupt activities were so huge that Nazarbayev decided to hold a recount of all the livestock in the Republic. He wrote two letters to the central committee of the Communist Party of Kazakhstan, requesting permission to start this recount. The permission was refused. Nazarbayev felt that Kunayev or his circle of top officials were protecting the wrongdoers. The Prime Minister and the First Secretary had a frank talk about the problem but nothing was ever done about it.

Another area of tension between Kunayev and Nazarbayev was the latter's growing importance as a well-connected networker in Moscow. For the previous 20 years Kazakhstan's relations with senior decision-makers in the Kremlin had been the preserve of the First Secretary. But from 1984 onwards, the Republic had a Prime Minister who knew his way around the corridors of power and was not afraid to speak boldly in them. Where Kunayev had been submissive in his dealings with the *nomenklatura*, Nazarbayev was assertive. One well-placed observer who noted this change of style was Kazakhstan's permanent representative to the USSR Council of Ministers, Sabit Zhadanov. He lived in, and was in charge of, the Kazakh Mission Residence; a hotel-style establishment in central Moscow which acted as a base for visiting delegations.

As Prime Minister Nazarbayev came here two or three times a month, so I saw a lot of him [recalled Zhadanov]. Unusually, he preferred to stay in our building rather than to accept one of the Kremlin's guest houses. He was a most effective operator in Moscow because he spoke perfect Russian and was a skilful negotiator with a combination of toughness and charm. He stood up for Kazakhstan's interests more vigorously than ever before. He was respected for that.

One mark of the growing respect was Kazakhstan's promotion in what was called "the constitutional order" at formal meetings of all 15 Soviet Republics. At these gatherings, which were held quarterly, the Prime Minister of each republic presented a report. For decades the opening order of reporting had been Russian, Ukraine, Belarus, Uzbekistan, Kazakhstan. From 1985 onwards, Kazakhstan was moved up two places in this batting order so that its reports were heard at No 3, immediately after the far more populous republics of Russia and Ukraine. This elevation was seen as a personal tribute to Nazarbayev. "His reports really impressed the Soviet Government", recalled Sabit Zhadanov. "Prime Minister Tikhonov of the USSR said that their meetings should hear from Kazakhstan as early as possible because Nazarbayev's presentation was such a good model of style and content that other republics should copy him."

As Prime Minister, Nazarbayev made many achievements which were of greater importance than being promoted in the speaking hierarchy of a Soviet Union constitution whose days were numbered. At home his most visionary policies were the development of the oil and gas industry, which was in its infancy in the early 1980s. "He took personal control of the large-scale projects to drill for oil and to build the natural gas installations", recalled the industry minister of the period, I. B. Yedilbayev. "It is because of the decisions he made over 20 years ago that Kazakhstan is today such a high energy-producing nation."

Some of the earliest decisions made by Nazarbayev in the energy sector of the economy were provoked by a disastrous blowout at an obscure oil-drilling borehole, No. T-37, in the Guriev district of the Caspian region. When drilling was in progress at this site in June 1985 at a depth of 4,000 metres, oil was not only struck, it exploded into a gusher which sent a gigantic fountain of raw crude shooting 150 metres above the surface and bursting into flames. For more than a year, the greatest experts and the most experienced fire-fighting units from all over the Soviet Union struggled unsuccessfully to bring this blowout under control. Although operational command of the disaster site was always in the hands of the First Vice Minister of the USSR Oil Industry, Nazarbayev made several visits to T-37 and was appalled by its environmental damage. Over 8 billion cubic metres of burning hydrogen sulphide were released into the atmosphere with catastrophic effects on the flora and fauna of the area. One oil worker died and dozens of fire-fighters suffered third degree burns. After 13 months of failed attempts to bring the flames under control, it was evident that the Soviet Oil Ministry lacked the technology and the expertise to cope with a blowout of this pressure. At one point in the drama, the Vice Minister from Moscow decided to suppress the blazing oil fountain by an atomic explosion. Nazarbayev, as Prime Minister of the republic, argued strongly against this plan on the grounds that it would bring radioactive fallout on the rural population living in farms and villages across the region. In the end, he won the argument. The atomic explosion plan was aborted. In its place the Texan oil blowout expert, Red Adair, was invited to implement his plan of drilling alternative pipeline routes into the T-37 well and pumping heavy chemical liquids into them. Four hundred days after the original explosion, the well was finally killed by this strategy. The worst blowout in the history of the Soviet Union's oil industry was over, although more than 34 million barrels of oil were lost in the disaster.

This episode left its mark on Nazarbayev in important ways. It was the first sign to him that the oilfield, known as Tengiz, on the Caspian shores of Kazakhstan, could have enormous potential. He also saw clearly that the oil ministry of the Soviet Union was far too backward in its technical and managerial expertise to exploit a field of this magnitude. "I realised that there was no modern technology in the USSR to develop a huge field such as Tengiz", said Nazarbayev. "I knew that one day we would have to turn to Western oil companies to reverse the neglect of our energy reserves."

Transport infrastructure was another neglected area. In 1984, 40 per cent of the republic's country towns could only be reached by dirt tracks. This inadequacy crippled rural communications and the movement of agricultural produce. Nazarbayev won budget battles in Moscow that allowed him to establish an infrastructure fund for transport links. With the new funding he has built over 2,000 kilometres of new roads. He also built airports with long runways near all the major provincial cities and industrial centres. "For the first time in our history we developed a proper road and aviation network", recalled Shamil Bekbolatov, the minister for transport from 1981 to 1992. "As a huge country we badly needed it but Nazarbayev was the first political leader to get it done."

"Getting it done" was Nazarbayev's trademark. In America he would have been called a "can-do" politician. Such a reputation was far harder to achieve in a centralised communist bureaucracy, but Nazarbayev was learning how to play the game with new initiatives. He was particularly interested in opening up the educational institutions of the republic to its native Kazakh people and to promoting the Kazakh culture. One of his key allies was the leading political lady in the republic, Manura Akhmetova, who served as Vice Chairperson of the Council of Ministers.

When he was Prime Minister, Mr Nazarbayev showed that he really cared about our cultural heritage [she had recalled]. Books, plays, and paintings by Kazakh artists and writers were dear to his heart. At that time the getting of an apartment was extremely difficult for people in the cultural world. So you can imagine what a difference it made when he issued a Prime Ministerial decree instructing that 260 apartments in Almaty should be allocated by the republic of Kazakhstan for writers, artists, composers, and people in the theatre.

Although Nazarbayev was breaking new ground with such political initiatives, his early years as Prime Minister were more notable for their setbacks than their successes. In the most important policy areas of heavy industry, agriculture and economic affairs he was frustrated by the general stagnation of the system and by the specific obstructionism of First Secretary Kunayev. One ray of light in the gloomy outlook was the appointment of Mikhail Gorbachev as General Secretary of the Soviet Communist Party on 11th March 1985. This vigorous 54-year-old, the first Soviet leader to have been born after the 1917 revolution, was a refreshing contrast to his decrepit predecessors. One of the key factors motivating Gorbachev's early calls for reform was his realisation that by all economic and industrial criteria, the Soviet Union had fallen badly behind its Western competitors. The new leader's understanding of this growing gap between communist and capitalist competitiveness derived from the overseas visits he had made in the early 1980s to the thriving economies of Helmut Kohl's West Germany, Pierre Trudeau's Canada and Margaret Thatcher's Britain.

Nazarbayev's frustrations over the sclerotic economic difficulties of Kazakhstan were similarly deepened by his awareness of international comparisons. In early 1985 he made his first official visit as Prime Minister to a country outside the Soviet Union – Austria. The day after he came back to Almaty from Vienna, he had lunch with his ministerial colleagues to report on his impressions. Nazarbayev described the prosperity of Austria's farmers who were growing so much grain that their production had to be limited to quota levels imposed by the government. "They are obviously very well off." He continued, "if that is rotting capitalism for you, it's not so bad."

The last few words were spoken as a humorous aside, but Nazarbayev was playing lightly on a well-known propaganda phrase to deliver a serious message. At that time one of the leading slogans of the Soviet Unions was: "Communism is flourishing. Capitalism is rotting." To have openly attacked this doctrine would have amounted to disloyalty.

All of us around the table knew that Nazarbayev was speaking the truth and meaning us to take his report on economic conditions in Austria in earnest [recalled Eric Gukasov, the Vice Chairman of the Council of Ministers]. But with Kunayev at the lunch it would have been dangerous to make such a criticism. That is why Nazarbayev presented it light heartedly as a throwaway line. Kunayev pretended not to understand the joke, but it was easy to notice that he was irritated.

The feelings of irritation between Kazakhstan's First Secretary and Prime Minister were becoming mutual. One of the tensions between them was Nazarbayev's refusal to play the annual game of plans and budgets by Moscow's traditional rules. His objection to the two most powerful budgetary authorities of the Soviet Union – the State Planning Committee and the State Supplies Committee – was that their methods were primitive and their ministers were corrupt. The way the system worked was that every rouble of revenue generated by state enterprises in the republics had to be sent upwards to Moscow, which then allocated resources downwards to the regional departments and projects favoured by the central planners. Their favouritism was often influenced by the personal gifts they received at the meetings when annual budget plans were decided.

Nazarbayev's first rebellion against these practices came soon after his appointment as Prime Minister when the chairman of Kazakhstan's planning department came to request a large allocation of funds for bonuses and overhead expenses for his staff to defend the plan.

"What are these payments for?", asked Nazarbayev.

"Don't you know that we're going to Moscow to defend the plan for next year?"

"So what?"

"Well, we will have to work with all the department heads at the State Planning Committee, invite them to our rooms, and offer them hospitality."

As this dialogue continued, Nazarbayev discovered that the word "hospitality" took on a far wider meaning than good wining and dining – important though this was in the rituals of planning the Soviet Union's budget. He was briefed on the backhander system by which presents were left for ministers on cloakroom shelves outside hospitality suites. He was also given detailed information on the specific gifts the recipients were expecting. "I'll never forget how I was told in all seriousness how one minister liked to be given piglets, another fresh tomatoes, and another chateau-bottled wines", he has recalled.

This minor venality at parties was matched by mega-incompetence at the planning meetings. No figure or statistic announced by ministers could be relied on. Indeed, it was widely known that there was always a shortfall of about 20–30 per cent below the officially declared resources and the budget allocations. So Moscow planning figures were fictions, distorted still further by cronyism and corruption. Nazarbayev despised this system but had to accommodate it before he began arguing for an alternative. According to his own scornful summary of the budgetary tactics he had to descend to in his first months as Prime Minister:

If you were on good terms with the minister of finance you could get a few extra million roubles. If you were friends with the chairman of the State Supplies Committee you could have cement, metal and timber. No one particularly cared that they were taking someone else's share out of the common pot, nor suffered any guilty conscience…. Whether you liked it or not, you had to follow the unwritten laws, so you had to fawn, give presents and offer hospitality. Otherwise not you, but your republic, your industry, your factory, would have to go on a starvation diet. The only way to get money was to be clever.

Nazarbayev was certainly clever but he could also be confrontational. Emboldened by Gorbachev's appointment as General Secretary and fortified by the new leader's clarion calls for transparency (*glasnost*) in public affairs, Nazarbayev made himself a nuisance to the *nomenklatura*. There was an aggressive streak in him as he began fighting his campaign to change the balance of economic power between the republics and the central government in Moscow. One of the Prime Minister's closest aides at the time of his early clashes with the old guard in Moscow over development funding for Kazakhstan was Nurtai Abikayev. "Mr Nazarbayev was the first Kazakh politician ever to fight for more decentralisation and local decision-making", he has recalled.

He criticised the party bosses in Moscow for exploiting Kazakhstan as a raw-material supplier to the rest of the Soviet Union. He would say that it is not fair that Kazakhstan sends 95 per cent of its mineral production to the other republics for *kopeks* [pennies], and that these republics are then allowed to process our materials and make a good profit from them. He made this point over and over again, often very sharply. I remember him saying "if this is Moscow's idea of a planned economy, the plans are wrong".

Senior officials in the highest echelons of the Soviet bureaucracy did not like being told they were wrong – particularly by a brash young Kazakh politician whose language could be strident. One or two of the ministers who had felt the lash of Nazarbayev's tongue called Kunayev in Almaty to say: "Please explain to your Prime Minister that this is not the way things should be done. It is the centre of the system in Moscow which knows what is best for the Soviet Union as a whole."

Kunayev was unsettled by these criticisms of his appointee. His former favourite was fast becoming an embarrassment. As a senior member of the Politburo, an intimate of Brezhnev, and the unassailable First Secretary of Kazakhstan, Kunayev had reigned supreme as controller of his republic's relations with Moscow. Suddenly those good relations were being threatened by Nazarbayev rocking the boat. It was a destabilisation of the united front between First Secretary and Prime Minister that was soon to widen into political conflict.

* * *

There were many signs of the growing tension between Nazarbayev and Kunayev. One of the most interesting of them came a few weeks after Gorbachev had become leader of the Soviet Union, when he visited the city of Tselinograd (later renamed Astana) in northern Kazakhstan. The local Communist Party leaders laid on a lunch in honour of the new General Secretary who was accompanied by his wife, Raisa, and a large entourage of

Moscow officials. Heading the welcoming committee were Kunayev and Nazarbayev, supported by the entire cabinet of the republic. Despite the presence of so many prominent politicians, it was the non-political figure of Mrs Raisa Gorbachev who did most of the talking. Her loquacity irritated Nazarbayev:

Raisa quickly began to dominate the conversation [he has recalled]. Within a few moments it became clear to me that she had an opinion on each and every subject under the sun which her husband always took very seriously. We sat listening in silence as she explained her categorical and often downright absurd opinions. At one point she declared that Kazakhstan, although an agricultural republic, did not produce its own wine. I dared to contradict her.

Nazarbayev's contradiction was provocative. He said that Kazakh wine was so good that everyone should taste a glass of it immediately. This was personally impertinent to Mrs Gorbachev and politically insubordinate to her husband who had recently made a major speech urging all good Soviet citizens to abstain from the temptations of alcohol. Kunayev kicked the Prime Minister under the table. Despite the blow to his shins, Nazarbayev became even more reckless. Not only did he order the waiter to bring in several bottles of the local wine, a few minutes later he sent for bottles of the local vodka as well, claiming that no one should be expected to make do on wine alone as it was such an unseasonably cold day. Kunayev was outraged by his Prime Minister's behaviour, but could do nothing about it because Gorbachev cheerfully concurred with Nazarbayev's suggestion. As the General Secretary downed his vodka it was evident that he had forgotten about his self-proclaimed role as the Soviet Unions' leading abstainer – at least for his day out in Kazakhstan.

Nazarbayev's defiance of his boss surfaced more publicly three months later when on 15th May 1985 he addressed one of the quarterly meetings of the republic's central committee. Instead of the usual anodyne Prime Ministerial report, Nazarbayev gave the committee a devastating 40-minute critique of what was going wrong with the administration of the state budget in several of the regions. The general thrust of his analysis was that essential services in rural areas such as housing, road-building, and welfare facilities were being denied funds because of overspending on what he called "building pompous structures" in Almaty. By this he meant spacious residences and offices in the heart of the republic's capital, constructed specially for officials. Even an exclusive city bathhouse had been built for their use. There was fierce moral indignation in the voice of the 44-year-old Prime Minister as he described how over 3,000 families headed by war veterans were having to endure primitive and squalid housing conditions while senior party officials openly jumped the waiting list queue by having three- and four-bedroomed apartments allocated to their relatives on a priority basis. "In the past two and a half years the city's executive committee has provided only 1 per cent of the capital's housing to people on legitimate waiting lists", claimed Nazarbayev, concluding with the charge that these losers were being denied their right to decent housing by the abuse of power on the part of senior officials. "They make these arrangements in all sorts of illegal ways. This demands a special investigation", he said.

Nazarbayev's speech was greeted not with applause but with stunned silence. As he walked away from the podium the ghostly hush that had fallen over the hall was broken by a final word from the chairman of the central committee, First Secretary Kunayev. "The information will be taken into account. The meeting is adjourned", he intoned in the deadest of deadpan voices. Within hours of this chilly ending "a wall of alienation arose between Kunayev's associates and myself", said Nazarbayev.

The alienation soon became a personal rift between the ageing First Secretary and the reforming Prime Minister. In September 1985, Nazarbayev sent his boss a memorandum recommending a massive house cleaning in the party bureaucracy, which would have resulted in the dismissal of many corrupt or incompetent officials. Kunayev summoned his subordinate and posed the question: "What do you want me to do about these ideas of yours?"

"Call a meeting of all the leaders of the regions and let's get it done", replied Nazarbayev.

After a long silence Kunayev said, "Look, you have been working with me for six years now. You know that in Moscow they think well of Kazakhstan. Do you want to ruin that good opinion? These irregularities are happening all over the Soviet Union. Do we want to be the first republic to start a campaign against all this past mess?"

The Prime Minister's answer to Kunayev's rhetorical question was "Yes". So in defiance of the First Secretary's resistance to the proposed clean-up, Nazarbayev began sweeping with his new broom. He soon found that his policy and personnel changes were blocked at every turn. Alert to the dangers of being at loggerheads with his immediate superior, Nazarbayev kept his lines of communication open with Gorbachev. At one of their Moscow meetings in November 1985, he told the General Secretary "Kunayev is getting very unhappy with me". After hearing a detailed account of the tensions between the two Kazakh leaders, Gorbachev responded "Do you remember me asking if you had enough backbone for a fight? Well here you go! These people in the old guard hate you and they probably hate me – but we have to fight them."

These words of reassurance were interpreted by Nazarbayev to mean that he had Gorbachev's protection. But the Soviet leader, who was at the height of his international acclaim in the mid-1980s, had neither the time nor the inclination to bother himself with internal squabbling in the Politburo of Kazakhstan. So although Nazarbayev continued to hear from senior Moscow sources such as Yegor Ligachev that Gorbachev liked and supported him, this backing from the top in Moscow was theoretical rather than practical when it came to the pressures on the ground in Almaty.

On his side of the power struggle, Kunayev seemed to recognise that while he could not remove his troublesome Prime Minister politically, nevertheless he could do serious damage to Nazarbayev psychologically. The First Secretary's principal weapon in this war of nerves was the KGB.

By the autumn of 1985, Nazarbayev became aware that a full-scale KGB investigation was being conducted against him. It took the form of bugging, personal surveillance by none-too-subtle watchers and, above all, an official inquiry into his finances.

It was a nasty business [said Nazarbayev's long serving personal aide, Vladimir Ni]. I was questioned myself in great detail. The KGB wanted to know if my boss had used state funds to buy his clothes, or if shopkeepers and food suppliers had been put under pressure to give him free gifts. There were even stories put in the paper saying that he had spent huge sums of government money building an elaborate tomb for his parents.

These allegations came to nothing because they were untrue. The graves of Nazarbayev's parents were simple memorials, paid for out of his own pocket. The inquiry into improper expenses collapsed when, to Nazarbayev's delighted surprise, Vladimir Ni produced a huge brown envelope of receipts for the KGB, covering every purchase made on behalf of the Prime Minister in the two years since he took office. The most recurrent expense was a far from costly weekly shopping bill for eggs and sausages, which Ni regularly fried up for his boss in a small office kitchen.

It was almost the only dish I ever cooked for him [recalled Ni]. He wasn't at all picky about his food. He was a workaholic who started at 8:45 sharp every morning, and often stayed in the office till after midnight. He usually wanted to eat as quickly as possible and get on with the job. He didn't have expensive tastes and he was very careful not to accept gifts. The KGB could not get anything on him.

Although Vladimir Ni felt that the investigations were running into the sand, Nazarbayev himself was more upset by the pressure than he admitted to his staff. Part of his concern was generated by his family. "My wife Sara was so worried by the surveillance and by the rumours that I would soon be taken off to prison that she became quite seriously ill", recalled Nazarbayev. "So she lay in bed for days at a time. At one point she said to me, "why don't we just give up and go back to Temirtau. You are still a good metallurgist." "Don't rush me, the steel plant will always be there", was Nazarbayev's reply.

For all the brave face he showed to his wife and to the world during the months of the KGB's operations against him in 1985–1986, Nazarbayev was becoming demoralised. In December 1985, he sent a private letter to Mikhail Gorbachev asking for permission to step down as Prime Minister of Kazakhstan. "It is no longer possible for me to continue to work in this way", wrote Nazarbayev. In response, Gorbachev despatched Dmitri Valavoy, who occupied an important position as Deputy Editor of *Pravda*, to talk to the beleaguered Prime Minister in Almaty. Valavoy urged Nazarbayev to hit back at the Kunayev regime by giving an interview to *Pravda* about the irregularities and corruption at the highest levels in the Communist Party of Kazakhstan.

"No, I don't want to spread this dirt all around the Soviet Union", said Nazarbayev.

"If you don't fight, these people will eventually get you", warned Valavoy.

"Well let them get me!", responded Nazarbayev, "but I will first speak out here in Almaty."

This conversation with Gorbachev's secret envoy, combined with the fears and frustrations that were undermining his spirits and those of his family, were the genesis for the gamble Nazarbayev took in an extraordinary speech he delivered at the 16th Party Congress of Kazakhstan in February 1986. A few days before the opening of the Congress, Nazarbayev's work patterns changed so unusually that his assistant, Vladimir Ni, realised that something must be up:

He shut himself up in his office and stayed there on his own until 3am [recalled Ni]. He would go for night strolls. He did not tell me what he was doing. I guessed he might be making some special preparations for his speech to the Party Congress, but there was nothing special about the text that was sent out in advance to Kunayev's office.

The official text was a decoy. The real text Nazarbayev had been preparing with such intensity contained bombshells of unprecedented criticism, savage humour and vitriolic personal attack. The custom of the Party Congress was that the Prime Minister carried out the traditional task of welcoming the annual report presented by First Secretary. Instead of performing this ritual in the usual sycophantic manner, Nazarbayev launched an attack. With a plethora of statistical detail he criticised what he called "the outrageous facts" of failure, waste and theft in agriculture and other key sectors of the economy. Then he returned to the crisis in housing for ordinary workers which he again said was caused by the budget being diverted into prestige projects, luxurious apartments and grand country residences for senior officials. "The working class from which many of these officials came has a right to be indignant about this kind of aristocratic behaviour" declared Nazarbayev.

Changing the tone of his speech, Nazarbayev deployed the weapon of humour when he ridiculed the incompetence of certain senior Politburo figures. His main victim was E. Jerembayev, who occupied a sinecure post in the cabinet with the horticultural title of Minister for Fruits and Berries.

Do you know what the Minister for Fruits and Berries does to earn his official salary? [asked Nazarbayev in playful tone]. All he does is to deliver baskets of fruits to the offices of members of the Politburo. In the season of watermelons, he comes round with a basket of the finest watermelons. When apples are on the trees, he delivers the finest apples. That's his only job, delivering gifts to other ministers.

The audience were laughing as Nazarbayev warmed to his theme.

In winter when there are no fruits and berries, the Minister has difficulty filling his day. But last week he did something. He delivered three glass jars of strawberry, raspberry and blackberry jam to my office. We sent them back. Did you get them back Minister?

Nazarbayev shouted this last question directly at the elderly politician who was being lampooned. This unfortunate Minister, who had been fast asleep in his chair throughout the proceedings of the Congress, suddenly woke up with a start. Hearing the laughter and applause, but not realising that it was at his expense, Minister Jerembayev clapped enthusiastically. His reaction made him look even more foolish, and doubled the decibels of laughter in the hall.

After the slapstick comedy, Nazarbayev moved towards his real target, Dinmukhamed Kunayev. However, he did not take his adversary head on. Instead, the object for Nazarbayev's most vitriolic criticism was Askar Kunayev, the notoriously alcoholic brother of the First Secretary. Askar was the President of the Academy of Sciences of Kazakhstan, responsible for the Research and Development programme of Kazakhstan's industries. His stewardship of this influential post was so nominal that it had become disgraceful. Askar Kunayev was a hopeless drunkard, who rarely visited his office, never turned up at cabinet meetings, and was regarded as a public nuisance for his nocturnal carousing around Almaty. His hangovers from these binges were so severe that he was unable to get out of bed on Mondays, and did not appear in his office on Tuesdays, Wednesdays and Thursdays; which at the Academy of Sciences were known as "The President's Yoghurt days". But because of his fraternal relationship to the First Secretary, this absenteeism was covered up. No open criticism was ever made of Askar Kunayev – until Nazarbayev went for his jugular on 16th February, in his address to the Party Congress.

The leadership of the Academy of Sciences, headed by it president, Askar Kunayev, is beset by inertia [declared the Prime Minister]. None of the Academy's institutes were included in the republic's industrial, scientific and industrial complexes. In the whole last five year plan period not one single license for an invention was signed.... Today at this Congress it is necessary to say that the Academy of Sciences is an organisation not subject to criticism. Apparently that is why the Academy's president does not attend meetings of the Council of Ministers. He is essentially not doing his job. I think it is time to compel him to do his duty.

By the standards of the time this was an unprecedented display of political insubordination.

It is hard to imagine an attack more calculated to infuriate First Secretary Dinmukhamed Kunayev than this personalised onslaught on his brother Askar. Nazarbayev knew this, but had thrown his usual caution to the winds. "I was just sick and tired of living under all this stress and pressure for more than a year. I just wanted to get it over with", he explained, "so I decided to bet the ranch on this speech."

The outcome of the bet was hard to read. Kunayev was predictably furious, but he could not make any immediate moves against a Prime Minister whose selection had been approved in Moscow by the General Secretary. Appointees at that level could only be dismissed on the orders of the Politburo of the USSR. So Nazarbayev had time on his side to wait and see how the after-effects of his speech played out.

In its short-term impact, the speech appeared to do Nazarbayev's cause more harm than good. Inside the Congress Hall, the attack on Askar Kunayev was greeted with stunned silence. Immediately afterwards, even the supporters of the Prime Minister appeared to think he had gone too far. "Surely you could have delivered your message more diplomatically", was the plaintive comment of one of his closest allies in the cabinet, the culture minister, Manura Akhmetova. However, in the next few weeks the tide of party opinion turned in Nazarbayev's favour, as regional leaders from all over the country came to see him privately, congratulating him on the speech and assuring him of their support. On the other hand there was outrage from Kunayev's circle of friends, who venerated the First Secretary with an almost religious reverence as the political patriarch of Kazakhstan. These loyalists turned on Nazarbayev, accusing him of "slandering the great son of the Kazakh people". Such recriminations created a poisonous political atmosphere in Almaty. Its most feverish symptoms were a rash of anonymous letters, smears, rumours and charges directed against Nazarbayev. In the three weeks following his speech, 53 official complaints were lodged against him. All of them were ordered to be formally investigated by the republic's prosecutors, various commissions of inquiry and the KGB. "This was a terrible time for us as a family", recalled Dariga Nazarbayev. "We felt the hostility of certain political leaders in most unpleasant ways. We were really under pressure."

The pressure increased on Nazarbayev during the summer of 1986, when Kunayev's political fortunes received an unexpected boost. It had been widely forecast that Gorbachev would use the 27th Congress of the Communist Party of the Soviet Union in June to initiate his reformist agenda and, as part of it, to retire certain members of the Kremlin's old guard, including the 74-year-old Kunayev. Instead, the veteran leader was reconfirmed as First Secretary of Kazakhstan and reappointed as a senior figure in the Soviet Politburo.

Strengthened by these developments, Kunayev decided to move against his Prime Minister. In October he flew secretly to Moscow for a meeting with Gorbachev with the intention of securing the General Secretary's agreement for the dismissal of Nazarbayev, who was described by Kunayev as "a dangerous man who must be stopped". This attack misfired. According to Gorbachev:

I was very surprised when Kunayev told me he had a big problem with Nursultan Nazarbayev, because in the past those two had been like a father and son. Of course I knew that there were difficulties in Kazakhstan but that was true of every republic in the Soviet Union by that time. It was a period when new leaders were evolving. Perhaps that was what made Kunayev so uneasy about his "son", because anyone who knew Nazarbayev soon realised that he was never afraid to confront and to challenge. When he saw a problem he took it head on. That was his style.

Since Gorbachev had himself encouraged Nazarbayev to develop his confrontational style in at least two exhortations about having "backbone for a fight", and since the Kazakh Prime Minister was well regarded in Moscow as a reliable ally in the struggle to implement *perestroika*, Kunayev's proposition that this ally should be summarily dismissed was not what the General Secretary wanted to hear. Perhaps realising that his Plan A, to remove Nazarbayev from office, was not getting a good reception, Kunayev introduced a bizarre Plan B, which was to send his Prime Minister on a world tour of permanent but impotent diplomatic discussions. "Halfway through the conversation Kunayev asked me if I could offer Nazarbayev a new job of being responsible for all the external trade and economic relations of the Soviet Union", Gorbachev has recalled. "Apparently, the purpose was to keep him travelling outside Kazakhstan for as long as possible."

This novel idea of sending Nazarbayev into exile by air tickets did not appeal to the Soviet leader. He, for quite different reasons, was becoming increasingly disenchanted with Kunayev. A few weeks earlier a deputation of three top officials from Kazakhstan, headed by Oleg Miroshkin, had been in Moscow describing the growing problems of economic and political stagnation in their republic. In a private meeting with Gorbachev, they had urged him to consider making changes in the leadership. That request was in itself the equivalent of a vote of no confidence by his colleagues in Kunayev, who was now confirming his perilous position by asking for the sacking of his Prime Minister. It was evident to the General Secretary that the top politicians of Kazakhstan were in turmoil.

I said to myself, something is seriously wrong here [recalled Gorbachev] so instead of agreeing to Kunayev's plan to get rid of Nazarbayev, I put forward an alternative. I told him about the criticisms made by the three visiting officials and then I said "Dinmukhamed Akemedovich, I take your words very seriously. What I would like you to do is to call a meeting of the leading officials of Kazakhstan, inviting them here to Moscow to sit down with all the members of the Politburo of the Soviet Union. Let's discuss the problems of Kazakhstan openly together, and together we will find the right solution."

When Kunayev heard these words, he realised that his days were numbered. If he agreed to a joint meeting in front of the USSR's Politburo, it would be an open admission that his own power was waning. It would also lead to a head-on confrontation with Nazarbayev, which the younger man might well win. To avoid such a humiliation Kunayev yielded immediately. "Mikhail Sergeyevich, if that is your suggestion then I will retire", he told Gorbachev, who formally accepted the First Secretary's resignation eight weeks later.

The Kunayev era had one last act of drama that was to leave behind a legacy of trouble for the Soviet Union and to usher in an era of change for Kazakhstan. This was the valedictory meeting in Moscow at which Gorbachev consulted the outgoing First Secretary on the appointment of his successor. It had a most unexpected outcome.

Passing the torch of leadership in Kazakhstan to Nazarbayev was the almost inevitable result once Kunayev had taken the decision to go into retirement. The strong expectation in the Kremlin was that the Prime Minister would become the new supremo in the republic. Nazarbayev was by far the strongest candidate in terms of experience, nationality, acceptability to Moscow and all-round leadership ability. Although he had made many enemies in the Kunayev circle with his criticisms of the economic stagnation and corruption, these frictions had never quite exploded into open personal combat between the two top politicians. Even though Nazarbayev's frustrations had led him into some considerable disloyalty to his boss during the past 18 months, nevertheless it was widely anticipated that there would be an orderly, if cool, transition from the First Secretary to the Prime Minister.

Mikhail Gorbachev was expecting the succession of Nazarbayev. So he was startled when at his farewell interview with Kunayev the following exchange took place:

Gorbachev: "May I now ask for your recommendation as to who should succeed you? After all, you have been running this country for the past 24 years. Who do you recommend?

Kunayev: "Right now there is no real candidate for the succession. There are several people intriguing and moving around, but none of them are really capable of leadership. So I advise you to send a good Russian strongman to lead Kazakhstan."

Gorbachev was surprised by this advice but was not averse to taking it. As a Russian strongman himself, he had faith in the notion that another member of the same club could be the right leader to sort out Kazakhstan's problems. But the General Secretary did not make the decision alone. He took it to the Politburo who agreed with Kunayev. No one present at the Politburo meeting seems to have suspected that the departing First Secretary might have been motivated by feelings of bitterness or jealousy towards Nazarbayev. Indeed, the general conclusion was that Kunayev's advice on the succession had been given for reasons of patriotic statesmanship. "The Politburo approved it because they could not believe that Kunayev would wish his republic ill", recalled Gorbachev. "That was why we followed his recommendation. We fell into the trap that the old fox had set for us. And we made a big mistake."

6

December 1986 and its Consequences

The big mistake made by Mikhail Gorbachev in December 1986 was to reject Nursultan Nazarbayev for the post of First Secretary of Kazakhstan. Instead, he sent a senior Russian official, Gennady Kolbin, to fill the vacancy left by the forced retirement of Dinmukhamed Kunayev. This was not merely an erroneous choice of appointee. It was a grave misjudgement which had profound strategic and historic consequences. This was because the demonstrations which followed the arrival of Kolbin proved to be the first sign of the nationalities problem which came to haunt, and eventually to destroy, the Soviet Union.

Nazarbayev was not surprised by the departure of Kunayev, since he had been anticipating it for several months. However, like everyone else in Kazakhstan, Nazarbayev was astonished by the appointment of Kolbin. This First Secretary of the Ulyanovsk region of Russia was a traditional Soviet apparatchik and a protégé of Gorbachev. Unfortunately, these were his only qualifications for his new job. Kolbin had no previous knowledge of or connections with Kazakhstan. He could not speak a word of the Kazakh language; he had never visited the republic; he was utterly unknown to its people. His appointment came as a shock because it was seen as a colonial-style reversion to the old "Moscow-knows-what's-best" mindset of centralised autocracy. This apparently contemptuous attitude towards the non-Russian republics seemed all the more intolerable in Kazakhstan because Gorbachev had been raising hopes of new political thinking which would give a greater degree of autonomy to the regions of the Soviet Union.

Nazarbayev learned that he had been passed over for the job of First Secretary on 15th December 1986, when Kolbin arrived in Almaty accompanied by Gyorgy Razumovsky, the secretary of the Central Committee of the Communist Party of the Soviet Union. The following day, a meeting of the Kazakhstan Central Committee was called with only one item on the agenda – "organisational questions". This was a well-known Soviet euphemism for senior personnel changes. At the meeting, Razumovsky announced the retirement of Kunayev and proposed Kolbin as the sole candidate to fill the vacancy. In stunned silence, Razumovsky's nominee was elected by a unanimous show of hands from all present. The meeting was over after 18 minutes.

Nazarbayev was inwardly upset, yet outwardly he gave no sign of his feelings. Although he thought that Kolbin's appointment was "old-style decision-making at its worst", he kept silent and made no attempt to criticise, let alone oppose, the decision. Like the rest of his central committee members and fellow ministers, Nazarbayev had been trained in the spirit of military-style obedience to Moscow. However, this subservient attitude was not shared by the younger generation of Kazakhstan.

It was the students of Almaty who made the early moves of protest against the imposition of a new First Secretary who was not a Kazakh. The most prominent student leader was Nurtai Sabilyanov, a 24-year-old graduate working on his doctoral thesis at the Institute of Economics. As he heard the official announcement on the radio of Kolbin's appointment, on the evening of 16th December, Sabilyanov was filled with passionate indignation:

I said to my fellow students in the dorm, "Who is this Mr Kolbin guy from Russia? How come there is not a single Kazakh in this huge republic worthy of this job? We have never before been asked to accept a leader who is not from this country, so why should we accept it now? If we allow Moscow to impose this outsider on us, it will be a blow to the heart and confidence of the Kazakh people!"

Sabilyanov was a handsome young man of considerable charisma and speaking ability. His words electrified his own dormitory. Before the evening was out he had addressed his student contemporaries at the nearby institutes of agriculture, veterinary training, engineering, teacher training, science and art. They were equally fired up with anger over the Kolbin appointment. "I persuaded them that we should all go to the square at 9 o'clock the next morning to present our arguments to the leaders from Moscow, and try to persuade them to change their bad decision", recalled Sabilyanov.

Nazarbayev knew nothing of these plans that were being laid in college dormitories. When he arrived in his office on the morning of 17th December, one of his aides told him that a young people's march had begun, and that several hundred of them were arriving in the open space outside the central committee building that was then known as Brezhnev Square. Many of the students were carrying banners and placards proclaiming slogans such as "We want a Kazakh leader", "Down with dictation", "Every nation needs its own national leader", "We're for a Leninist nationalities policy" and "We have *perestroika* but where's democracy?" Apart from the waving of these banners and some occasional chanting the demonstrators were peaceful and good-natured. The initial marchers were no more than 300 in number, predominantly from universities and educational institutes.

Nazarbayev could not see the demonstration from his government office but, having been given eyewitness descriptions of it from other colleagues with offices overlooking Brezhnev Square, he decided to move to the scene of the action. Calling his driver, he set off in his official car but was soon surrounded by many more hundreds of young people and workers marching through the streets of central Almaty. Nazarbayev decided to get out of his car and walk with the protestors. Soon, he was talking to the student leaders. "Nazarbayev's main concern was to warn us that we could easily be hurt", recalled Nurtai Sabilyanov. "He kept saying, 'don't let this get out of hand. I will report your views, but be patient. Moscow always chooses the leader and they are not going to change their minds'."

By the time Nazarbayev arrived in Brezhnev Square, the size of the demonstration had grown to about 2,000 young men and women. But the atmosphere was good-natured. Although there were increasing numbers of banners in the Kazakh or Russian languages, and more slogans being chanted through megaphones, the mood of the gathering was relatively calm. This tranquillity was not to be found at Nazarbayev's next port of call, which was the office of the ideology secretary of the Communist Party. Because it had large windows overlooking the square, many senior party officials, including the new First Secretary Gennady Kolbin, had gathered there to observe the demonstration.

The atmosphere among these watching party officials was close to panic. Protest demonstrations of this size and nature were almost unknown in the Soviet Union, particularly in Kazakhstan which had the reputation of being the most peaceful and ethnically harmonious of the republics. The Moscow representatives who had flown down for the installation of Kolbin had no idea how to handle the situation. Looking wildly around for someone to blame, they made vague accusations in the direction of the local Kazakh ministers for allowing such nationalist feelings to get out of hand. However, the local ministers were themselves upset and divided about what to do. Nazarbayev urged caution and said that the situation should be analysed carefully before any action was taken against the demonstrators. He suggested that officials should go and mingle with the crowds and engage in a dialogue with them. This advice was initially ignored.

Gennady Kolbin, on his first day in office as First Secretary, was listening to many sources of advice, some of them contradictory. His Moscow handlers, principally from the KGB and the Central Committee of the Soviet

81

Union, recommended the authoritarian approach of suppressing the demonstrators by force. To this end, the Almaty garrison of the Soviet army was put on full alert, the police were ordered to cordon off the square, and all police reserves were called out. However, difficulties in this strategy soon began to emerge as it became clear that many of the police, particularly the reserves, were sympathetic to the demonstrators. For example, in the key district of Frunze, adjacent to Brezhnev Square, the police reserves were lined up in preparation for a baton charge against the protestors. For this purpose two lorryloads of steel batons were delivered to the Head of Frunze district, Nurtai Abikayev, a former aide to Nazarbayev. But Abikayev had misgivings as to whether his volunteer police reserves, many of whom were academics and members of the intelligentsia, would actually wield their batons in anger against the students. "I thought, this is all wrong. We are not going to do this", recalled Abikayev, "so I did not arm our volunteer policemen with steel batons, even though this meant defying an instruction that had been issued by a senior member of the Central Committee."

Similar confusions of order, counter order and disorder prevailed through-out the day of 17th December in Almaty. The commander of the Soviet troops of the Central Asian military district, General Vladimir Lobov, refused to send his soldiers out into the streets, telling Kolbin: "By law I am not allowed to involve the army in a civil conflict." This was a courageous decision that undoubtedly prevented a far worse bloodbath than the one which did eventually occur. At the time, however, the military's resistance to requests for help in suppressing the demonstration only increased the panic factor in the leadership. One of their major concerns was the number of workers supporting the students. To alleviate that problem, Nazarbayev was told by Kolbin to ensure that the unrest did not spread to the major factories in the city. Having carried out this mission, he was then asked to implement his original suggestions of entering into a dialogue with the demonstrators. So Nazarbayev, accompanied by Kamalidenov, the ideology secretary; Mendy-bayev, First Secretary of the Almaty regional party committee; and Mukashev, the chairman of the Supreme Soviet Praesidium, went down to the podium in Brezhnev Square. This quartet was given a rough ride by the increasingly boisterous crowd.

When the officials tried to speak, they were initially interrupted by whistles, catcalls and demands to share the microphone with the protesters. After a while a dialogue of sorts did develop. Nazarbayev seemed to be building a rapport with the students, many of whom were chanting his name as a can-didate for the post of First Secretary. However other names, including those of ethnic Russian members of the Kazakhstan cabinet, were also being shouted; so the crowd's choices seemed to be local rather than nationalistic. The main fervour of the demonstrators was directed to complaining noisily about the appointment of the unknown Kolbin, although there were other protests, particularly against the recently resigned Kunayev for the favouritism he had shown to his relatives and to his own clan members.

The increasingly chaotic scene unnerved the senior party officials who were watching from their offices overlooking the square. An order was given to drown out the speeches by playing music at high volume through huge government loudspeakers, which had been set up around the edge of the cordoned off area. This enraged the crowd who began throwing lumps of snow, ice and stones towards the podium. One large stone struck the microphone as Nazarbayev was speaking. It ricocheted off the loudspeaker and grazed him on his cheek, leaving a nasty scratch. The injury and the worsening mood of the crowd forced the Prime Minister and his colleagues to beat a hasty retreat.

The tactic of playing the mega-loud music had been ordered directly by senior figures in Moscow, who were in continuous telephone contact with Kolbin. At their instigation, he ordered water cannons into action, but their soaking of the students seemed to increase, rather than quench, the ardour of the protests. With vodka drinking in the crowd noticeably on the increase too, someone let off a home-made firework, which hit the window of Kolbin's office. This was reported back to Moscow as "a rocket attack". The news of it brought Mikhail Gorbachev into direct contact with Almaty on the evening of 17th December. "I was told by our secret sources that this demonstration was being carefully orchestrated from the universities by ethnic Kazakhs", he has recalled. "It was reported to me that they might be going to storm the government buildings. So I decided to act personally. I asked to be connected immediately to Kunayev."

The recently retired First Secretary was tracked down to his private apartment, which was still equipped with a direct telephone line to the Kremlin. Using this line, Gorbachev became angry with his former Politburo colleague. "Dinmukhamed Akhmedovitch, what is happening? What are you doing? Have you done this on purpose? Are you behind all this?"

"No, no, no! It is the young people", replied Kunayev, adding the damaging assertion, probably aimed at Nazarbayev: "they are being encouraged by those who are fighting between each other to secure positions in the government."

Gorbachev took no notice of this attempt to put the blame for the demonstrations on the man he had just passed over for the post of First Secretary. Instead he kept the heat on Kunayev, issuing him with an impossible ultimatum: "I know how much your words mean to Kazakhs", said Gorbachev. "I know how much your people respect you. So I will give you 40 minutes. If you will not stop these young men from marching towards the government buildings, then after that I will give my orders to the law enforcement agencies to stop them by force. That's it!"

These words from the General Secretary of the Soviet Union sounded menacing but they made no discernible impact on Kunayev. He did not try to exert his influence with the demonstrators. They were beginning to disperse anyway, because darkness was falling and the night air was cold. However, their anger had not dispersed, as events the following day were to prove.

Overnight, a new group of senior Kremlin officials flew down from Moscow to Almaty on a special flight. They were led by Mikhail Solomentsev, a member of the Politburo, and Yevgeny Razumov, the first deputy chief of the organisational department of the Communist Party's central committee. Also on the flight were high-ranking officers from the KGB and from the Interior Ministry. They made an assessment of the situation and reported back to their boss in Moscow, Interior Minister Alexander Vlasov. Reversing the cautious approach of the army commander, General Lobov, the previous day, Vlasov ordered units of the Ministry of the Interior's elite *Spetznaz* special forces into action. These troops were flown to Kazakhstan during the night of 17th December from their barracks in Russian cities as far away as Sverdlovsk, Moscow and Leningrad.

By mid-morning on 18th December, the streets of Almaty were filling up with some 15,000 demonstrators. Their mood was characterised by mass singing of Kazakh songs, particularly "Elimai", a 17th-century marching tune about nomad warriors needing courage to resist the Jungar invaders. The 20th-century protestors needed similar courage, for as they converged on Brezhnev Square the police and the Spetznaz forces unleashed a carefully planned attack, code-named *Operation Snowstorm.*

Nazarbayev was kept in the dark about the covert plans for Operation Snowstorm. Although he was the Prime Minister of the republic, he was excluded from the decision-making process in the hands of the group from Moscow because his name had been chanted by the demonstrators the previous day as an alternative candidate to Kolbin.

So Nazarbayev had to watch with growing horror as the police and *Spetznaz* troops attacked the protestors using steel batons, truncheons, army spades and police dogs. An independent young observer of these events was a 16-year-old schoolboy, Nurlan Kapparov, who witnessed the turmoil from the balcony of his parents' apartment overlooking Brezhnev Square: "It was very messy with lots of blood flowing" he has recalled. "I was terribly shocked as the soldiers and military police tore into the students".

In the short term these tactics did disperse the demonstrators, although at the cost of two deaths and 200 serious injuries. Another painful cost was the violence used by the heavy-handed security forces as they made over 8,000 arrests. Since there was no room in the prisons or police stations for such huge numbers, almost all those detained were released late on 18th December. However, many of them were beaten and stripped semi-naked before being sent out into the bitterly cold winter night. These ruthless moves had the effect of putting an immediate end to the protests in public. However, in the longer term a private legacy of bitterness spread throughout Kazakhstan and far beyond it. This was to have profound consequences throughout the Soviet Union over the next four years, as other nationalities and nationalistic movements followed the example of the Almaty protesters and took to the streets in their own rebellions against centralised rule from Moscow.

In the aftermath of the December 1986 events, which became collectively known as Jeltoqsan (the month of December in the Kazakh language), Kazakhstan was a restless republic.

The tragedy was the misuse of force against the young people [said Nazarbayev]. Ironically, the demonstrations began because most of them sincerely and truly believed what Mikhail Gorbachev had been saying about *perestroika* and *glasnost*. After the violence they lost all respect for the Soviet system of government.

* * *

Nazarbayev was still the No. 2 man in the government of the Soviet Republic of Kazakhstan, but he had many difficulties working in uneasy harness with the new No 1, Gennady Kolbin. Instead of calming people down after the trauma of Jeltoqsan, Kolbin wanted to launch a witch hunt against the people he blamed for the demonstrations. Nazarbayev tried to restrain his boss from this course of action. In the early weeks of 1987, much frank talking was done over glasses of vodka by the two leaders. Initially, Kolbin seemed willing to listen to his Prime Minister's advice. However, their working relationship was gradually undermined by three factors: interference from Moscow; a declaratory style of leadership which made too many empty promises; and an atmosphere of backbiting and backstabbing which revealed cracks in the façade of mutual loyalty.

Moscow's approach to the problems revealed by the demonstrations of December 1986 was to blame them on "erupting nationalism", and to take the hard line that those responsible for encouraging the protesters should be purged and punished. So an investigation was carried out to discover which colleges had been the main sources of the students who marched in Brezhnev Square. The lecturers and directors of those colleges were fired from their jobs. The most spectacular victim of the purge was the cabinet minister responsible for higher education, Kupzhasar Naribayev. He was accused of encouraging the cause of Kazakh nationalism by having allowed the enrolment of too many ethnic Kazakhs into the universities. This charge was levelled against Kupzhasar Naribayev in a detailed presentation at a cabinet meeting by Gennady Kolbin, who demanded the immediate dismissal of the education minister.

To his credit, Nazarbayev spoke up in defence of his beleaguered colleague, arguing that the increase in the numbers of ethnic Kazakhs going to university was partly a product of their high birth rate in the demographics of Kazakhstan, and partly due to an across-the-board policy of encouraging the recruitment of Kazakhs by all ministries and industries.

Mr Naribayev has only been a minister for three years [said the Prime Minister]. He has been implementing a policy which has been going on for a much longer time, so why should he alone be blamed? The ideology of the republic was agreed by all of us. He has merely been executing instructions. So I think we should not strip him of his minister's position. Why don't we just give him a written warning and let him stay in his department to help us correct the faults and weaknesses in higher education.

Nazarbayev's plea fell on deaf ears. No one else in the cabinet voiced similar support. Realising that the vote was certain to go against him, the education minister chose to jump before he was pushed, and offered his immediate resignation. Soon after the meeting, he was clearing out his personal belongings from his office when a call came in from the Prime Minister. "I am sorry this has happened", said Nazarbayev, "but don't take it too hard. Please stay in touch. One day I believe we will be working together again." These words were not just a gesture of human kindness. They were also an accurate political prophecy. For three years later, Nazarbayev and Naribayev were again working together when the sacked education minister was brought back into a high official position as President of the Kazakh National State University.

Kolbin's purges of Kazakhs in senior posts were bizarrely balanced by political concessions to the Kazakh population. He ordered all government officials who did not speak Kazakh to learn the language immediately. Kolbin himself announced that he would present the First Secretary's report to the next Central Committee plenary meeting speaking in Kazakh. Neither of these promises were carried out. They were part of a growing pattern of gesture politics with no results. Kolbin put great emphasis on holding big regional meetings ending in policy initiatives that were announced with much fanfare but never followed through. For example, there was the announcement that Kazakhstan's housing shortage would be solved in five years – but with no increase in house building. There was the announcement that food shortages would be ended – but with no increase in agricultural production. There was the announcement of the war against alcoholism and the setting up of sobriety zones – but with little or no enforcement, although the announcement of the rules themselves had the unexpected effect of increasing alcohol abuse. Meanwhile, the economy continued to decline and absenteeism from work soared. The age of ordinary people being afraid of the government was over. The era of resenting and ridiculing the centralised power of the Soviet Union had begun.

∗   ∗   ∗

Gennady Kolbin accelerated the twilight of Soviet authority. In appearance he was the stereotype of a Russian apparatchik – thick-set, red-faced, blustering in his tone of voice and an obvious heavy drinker. In attitude he was a rigid administrator of the old school, who could not understand that the old methods would no longer work. Some of his orders were a farce, such as his instruction to hold a national goose-shooting day in order to alleviate meat shortages in the shops. It was a failure, producing Kazakh jokes about how the only casualty of the operation had been one fat goose who shot himself. His name was Goose Kolbin.

The First Secretary's failures soured his relationship with his Prime Minister. Kolbin followed the example of Kunayev by ordering KGB investigations of his subordinate, and by trying to get Nazarbayev "promoted" into some senior position in the Moscow bureaucracy. Gorbachev, however, would not countenance such suggestions. Yet, even with the General Secretary's protection, 1987 was a year of difficulty and despondency for Nazarbayev. Its lowest point was the publication in June of the official inquiry by the Central Committee of the Soviet Communist Party into the demonstrations that had taken place in Almaty eight months earlier. The main thrust of the report was to blame Kunayev and his ministers for unfairly promoting young Kazakhs into key posts at the expense of ethnic Russians; for rehabilitating "bourgeois nationalists"; and for encouraging a growth in "nationalistic manifestations" which culminated in the protests against Kolbin's appointment. There were also harsh criticisms of Kunayev for having created "an unhealthy atmosphere" in the political life of Kazakhstan, which had led to the lowest economic growth of all the Soviet republics.

A week after the report had been issued Kunayev was stripped of his remaining official positions. In his formal retirement speech to the Central

87

Committee of the Communist Party, the former First Secretary lashed out with a furious attack on Nazarbayev for causing all the troubles in Kazakhstan and for encouraging the December events by his "thirst for power". Gorbachev intervened in the proceedings of the Central Committee to silence Kunayev and to deny his accusations. However, the fact that the accusations had been voiced so publicly caused Nazarbayev immense distress. Under the emotional pressure of the attack, his blood pressure shot up and he had to be rushed into the emergency cardiology unit of the Kremlin Hospital. Many witnesses of his dramatic exit from the Central Committee thought that Nazarbayev's career would be over too. Only one of his cabinet colleagues from Kazakhstan took the trouble to call him in the hospital. This sole inquirer after his health was his old political ally from Almaty, Madame Manura Akhmetova. "He told me that his heart was fine and that his blood pressure problem was just a temporary reaction", she has recalled. "He told me 'don't get nervous, calm down, everything will be OK'."

Everything was not OK in Kazakhstan, even though Nazarbayev quickly recovered his health, stopped smoking and returned to full Prime Ministerial duty. The economy continued its decline, and the nationalistic rumblings of discontent against Gennady Kolbin increased. They were exacerbated by other manifestations of the nationalities problem elsewhere in the Soviet Union, such as unrest in the Baltic states and demonstrations in Moscow organised by Pamyat, a Russian nationalist group with links to Boris Yeltsin. In November, Mikhail Gorbachev released his book *Perestroika: New Thinking for Our Country and the World*. Nazarbayev was a strong supporter of the reformist philosophy set out in the book. However, he was worried about the absence of specific proposals for reform. His main concern was that since the Communist Party had no agenda for changing itself, how could it change the economy of the Soviet Union?

We continued to see the same flaws in the party leadership [Nazarbayev has recalled]. There was a total absence of self-criticism, and an unwillingness to listen to criticism and warnings. The party was really incapable of making serious proposals for change since it didn't have an adequate think tank.

Within Kazakhstan, Nazarbayev was the only heavyweight political figure to be doing any serious thinking about how to apply the ideas of *perestroika* and *glasnost*. He wanted greater autonomy for his republic, he was intrigued by the possibility of experimenting with Western-style market-economy freedoms in some limited areas, but he saw these potential changes in the context of Kazakhstan remaining within the Soviet Union. "I regarded Nazarbayev as a loyal ally at this time", Mikhail Gorbachev has recalled. "He was always absolutely candid with me. He wanted reform, but saw that the break-up of the Soviet Union would be a big disaster. And he was absolutely right about that."

The seeds of break-up were germinating far too quickly, not least in Kazakhstan in 1987–1988. Kolbin was proving to be an incompetent and unpopular manager of decline. The January 1988 Party plenary meeting in Almaty was a disaster for him. He tried to stay above the barrage of criticism on economic matters by adopting a lofty "divide and rule" posture as First Secretary. But his attempts to pit one minister against another back-fired, as did his efforts to isolate Nazarbayev by promoting his potential rivals in the cabinet. The reality was that Kolbin was losing authority not gaining it. Events were undermining him, not disloyal subordinates or dissident students. Nazarbayev's stance in the cabinet was ambiguous. Publicly he did his best to shore up the floundering First Secretary while privately admitting that Kolbin's days were numbered. The Communist Party leadership in Moscow gradually came to the same conclusion. In May 1989, the USSR Congress of People's Deputies voted to promote Gennady Kolbin to a new post in the Kremlin with the Orwellian title of Chairman of the Committee of People's Control. This meant that the leadership position of First Secretary of the Soviet Republic of Kazakhstan was now vacant.

In theory, the vacancy could be filled by diktat from the Kremlin. In practice, any attempt by Moscow to impose another high-handed appointment of a non-Kazakh outsider would have been politically disastrous after the experience of the December 1986 demonstrations. No one understood this better than Mikhail Gorbachev.

We had to fix the error we had made with Kolbin [he has said]. That was our first big mistake in inter-ethnic relations, and I was determined not to repeat it. We had all come to accept that Kazakhs should run their own republic, and we gave them the right to decide who should be their new leader.

So colonial rule from on high was replaced by a surprisingly democratic consultation process at the grass roots before the new First Secretary was chosen. This time, suggestions for the appointment were solicited from a wide cross-section of society in Kazakhstan including people's deputies, regional officials, municipal leaders, opinion formers in the intelligentsia, workers' groups from various industries and even ordinary citizens in the street. Only after these extensive soundings had been taken was a meeting of the Central Committee of the Communist Party of Kazakhstan convened to decide on the choice of its First Secretary. The decision was made to hold the first ever free vote in a secret ballot in the history of any Soviet republic. This election was held on 1st June 1989. By an overwhelming majority, and with the support of many of his former opponents, Nursultan Nazarbayev won the vote and became the new leader of Kazakhstan.

* * *

The new First Secretary was pleased but not euphoric about his victory.

I knew that I had little time to carry out all the changes that were required [he has recalled]. My three highest priorities were to strengthen stability and inter-ethnic accord; to work out and implement a programme of economic reform; and to determine exactly what would be the division of powers between the republic authorities and Moscow.

Healing the wounds of December 1986 was Nazarbayev's most immediate challenge. He showed skill in rising to it both personally and politically. One of his first breakthroughs was a reconciliation with Dinmukhamed Kunayev, brought about by the death of the former First Secretary's wife. In accordance with Kazakh tradition, Nazarbayev visited the home of the bereaved husband. Kunayev greeted his visitor with an emotional embrace, whispering "Forgive me, please forgive me". Nazarbayev, equally moved, replied "No, it is I who should ask your forgiveness. Please will you forgive me?"

This exchange, witnessed by Kunayev's relatives and many supporters, ended the rift between the two Kazakh leaders. From that time on, they had good relations. Nazarbayev provided his former boss with small kindnesses denied him under the Kolbin regime, including a car and driver, and a small apartment for his housekeeper. A greater challenge of healing was how to calm the seething resentment among many Kazakhs about the Soviet treatment of the Jeltoqsan demonstrators. Some of them had been convicted in show trials and sentenced to long periods of imprisonment. One of the defendants had died in custody, becoming a national martyr. There was also widespread anger over the official Soviet report of the events of December 1986. This mood built up into intense political pressure for a new inquiry into the demonstrations in Brezhnev Square. Nazarbayev agreed to this demand and did his best to shape the commission's terms of reference in the spirit of *glasnost.*

I realised from the start that if the commission was to deal with the problem then it had to be created in the most thorough and open way [he has stated]. It also had to be entitled to have access to all official papers and to interview any officials it wished. However harsh its conclusions, this was the only way it could do any good.

While the new commission of inquiry began its investigations, Nazarbayev was trying to introduce *perestroika*-type reforms into Kazakhstan's economy.

90

One of his initiatives was the introduction of an experiment in free-market prices at food shops in Almaty. This was known as "the rental system", under which private businessmen were allowed to rent shops, to stock them with good-quality produce which they purchased directly from local farmers, and then to sell this produce at market prices. This was a controversial system because it resulted in higher prices for noticeably better goods. Nazarbayev was immediately criticised for "introducing capitalism", and for "exploiting the poor and the pensioners". However, he was firm in his resolve and willing to defend his policy. The Vice Chairman of the Kazakhstan Council of Ministers with responsibility for agriculture, Erik Gukasov, recalls Nazarbayev telling the cabinet: "This is a first step towards a market economy. We have to start moving forward in this direction to give the people better quality, better supplies and better service."

While Nazarbayev was moving forwards, attempts were being made in Moscow to force Gorbachev to move backwards. In July 1989 the General Secretary announced that he wanted to purge the Politburo of conservative hardliners who opposed *perestroika*. In the first of a series of escalating challenges to Gorbachev's authority, the hardliners turned against him and argued that it was *perestroika* itself which was to blame for the increasing manifestations of dissent across the Soviet Union. The standard bearer for these views in the Politburo was Yegor Ligachev, who called for curbs on the media and a crackdown on what he called "anti-Communist groups". Nazarbayev was forthright in his opposition to Ligachev, whom he accused of being "afraid of democratisation" and "full of the traditionally negative attitude towards dissent".

Dissent was breaking out all over the Soviet Union in 1990–1991. There was constant turmoil on the streets of the Baltic republics; riots in Tbilisi over the resignation from the Politburo of Eduard Shevardnaze, the Georgian leader; and eruptions of nationalist demonstrations in both Ukraine and Russia. Kazakhstan was not immune from these movements which Mikhail Gorbachev called "the dark forces of nationalism". In Almaty, which had been the scene of the earliest manifestations of nationalistic discontent in December 1986, protesters took to the streets again in February 1990. Even though the commission of inquiry into the 1986 events was well advanced in its work, the impatient demonstrators noisily demanded the immediate and full rehabilitation of those who had been dismissed, punished or jailed in the aftermath of the original upheavals in Brezhnev Square. Nazarbayev was sympathetic to these demands. He sent the commission a letter stating his agreement with them and setting out his personal assessment of the cause of the crisis.

When the commission of inquiry published its report in September 1990, the findings amounted to a vindication of the protesters and a condemnation of the Soviet authorities and the security forces that had suppressed the demonstration. Nazarbayev welcomed these conclusions and later issued a decree formally rehabilitating those who had been prosecuted for their participation in December 1986. He also made 17th December the annual commemoration day of those events, naming it "Day of Democratic Renewal of the Republic of Kazakhstan".

What happened should never be forgotten [says Nazarbayev]. More than anything, those terrible hours in Brezhnev Square serve as a permanent warning of how the powers-that-be should not behave with regard to the people and public opinion.

*　*　*

Nazarbayev's response to public opinion after the commission of inquiry's report into the Jeltoqsan events of December 1986 earned him the reputation of being "a democrat". The same label was applied to Boris Yeltsin, who had emerged from the party hierarchy to become an increasingly popular figure in Russia. It is doubtful whether either of these two leaders held deepseated beliefs in the democratic process at this time. Nevertheless, their democratic supporters hailed them as kindred spirits who had been bold enough to criticise the failures of the centralised Soviet system.

By the summer of 1991, the tide of discontent against those failures reached a new peak with the election of Yeltsin as President of the Russian Soviet Republic. Gorbachev's authority was waning by the day.

This was the time when Yeltsin and I became really close [recalled Nazarbayev]. We had known each other since 1986, but now he was the No. 1 in Russia and I was the No. 1 in Kazakhstan, we began to meet regularly outside the Kremlin. We both said to each other that the Soviet Union as we knew it was about to end. But we conferred about a plan to preserve a new USSR as a federation of autonomous republics.

This was the Novo-Ogarevo plan that Gorbachev had put forward some months earlier. Nazarbayev had supported it at the first meeting because he strongly believed that some form of voluntary federation was essential in the best economic and political interests of all the Soviet republics. At the end of July, Gorbachev convened a second meeting at Novo-Ogarevo. The most important part of these discussions between Nazarbayev, Yeltsin and Gorbachev revolved around the changes in the Soviet government that would be required after the new Union treaty had been signed.

The three leaders agreed that some of the conservative hardliners in the Politburo would have to be replaced. The prime candidates for dismissal were the Minister of Defence, Dmitri Yazov; the Chairman of the KGB, Vladimir Kryuchkov; and the Prime Minister, Valentin Pavlov. Yeltsin proposed that Nazarbayev should take Pavlov's place as the new Prime Minister of the reconstructed Soviet Union. Gorbachev accepted this suggestion, but Nazarbayev insisted on reserving his position. During a break in the main discussions, Gorbachev requested a private word with the Kazakh President, asking him to explain his hesitation about taking on the post of Prime Minister of the USSR. "I have some conditions", said Nazarbayev. "First, I will have to travel around all the republics, including Kazakhstan, asking them to endorse my nomination by votes in their own Parliaments. If they do endorse me I will have to take some extraordinary measures. So I will have to be in charge of all economic policy, and you will not interfere in those matters."

"But what is left for me to do?", asked Gorbachev.

"You will still be the President. You will deal with international affairs", replied Nazarbayev.

Gorbachev was unable to agree with this reduction in his Presidential authority. However, as power was inexorably slipping from his hands it was an argument that Nazarbayev would probably have won in the end had not other, at the time invisible, forces intervened. Only one of the three leaders had an intuitive feeling about these invisible forces. For when the discussions resumed at Novo-Ogarevo about the restructuring of the KGB, Yeltsin suddenly made melodramatic gestures towards the ceiling as if to warn his fellow Presidents that their conversation might be bugged. Gorbachev dismissed these fears as an absurdity. "How can you think of such a thing? I am the President of the Soviet Union", he said indignantly. But Yeltsin was right. Unknown to the three principals, KGB eavesdropping devices were indeed taping every word of their conversation. So it was hardly a coincidence, after hearing of the plans for their own dismissals, that KGB chairman Kryuchkov, Prime Minister Pavlov and Defence Minister Yazov should have begun organising a coup to overthrow the Soviet government and its President.

* * *

Unaware of any plot against him, Gorbachev set off on 4th August for a two-week vacation in a dacha at Foros on the Crimean coast. Yeltsin, having forgotten his fears about eavesdroppers, decided to pay an August weekend visit to his new best friend in Soviet power politics, Nazarbayev. The two Presidents were in festive spirits, but first they had some serious business to do. On 16th August, they signed a treaty of bilateral friendship between Russia and Kazakhstan, which included an accord on trade and economic cooperation between their countries. They proposed a joint initiative to resolve the Armen-ian–Azerbaijan conflict. Most important of all, they signed agreements designed to strengthen the practicalities of cooperation and coexistence between the republics under the impending new Union Treaty. The titles of these agree-ments "On a Single Economic Territory" and "On Guarantees of Stability in the Union of Sovereign States" seemed to show that the two Presidents were serious about implementing the *Novo-Ogarevo* principles. In their private conversations, Yeltsin and Nazarbayev were optimistic that the treaty would give the signing states maximum autonomy while preserving the minimum structure that would save the Soviet Union from break-up and maintain orderly economic activities between the republics.

Congratulating themselves on a job well done, the two Presidents then decided to enjoy themselves. On the first evening of the visit, they travelled to the district of Medeo in the Alatau Mountains. After touring the town's famous museum of musical instruments, the leaders toasted each other and sat down to enjoy an informal Saturday night concert. On impulse, Yeltsin decided he would like to join in. "Bring me my spoons", he called to one of his aides. A set of long-handled spoons was produced and the Russian leader joined the percussion section of the orchestra, tapping away first on the instruments and then on the heads of local girls with enthusiasm if not always with good timing. The next day, Yeltsin's *joie de vivre* increased. First stop was the Panfilov state farm racing stud, where Nazarbayev presented his guest of honour with a magnificent black stallion. After many toasts to its strength, speed and beauty, Yeltsin announced that he would like to try out his new steed then and there, ordering it to be saddled up immediately.

"But has he ever ridden a horse before?", Nazarbayev asked the Russian President's head of security.

"No", was the reply, "but there's no way of stopping him."

It took four strong aides to lift the burly Yeltsin into the saddle, another two on each side to prop him up, and two more to hold the stallion steady. The horse was not entirely cooperative with his uneasy rider. "I have never seen anything like it", recalled Nazarbayev. "Yeltsin was well and truly drunk. He kept rolling out of the saddle first one way, then the other, while his security men did their best to keep him from falling as the stallion kicked out and reared up. It was quite dangerous."

More vodka gave Yeltsin the taste for greater dangers. The next stop on Nazarbayev's scenic hospitality tour was the Talgar gorge, a spectacular con-fluence of mountain rivers high above Almaty. The ice-cold waters in the gorge were fast and foaming. Yeltsin insisted that he wanted to swim in them, dismissing all calls for caution on the grounds that he took regular dips in the Moscow river when the water temperature was barely above freezing. As the Russian leader began to disrobe, Nazarbayev became alarmed. He knew, better than his visitor did, the perils of the strong current and the jagged rocks just below the surface. "Although Kazakh tradition means that the wish of a guest is law for the host, I permitted myself on this occasion to violate custom", he has recalled. These words do not adequately recapture the clash of Presidential wills that took place beside the waters of the Gorge.

"You can't swim here. You will be pulled to the rocks", protested Nazarbayev.

"No, I will go", shouted Yeltsin.

As the argument between the two leaders intensified, their combined security details devised an ingenious diversionary tactic. Hastily, they built a dam in the shallows of the water, cordoning off a calm area in which the current would not sweep swimmers away. The temperature was still a bone-chilling 8 degrees, and the waters of the gorge remained rough, but Yeltsin took the plunge, surviving not only to tell the tale but to demand more shots of vodka to warm himself up.

The excitements of the riding and swimming exploits created serious post-ponements in Yeltsin's schedule. So did the farewell lunch party. Nazarbayev thoughtfully provided his guest with a yurt for a prolonged post-prandial nap. When he eventually emerged from it, Yeltsin called for more toasts. By the end of them, he could no longer stand up. "I had to order the police to keep everyone away from the airport so that nobody could see the President of Russia in such a condition", recalled Nazarbayev. "We had to push him up the aircraft steps to get him on his plane."

By the time Yeltsin took off for Moscow, it was 8 pm on the evening of Sunday 18th August, three hours later than the carefully scheduled original departure time of 5 pm.

This three-hour delay may have saved Boris Yeltsin's life. For, according to the story that the Russian President told several of his associates in later years, at the time when he had been swimming at Talgar gorge, the coup plotters were making their first moves in Moscow to overthrow the government of the Soviet Union. By Yeltsin's account, one of the earliest and most sinister commands from the conspirators was received by the Soviet air defence force at Aktyubinsk military base in western Kazakhstan, on the morning of 18th August. The order said that an aircraft, taking off from Al-maty at 5 pm on a flight plan to Moscow, must be shot down.

The soldiers at the base duly prepared to obey the order to fire their ground-to-air missiles. But no Moscow-bound aircraft took off from Almaty at 5 pm. After an hour or two of waiting, the soldiers stood down and de-activated their missiles, since the coup leaders had issued no contingency orders for delays. As a result, Boris Yeltsin flew safely back to Moscow on the night of 18th August and Nursultan Nazarbayev slept soundly in his bed at his official residence in Almaty. Neither of them had any inkling of what was being planned by the coup leaders, so they both awoke to a day of high drama and political upheaval.

7

The Coup and the Breakup

On the morning after Yeltsin's departure from Almaty, Nazarbayev was fast asleep at the unusually late hour, for him, of 9 am. Suddenly his wife, Sara, rushed into the bedroom and woke up her husband with the astonishing words "I've just heard that Mikhail Gorbachev is sick. He has stepped down. Vice President Yanayev has taken over."

Switching on his bedside radio, Nazarbayev listened to the early morning news bulletin from Radio Moscow. The announcer said he was speaking on the authority of "The State of Emergency Committee". The ensuing statements issued in the name of this committee (a hitherto unheard-of body) declared that drastic measures were being taken to prevent the breakup of the Soviet Union. According to these broadcasts, Gorbachev was too ill to take charge of events so his Vice President Gennady Yanayev had assumed control.

Nazarbayev was immediately suspicious. His foreboding about a coup multiplied when he found that his hotline to the Kremlin was not working and that his official car and driver had not arrived to take him to his office. Old memories of Stalin's terrors and other Soviet purges started to haunt him. Nazarbayev asked his wife: "Do we have anything in the house which is compromising, which they could somehow use against me?" By "they", he meant the KGB whose operatives Nazarbayev now expected to appear to arrest him as part of the putsch.

This tension diminished slightly when the official presidential limousine arrived with the driver apologising for delays caused by a simple mechanical problem. On arriving at his office, Nazarbayev found that his staff knew no more than he did. The announcements on Moscow radio were their only source of information.

Shortly before 10 am (7 am Moscow time) on the morning of Monday 19th August, Boris Yeltsin called. "What is happening there, Boris Nikolayevich?", asked the President of the Republic of Kazakhstan. "I don't know", replied the President of the Russian Republic, in a voice still blurred by his alcoholic excesses of the previous day. "But I think this is a real coup and we must prepare ourselves for the worst. Gorbachev has been arrested. Tanks are moving into Moscow." "Where are you?", asked Nazarbayev. "In my dacha", replied Yeltsin, adding that he was going to go to the Russian Parliament building, popularly known as the White House. "Anything could happen", he continued. "The main thing is that we should take a stand together against this State of Emergency Committee."

A few minutes later, Nazarbayev was telephoned by the leader of this mysterious committee, Vice President Gennady Yanayev, who wanted to know the reaction in Kazakhstan to the news from Moscow. Instead of giving a reply, Nazarbayev fired off a fusillade of questions about Gorbachev. Where was he? How was he? What had happened to him? The answers were evasive, but at least they provided the reassurance that Gorbachev was still alive at his dacha in the Crimea. However, Yanayev then strained his own credibility past breaking point by insisting that Gorbachev was in agreement with the new measures being implemented by the State Emergency Committee and supported its view that "order had to be restored in the country". Under further questioning, Yanayev declared that Gorbachev had given the State Emergency Committee his full approval for their plan of action.

"I had never had a high opinion of Yanayev, but I had never imagined that he was capable of such barefaced deceit", was Nazarbayev's recollection of his shocked mood as he listened to this unbelievable account from the Vice President. Having had a long conversation with a perfectly healthy Gorbachev about various issues relating to the new Union treaty only two days earlier, Nazarbayev knew that the story he was being told about the Soviet President's abandonment of all the policies for which he had been fighting must be a travesty of the truth.

The real truth about the new self-installed government of the Soviet Union was difficult for Nazarbayev to discover on the first morning of the coup. He became increasingly apprehensive of the implications for Kazakhstan after his next telephone call from Moscow, which was from Kryuchkov, the head of the KGB. He addressed the President of Kazakhstan in "a condescending not to say haughty tone", making hints that he would in due course offer the Kazakh leader a senior position in the "new leadership set-up", as Nazarbayev later described it. The KGB chief presented the situation as a constitutional fait accompli beyond discussion, saying that all the powers of the central authority of the Soviet Union had been legally transferred to the State Emergency Committee. As this authority held the power to move Soviet troops to any of the republics, Nazarbayev feared that the new leadership might respond to any national demonstrations or disturbances with a show of military force.

With these fears uppermost in his mind, Nazarbayev convened an emergency meeting of the Kazakhstan cabinet at 2 pm on Monday 19th August. He gave the ministers a full briefing on all the information he had been able to obtain in his morning of telephone calls from Vice President Yanayev, KGB Chairman Kryuchkov and Prime Minister Pavlov. One of the most disturbing features of these conversations was that none of the callers would answer Nazarbayev's questions as to *where* the state of emergency was going to be introduced in the Soviet Union. According to the radio broadcasts, the emergency powers would be introduced "in certain regions of the country". This vague description, in Nazarbayev's view, was dangerous to Kazakhstan because it effectively gave the so-called State of Emergency Committee carte blanche to blackmail any republic, region or city.

At the cabinet meeting in Almaty, opinions were divided. Some ministers were clearly frightened. Others took a subservient line, saying that orders from the new leadership in Moscow should be given unquestioning obedience. However, the majority were in favour of adopting a political stance that was independent of any instructions issued by the new "Soviet government" – at least until its constitutional legitimacy had been established.

Both at the cabinet meeting and in his TV and radio broadcast a few hours later to the people of Kazakhstan, Nazarbayev had two paramount priorities. The first was to protect his republic from any abuse of power by the coup leaders in Moscow. The second was to prevent any signs of ethnic or nationalistic rebellion which could be used as a pretext for bringing in troops on the orders of the State of Emergency Committee.

In his broadcast on the evening of 19th August, Nazarbayev began by appealing for restraint, saying that this was imperative at such a critical time "since any emotional, ill-considered action by any one of us may become the spark that sets off social upheavals". He was clearly warning against any repetition of the December 1986 demonstrations in Almaty as he urged all political organisations to "put aside tactical differences, adopt a rational and responsible position, and not allow confrontation to develop". Having made this request to keep the domestic population of Kazakhstan calm and off the streets, Nazarbayev then addressed a different section of this audience, namely the various military and paramilitary units based in the republic. "I appeal to those serving with the armed forces and in units of the KGB and Ministry of Internal Affairs stationed on the territory of Kazakhstan to adhere to constitutional norms", he said. "I would like in particular to stress the fact that a state of emergency is not being introduced in Kazakhstan." He rounded off his message by declaring his support for "strengthening the sovereignty of the republic, for the principles of democracy and the preservation of the Union".

This was a skilful broadcast which achieved its objectives of buying time and reducing tension. Nazarbayev appealed to the innate sense of caution that was prevailing both on the domestic political scene and among the military and KGB commanders in the area who must have been watching the events in Moscow with some confusion. For the organisers of the coup were not having an easy ride. This became clear to Nazarbayev on the evening of 19th August when Vice President Yanayev called him for the second time in an effort to solicit Kazakhstan's support for the State of Emergency Committee. The effort failed. Nazarbayev, in a robust spirit of defiance, told the Soviet Vice President that his action in taking over the role of head of state from Gorbachev was an illegal violation of the constitution of the USSR. Yanayev replied with cynical candour that he accepted the point but politics were not about keeping your hands clean, and the ends justified the means. He added that the powers taken by his committee would be retrospectively legitimised by the Supreme Soviet in one way or another.

Nazarbayev was shocked by this blatant admission of breaking the constitution, and redoubled his efforts to thwart the coup. The following day, he composed a strongly worded personal statement that attacked the legitimacy of the State of Emergency Committee's actions and concluded:

If we continue along the crooked paths of lawlessness, the people will not forgive us. Above all in these difficult days, we wish to hear the opinion of Mikhail Gorbachev himself. He must personally confirm his incapacity to perform the duties laid upon him.

This statement was read out by Nazarbayev on Kazakhstan radio and television on 20th August. It made Kazakhstan the second republic after Russia to condemn the coup. Although the news of Nazarbayev's opposition was suppressed in Moscow, his statement was broadcast to the world by the international media. Kazakhstan's uncompromising position of hostility to the coup plotters was a great encouragement to Boris Yeltsin and his followers, who were now demonstrating in large numbers on the streets of Moscow.

On the afternoon of 20th August, Yeltsin telephoned Nazarbayev on the only uncut high-frequency communication line between Moscow and Almaty. Speaking from the Russian Parliament building known as the White House, Yeltsin was in a highly emotional state. He said that the coup leaders were planning to storm his headquarters with tanks. He begged Nazarbayev to do all in his power to prevent this bloodshed. Nazarbayev immediately offered to fly to Moscow and confront the coup leaders, but Yeltsin categorically opposed this suggestion. "Don't take a step outside your own republic, Nursultan!", was the advice of the Russian President. "In the present situation, your home is your fortress."

The shaken tones in which this warning was delivered disturbed Nazarbayev.

I could tell that Yeltsin was really scared [he has recalled]. I know he told everyone after the coup was over that he was never afraid, but in that call I could hear the fear in his voice, especially when he repeatedly asked me to "do whatever you can to stop them attacking me".

The only action Nazarbayev could take from Almaty was to telephone the leading figures of the State of Emergency Committee with strong warnings against their alleged plan to attack the White House. His first call was to Vladimir Kryuchkov, the head of the KGB.

"What is happening? I demand to know as one of the leaders of the Soviet Union!", was Nazarbayev's opening to the call.

"We are re-establishing law and order", replied Kryuchkov. "You know how bad the condition of the country is. Here in Moscow, criminals and looters are roaming the streets. We have to get the situation under control. That is what we are doing."

"Where is Gorbachev?", asked Nazarbayev.

"Gorbachev knows all about this", was the KGB chief's answer. "He will come back to Moscow when we have restored law and order. If only a strong man like you had been in charge here instead of Gorbachev, all this would never have happened."

"Don't try that one on me", snapped Nazarbayev, who was getting angrier by the minute. "Let me ask you one question: Are you planning to attack the Parliament building?"

Kryuchkov denied he had any such plan, but in less than convincing terms. "No, there won't be an attack", he said, "but people there are killing one another and we have to restore order." Nazarbayev became angry. "If you kill innocent people, then all the other Soviet republics will rise up against you", he shouted, adding that he had already spoken to the leaders of the other republics, and that they were united in their opposition to the coup.

Nazarbayev's next call was to Gennady Yanayev, but the Vice President did not seem to be exercising any control over the situation. So after repeating his warning about the hostility from the republics, Nazarbayev reached the vital member of the Emergency Committee who was controlling the tanks and soldiers on the streets of Moscow – Defence Minister Dimitry Yazov.

Nazarbayev and Yazov were friends. Their families knew each other well and had exchanged visits. "I regarded him as a good and honest person", recalled Nazarbayev, who used the call to plead with the Defence Minister on a level that combined political intensity with personal intimacy. After once again describing the fierceness of the opposition to the coup in Kazakhstan and all the other republics, Nazarbayev asked: "So what are you doing getting involved with this, Dimitry Timofeyvich? And what are you going to do now?"

"I don't know", replied the Defence Minister of the Soviet Union in a tone that was almost a wail of despair. "I have got myself caught up with these fools. What do you suggest?"

Nazarbayev seized his opportunity. His voice rising in passion, he did all in his power to persuade his old friend to avoid bloodshed.

"You are a great hero of the war. You fought as the commander of a special forces battalion. You are also a father and a grandfather" began Nazarbayev. "Are you now going to give an order to shoot women and children on the streets of Moscow? Are you going to stain your hands with the blood of young people whose only crime is that they are standing in front of the White House in order to protect their President from an attack on the White House?"

Yazov replied: "I have brought tanks into Moscow, but I have no further orders."

"Forget about orders. You should arrest the people who organised this coup", advised Nazarbayev. "But first you should pull your tanks out of Moscow immediately."

It appears that this advice was taken. For less than 20 minutes later, one of Yeltsin's closest aides called Nazarbayev to report that the tanks which had been moving towards the White House had halted their advance. In the next four hours, as more and more demonstrators poured onto the streets, soldiers deserted from their regiments. As Yeltsin clambered onto one of the tanks to make a memorable speech to the crowd, it became more and more clear that public support for the coup was collapsing.

Although Nazarbayev was elated that the moment of maximum danger for Yeltsin and his supporters inside and outside the White House appeared to have passed without bloodshed, there was no certainty about what might happen next. In Kazakhstan, all telephone lines to the outside world had been cut off by Moscow. So Nazarbayev could only follow events by watching satellite reports from CNN on the TV set in his office. The questions uppermost in his mind were: What were the coup leaders going to do? What was the fate of Gorbachev? The idea that the two answers could be combined in one destination did not occur to Nazarbayev. For the notion that the plotters might fly to the Crimea to seek protection from the very President they had been trying to overthrow was far too fantastic an idea to enter Nazarbayev's head. Yet that was precisely what happened.

Late in the afternoon of 21st August, Mikhail Gorbachev telephoned Nazarbayev from his dacha at Foros in the Crimea. Nazarbayev's eyes filled with tears of joy as he heard the living voice of the Soviet President he feared had been killed by the coup leaders. The emotions that overcame Nazarbayev were heightened by the unusual sound of Gorbachev's voice. Instead of his usual forceful rasp, the Soviet leader spoke in a low and shaken monotone. As Nazarbayev recalled: "I will never forget the unusually intimate tone of his agitated voice, which made it impossible not to appreciate the enormous shock which this man had suffered."

Gorbachev was not too shocked to express his gratitude to Nazarbayev. With tremulous eloquence, he thanked the President and people of Kazakhstan for their steadfast support to the principles of freedom and democracy. He also praised them for their constitutional loyalty to the lawfully elected authorities of the USSR. Then, in a surreal touch of surprise, Gorbachev said that several of the leaders of the coup attempt against him, including Yazov and Kryuchkov, were in an ante-room of his dacha waiting to see him. He had agreed to meet them, but only on the condition that he first spoke to the two Presidents who had opposed the coup from the beginning – Yeltsin and Nazarbayev.

At the end of this historic call, which lasted less than 10 minutes, Nazarbayev began to relax for the first time in three days. To his aides he seemed to have fallen into some sort of temporary trance, for he sat motionless in his office apparently hearing and seeing nothing even when his staff entered and tried to talk to him.

At 9:30 pm Nazarbayev snapped out of his trance when the thought suddenly struck him that he was the only individual in Kazakhstan who knew for certain that the coup was over. A glance at his watch and at the TV screen made him realise that the republic's prime-time evening news programme was on the air. What a great opportunity, he thought, to make a Presidential broadcast breaking the news of Gorbachev's reinstatement and the collapse of the coup.

Arriving in haste at the central TV headquarters in Almaty, Nazarbayev and his aides at first received an incredulous reception from the technicians and floor managers, who were in mid-transmission of the evening news programme. Interrupting a live broadcast was out of the question, they said, swiftly changing their minds when a live President arrived in the studio. As the cameras swung on to him, Nazarbayev delivered his sensational message. "I have just spoken to Mikhail Gorbachev. He is in good health, and has resumed his duties", began the President. In his brief, impromptu remarks, Nazarbayev summarised his conversation with the restored Soviet leader, putting particular emphasis on Gorbachev's expressions of gratitude to the people of Kazakhstan for their resolute loyalty. Nazarbayev also thanked viewers for their calm and steadfast response to the crisis. He assured them it had now ended in a great victory.

As Nazarbayev left the studio immediately after his impromptu broadcast, he was chased after by TV producers confessing that in the haste of his unexpected appearance, they had forgotten to record him. The President was easily persuaded to come back in front of the cameras and to repeat his message. This time, it was safely videotaped and replayed on numerous news bulletins. Nazarbayev then returned to his office.

I was in high spirits when I got back [he has recalled]. Despite the late hour, almost all the members of the government and my aides were there. I have always made a point of never keeping alcohol in my office, but a bottle of champagne appeared out of nowhere and this time I did not refuse.

Nazarbayev deserved his champagne. Throughout the three days of potentially explosive crisis he had made the right calls of political judgement. He had defied the coup leaders at the earliest opportunity. He had backed the winners, the people of Russia led by Boris Yeltsin, with instinctive conviction. Perhaps Nazarbayev's finest achievement was the bond of trust he established with the people of Kazakhstan at every stage of the turmoil. They had responded to his leadership, accepted his advice, stayed calm and trusted in his broadcasts. In the deeper, if less dramatic, crises that lay ahead for the republic, this bonding between President and people was to serve Kazakhstan well.

On the wider stage of Soviet Union politics, the bonds of trust were falling apart as the relationships between the Kremlin and the republics disintegrated at ever-increasing speed. Gorbachev returned to Moscow, but soon discovered that he was in office but not in power. After arresting the coup leaders, some of whom had already removed themselves by suicide or flight, filling their vacant places at the Politburo proved to be a demonstration of Gorbachev's impotence. Virtually all the new appointments were dictated by Yeltsin. In some cases, Gorbachev would choose a Politburo member only to see him removed a few days later at Yeltsin's insistence. Nazarbayev was sometimes a mediating influence in these power struggles. For example, when Gorbachev appointed General Mikhail Moiseyev to the key post of Chief of Staff of the Soviet Army, Yeltsin promptly forced his dismissal because he wanted his own man, Marshal Shaposhnikov. It was Nazarbayev who ended this particular clash of wills by securing the compromise appointment of General Vladimir Lobov. "He was a good man who had shown his courage in Almaty during the events of December 1986, when he had been under pressure to use soldiers to put down the students and had refused", recalled Nazarbayev. His choice of Lobov, far from being a compromise in his eyes, was a telling indicator of how Nazarbayev's own judgement and decision-making process had been deeply impacted by the demonstrations in Brezhnev Square some five years earlier.

Personnel issues, difficult though they were inside the Kremlin after the coup, became secondary to the constitutional crises that were erupting in every republic of the Soviet Union. Nazarbayev's attitude to the problems faced by the USSR was initially constructive, not destructive.

It was obvious that the empire had collapsed and that now we had to climb free of the ruins with as little loss as possible in order to begin the construction of a radically new kind of state [was his view of the situation in the weeks following the defeat of the coup]. In my opinion, we had at that time a good chance of success.

The chances of successfully rebuilding a new kind of Soviet Union were wrecked by Boris Yeltsin. Not only did the Russian government systematically take over the power structures and ministries of the Union government, Yeltsin himself issued a series of inflammatory and ill-considered statements about the future of the Union which were bound to cause the greatest possible anxiety in neighbouring capitals. By far the most explosive of these statements was Yeltsin's ultimatum that Russia reserved the right to make territorial claims against other republics, specifically the Ukraine and Kazakhstan.

Nazarbayev was horrified by the implications of this apparent threat to the very existence of Kazakhstan. He made a series of urgent telephone calls to Yeltsin, whose responses to his friend's concerns oscillated between the incoherent and the incredible.

To be frank, Yeltsin was not able to offer any comprehensible explanation for his move, and in the end passed it off as an unfortunate statement by his press secretary [recalled Nazarbayev]. Naturally, I was not satisfied by this diversionary tactic over an issue of such vital importance to the republics as borders.

In the atmosphere of high tension created by Yeltsin's statement, the USSR's Supreme Soviet – the Parliament of the entire Union – met in extraordinary session on 26th August. Ironically, this session had been convened by the leaders of the abortive coup a few days earlier in order to legalise the seizure of power by the State of Emergency Committee. Now the deputies of the Parliament had to deal with a completely different emergency, namely the attempt by Yeltsin to exploit the post-coup chaos for the benefit of Russia. In the view of Kazakhstan and most of the other republics, it looked as though

Yeltsin was trying to create a Russian-dominated Federation that would not respect either the territorial integrity or the sovereignty of neighbouring states.

On the second day of the Parliamentary session on 27th August, Nazarbayev made a bold speech which amounted to a head-on challenge to Yeltsin's imperialist plans for a Russian-led Federation. Having reminded his audience of fellow deputies that he had always been a supporter of Gorbachev's proposals for a new Union treaty based on the Novo-Ogarevo principles, Nazarbayev swung into the attack. After citing Andrei Sakharov's vision that the Union should be a community of equal republics, he declared:

Now the time has come for us to appreciate the truth of those words. For me, it is clear that the renewed Union can no longer be a Federation…. The new Union should not have any Union cabinet, no Union parliament, nothing except the agreed relations the republics have entered into. Today, we face the moment of truth and I cannot imagine any other basis on which Kazakhstan will enter a Union with other republics…. We will never consent to be "the appendage" of another region, and will never be anyone's "little brother". We will enter the Union with equal rights and opportunities.

After Nazarbayev sat down, the chairman of the Parliament, Anatoly Lukianov, made the pessimistic comment: "That's it! If that is the position of Nazarbayev, who has always been in favour of integration, then that is the end of the Soviet Union."

In fact, Nazarbayev was doing his best to save the Soviet Union, although he wanted it to survive in a very different form with its acronymic name changed from USSR to FUSR – the Free Union of Sovereign Republics. He was a passionate believer in the right of Kazakhstan and all the other republics to have their independence. However, he believed that the republics should remain united as an economic commonwealth of nation states with a single currency, the rouble, and with a common trade policy. "Perhaps more than any other of the leaders, I understood the extent to which all our economies were intertwined", said Nazarbayev. Another of his major concerns was the future of the Soviet Union's nuclear weapons, many of which had been secretly tested and stationed in Kazakhstan. The magnitude of these military, economic and sovereignty issues which were dominating Nazarbayev's agenda in August 1991 can scarcely be exaggerated. With events moving at breakneck speed in unpredictable directions, he was the most clear-sighted of the principal players in the gathering storm which was destined to end in the collapse of the Soviet Union before the year was out.

One foreign observer who met Nazarbayev at this time and formed a favourable impression of his vision and political skills was Margaret Thatcher. On 31st August, the former British Prime Minister made a stopover at Almaty on her way to a lecture engagement in Tokyo. Nazarbayev briefed his visitor on the momentous changes sweeping through Kazakhstan. He told Thatcher about his republic's moves towards a free market economy and added that a few days earlier he had resigned from the Soviet Politburo, and from the post of First Secretary of the Communist Party of Kazakhstan. "Mr President, you seem to be moving from Communism to Thatcherism", said the Iron Lady, as she briefed him on her government's privatisation policy. The comment was a prescient description of the political road on which Kazakhstan and its President were travelling.

On 2nd September, the Soviet Congress of Peoples' Deputies met in full session but without the three Baltic republics of Estonia, Latvia and Lithuania, which had already declared their independence, with widespread diplomatic recognition from the international community. The political atmosphere in the Kremlin resembled a sinking ship, for other declarations of independence were strongly rumoured. Nazarbayev, however, was still struggling to keep the ship afloat. "As I saw it, the main task was to salvage what we could from the wreckage and to prevent the growing centrifugal forces from breaking the economic ties which had bound our republics together for decades", he said. In practice, this meant an attempt to create structures and procedures for moving towards some form of economic union. So an Inter-State Economic Committee was set up which agreed that a draft treaty of economic union should be prepared for discussion at a meeting in Almaty on 12th October. As the host and chief coordinator of this meeting, Nazarbayev achieved some short-lived success. Of the 12 republics still within the Union, 11 turned up and made encouraging progress. Over 25 detailed treaty documents were agreed on subjects such as the creation of a customs union, a unified economic space, a payments union and a single currency. Such was the accord that the heads of state of the republics arranged to meet in Moscow on 18th October to sign the final version of the treaty.

Unfortunately for Nazarbayev, the agreements reached in Almaty did not last for a week. When the Moscow meeting took place six days later, only eight of the previous eleven heads of state turned up. The most important of the three dropouts was the President of the Ukraine, Leonid Kravchuk. He was in the middle of a Presidential election which he could only win by following the tide of militant nationalism. In that atmosphere, he was unable to sign any kind of agreement that could be interpreted by his domestic electorate as a throwback to the days of subservience to the old colonial masters of the Soviet Union. Nazarbayev was disappointed by Kravchuk, but he was equally dismayed by the attitude of Yeltsin, who became increasingly antagonistic towards Gorbachev both politically and personally. Despite these difficulties, Nazarbayev kept on arguing for some form of economic union, along the lines of the European Union, by which national sovereignty was preserved within a community of economic cooperation.

We worked on through October and November 1991, but we were unable to agree anything [he has recalled]. I could see that the key issue was to reconcile Gorbachev and Yeltsin and I tried personally to narrow their differences. I advised them to meet separately and to try to get over their personal antipathy for each other on the grounds that the whole country expected it. However, Gorbachev's relationship with the Ukrainian leadership was almost as bad. It was becoming increasingly clear to everyone that there was no way that these three sides could agree on anything.

The divisions between the antagonistic trio of Gorbachev, Kravchuk and Yeltsin became hopelessly irreconcilable when a referendum, held in the Ukraine on 1st December, committed that country to all-out independence. On that same date Nazarbayev was re-elected President of Kazakhstan, yet with a commitment to the plan for a union of sovereign states. "But I warned my people that we must be ready for complete autonomy if the plan broke down", he has recalled.

In one last effort to salvage the plan for an economic union of sovereign republics, Gorbachev called a summit meeting in the Kremlin on 9th December, to be attended by the Presidents of the Republics of the Soviet Union, including Russia, Ukraine and Kazakhstan. Nazarbayev, still hoping for a miracle that would bring about this proposed union, flew into Moscow the day before the meeting on 8th December. But soon after arriving at the airport, Nazarbayev was telephoned by Yeltsin who was on a visit to Belarus. He was passing through that republic for talks with its President, Stanislav Shushkevich, and also with the President of Ukraine, Leonid Kravchuk, ostensibly for the purpose of working out a common Russian–Belarussian–Ukrainian negotiating position for the next day's summit with Gorbachev.

Yeltsin began the call by explaining that he, Kravchuk and Shushkevich were together in Belarus, about to have dinner in Brezhnev's old hunting lodge called "Belovezhskaya Pooshia".

"Come on over and join us", said Yeltsin.

For a fleeting moment, Nazarbayev thought he might accept the invitation, as he had his aircraft on the runway and could fly to Belarus within an hour. But first he wanted to understand the purpose of the dinner.

"Why?", he asked.

"Because we have just created a Commonwealth of Independent States", replied Yeltsin.

Nazarbayev was astonished.

"But we were meant to be discussing all these matters together in Moscow", he objected.

"Come on, fly over and we'll talk about it", replied Yeltsin. "We're all sitting here, everything is ready, but we just need your signature."

Nazarbayev became even more astonished.

"Hold on a minute!", he said, "You want me to sign it just like that? I have to study it first."

"We did not really read it ourselves", replied Yeltsin, in the nonchalant manner of a man who has not bothered to look at the small print of a restaurant bill. "We just sat down and signed it."

From the jovial tone of Yeltsin's voice and the background noise of laughter and clinking glasses, Nazarbayev realised that a pre-dinner drinks session must be well in progress. He asked to be briefed on the agreement to create a Commonwealth of Independent States. Yeltsin put the Belarussian Prime Minister, Vyacheslav Kebich, on the line, who opened with the superfluous comment: "The atmosphere here is all very warm and friendly."

Nazarbayev became cool and formal. With some difficulty he persuaded Kebich to read out the documents the three other Presidents had just signed. As he listened to the terms of their agreement, Nazarbayev was horrified by the complete elimination of any role for the federal authorities of the Union. He was unconvinced by the explanation that the disappearance of these ties was due to pressure from the Ukraine. Nazarbayev believed there was a hidden agenda driving the deal that had been struck. "At the heart of it was the personal antipathy between Yeltsin and Gorbachev", was his assessment. "The main aim seemed to be to ensure that the unfortunate Soviet leader was completely deprived of his powers, that he was left with absolutely nothing."

With increasing antipathy for the motives of the members of the cabal who had signed the agreement, Nazarbayev asked how they justified the legality of their action. Their response was that the Soviet Union had been formed in 1922 by four parties – Russia, Ukraine, Belarus and Transcaucasus (which no longer existed as it had been split up into individual republics). So as the three surviving members of the original founders, they considered that they had the constitutional right to dissolve the legal entity which their countries had created. Nazarbayev said this could not be a valid justification because between 1922 and 1940 another 12 republics, including Kazakhstan, had joined the union. How could Russia, Belarus and Ukraine possibly give themselves the right to dissolve the wider structure without consulting all the other parties who had agreed to it?

Whatever the correct constitutional legalities might be, arguments about them were making no impact on the "warm and friendly" trio of Presidents at Brezhnev's hunting lodge in Belarus. So Nazarbayev gave up his attempts to enter into a dialogue with them. Instead, he telephoned Yeltsin's Vice

President, Alexander Rutskoi, and tried to remonstrate with him. This was useless because Rutskoi was completely in the dark about the agreement signed by his boss. The furious Vice President complained bitterly that he had been left behind in Moscow by Yeltsin who had gone to Belarus secretly accompanied only by Gennady Burbulis, the first Deputy Prime Minister, and Andrei Kozyrev, the Foreign Minister. They were responsible for the text of the agreement, but they had told Rutskoi nothing about it.

Nazarbayev's next caller was an even more furious but equally unsighted Gorbachev. He wanted to know what the three Presidents were getting up to in Belarus and became incandescent when he was briefed on the bad news. Nazarbayev himself was indignant about the clandestine nature of the deal, but ever the realist, he could see some merit in the deal itself. A Commonwealth of Independent States (CIS) was not so different from the Free Union of Sovereign Republics (FUSR) he had proposed some weeks earlier. As he put it:

It was now clear that the Soviet Union was at an end, but something was still needed to replace it. The agreement reached between the three Presidents in Belarus was a potential solution. But I insisted that it had to be an open kind of pact, which the other former Soviet republics would be free to join. It had to be fair. For this reason, I believed that we should tell the leaders of the other republics and Gorbachev what we were doing. A secret deal had no appeal for me at all.

On the morning of 9th December, the date originally set for the summit meeting in Moscow between the leaders of the republics of the Soviet Union, Nazarbayev received a message that Yeltsin alone was flying in from Belarus. Apparently the other two signatories of the hunting-lodge agreement had decided that the Russian President would represent their joint position.

Nazarbayev telephoned Gorbachev with this news and asked him, "So what do I do? Go home?"

"No, come!", insisted the Soviet leader.

So Nazarbayev joined Gorbachev in his Kremlin office. They sat there on their own for some minutes, reading the text of the agreement that had been reached in Belarus without their participation. Eventually, Yeltsin arrived. With barely suppressed anger in his voice, Gorbachev immediately began to question him.

"So you have agreed all this. But what is going to happen about nuclear weapons?"

Yeltsin kept silent.

"And what about the army?", demanded Gorbachev. "And what about the matters of citizenship?"

There was no reply from Yeltsin.

With the temperature rising, the Soviet President fired a fusillade of questions. How were the CIS republics going to cooperate as trading nations? Were they going to erect frontiers and extract customs duties from one another? Would the rouble remain their currency? Would people be allowed to move freely between these newly independent states? If not, what would become of the many families whose relatives lived in different republics?

Unable to respond to any of these issues, Yeltsin eventually lost his temper. "What is this, some kind of interrogation?", he roared. Nazarbayev took upon himself the role of mediator. He did not achieve peace but at least he prevented his two furious fellow Presidents from coming to blows. Calm was gradually restored but the divisions between Gorbachev and Yeltsin had grown wider than ever. Although the discussion ended with Gorbachev saying he would study everything and that they would meet again soon, Nazarbayev saw clearly that the split was now irrevocable and irreconcilable. There was no longer a role for the President of the Soviet Union in the future of the former Soviet republics.

Nazarbayev now began to focus on an even worse problem than the breakup of the union. This was the very real possibility that a bitter Slav versus Moslem confrontation could erupt in the space vacated by Soviet authority. The agreement for a Commonwealth of Independent States consisting of Russia, Ukraine and Belarus meant that there would come into being a powerful Slav bloc of states. It would only be a matter of time before the Turkic-Moslem republics of Central Asia of Turkmenistan, Uzbekistan, Kyrgyzstan and Tajikistan formed their own bloc.

There was an obvious danger that this situation could lead to some kind of open confrontation between the two blocs [said Nazarbayev], and it could have potentially catastrophic consequences for Kazakhstan because our population consisted of both ethnic Russians, who were Slavs, and our native Kazakh peoples who came from Turkic, nomadic and Moslem backgrounds. The people themselves would want to live peacefully together but their differences could be exploited by Russian nationalists.

Nazarbayev moved with speed to head off the possibility of a Slav-Moslem split among the republics. He called the leaders of all four Central Asian republics and asked each one of them to join him at an urgent meeting. He was anxious to avoid the impression that this was his initiative, or that the meeting would be dominated by Kazakhstan, so he persuaded the President of Turkmenistan to host the meeting in his capital, Ashkhabad, on 13th December. However, the Turkmen leader put at the top of his agenda at this meeting a resolution calling for the creation of the "Turkestan Union", a Federation of the Central Asian republics and Kazakhstan. The first move towards the Slavic–Turkic/Moslem split that Nazarbayev had feared was now on the table.

The discussions at the Ashkhabad summit went on until 4 am on the morning of 14th December. Nazarbayev's participation was frequently interrupted by telephone calls from Yeltsin, who kept urging him to persuade the four Central Asian republics to join the CIS. This pressure from Yeltsin was a welcome antidote to the Turkmenistan pressure for a Central Asian Federation. Nazarbayev played his cards skilfully, presenting the CIS membership offer as a preferable alternative to setting up a separate federation. Eventually, as the dawn calls to prayer began ringing out from the minarets of Ashkhabad, the Asian leaders made their decision. They opted to join the CIS on condition that they were all considered to be equal founder members with Russia, Belarus and Ukraine. It was also a requirement that Presidents Yeltsin, Kravchuk and Shushkevich should come to Almaty for a formal ceremony on 21st December, at which the heads of state of all the founding members would sign the treaty creating the CIS.

21st December was a historic day for Nazarbayev. The date not only inaugurated Kazakhstan's formal independence as a nation state, it also provided the international stage on which the Soviet Union was consigned to history and replaced by the CIS. Aware of the political and diplomatic importance of the event, nearly a thousand foreign journalists, cameramen and TV crew flew into Almaty to report on the ceremony. As Nazarbayev described the occasion: "We were implementing one of the most momentous decisions of the 20th century. The Soviet Union was dead. In its place were 15 fully fledged independent states."

The most notable absentee from the celebrations in Almaty was Mikhail Gorbachev. 72 hours later, on Christmas Day 1991, he resigned his Presidency of the Soviet Union, and gave up the still enormous military powers that were in his hands, without any sort of fight or serious protest. Perhaps Gorbachev is the most objective participant in these drama to offer, in an interview for this biography, his retrospective assessment of the role played by Nursultan Nazarbayev in the breakup of what had been one of the most feared and most dominant power blocs in the history of the modern world.

We had our differences, but I honour Nazarbayev as the one leader who was consistently right on the big issues [recalled Gorbachev]. He was one of the first to see that the reform of the Soviet Union was a necessity, and he was one of the last to keep fighting to prevent its complete collapse, because he knew that would be a disaster. He was absolutely correct on both counts. We are still struggling with the after-effects of that disaster. But I can also say of Nazarbayev that he handled the disaster better than any of the other newly independent countries of the former Soviet Union.

8

The Birth Pains of Independence

Kazakhstan's independence started disastrously. The majority of its multi-ethnic population were shocked rather than joyful on learning that they were no longer citizens of the Soviet Union. As the New Year of 1992 dawned, the problems facing the first President, Nursultan Nazarbayev, were so overwhelming that the country's chances of survival looked at best fragile and at worst negligible.

Among international observers, the optimists were those who thought Kazakhstan might last for 10 years. The pessimists feared it would collapse much sooner. The threat was not military invasion by an external predator, it was internal implosion brought about by any one of several causes of chaos. The sources of instability ranged from hyperinflation to a home-grown constitutional crisis. They included the government's inability to pay wages and pensions; bellicose behaviour by Moscow; the exodus of more than two million ethnic Russians; paralysis of the President's reform programme by an inexperienced Parliament; insecurities about international borders; and unprecedented demonstrations against the Semipalatinsk nuclear testing grounds and nuclear arsenals in the country. Nazarbayev's struggles to come to terms with these early challenges tell the story of Kazakhstan's birth pains as a nation state.

The epidemic of hyperinflation that swept through Kazakhstan in 1992–1994 was a brutal illustration of the old saying "When Russia sneezes, her neighbours catch pneumonia". Nazarbayev had hoped that the health of his country's economy might be an issue for cooperation with the government headed by his friend Boris Yeltsin. This optimism was misplaced. Even though over 90 per cent of Kazakhstan's trade remained with Russia, collaboration with Almaty was a matter of complete indifference to the new ruling élite of Moscow. The first manifestation of their attitude came on 2nd January 1992, when the acting Russian Prime Minister Yegor Gaidar lifted all price controls at a stroke. Nazarbayev was himself moving towards free-market economic thinking but the speed, secrecy and magnitude of this initiative shocked him.

He accused Gaidar of being "better at destroying than building…, he is essentially academic. He has not spent any time working in industry … he does not understand the psychology of industrial managers."

The psychology of the consumers of Kazakhstan moved towards panic as prices in the shops skyrocketed. For a few weeks after Gaidar's bombshell Nazarbayev attempted to maintain a price-controlled economy, but with speculators on the rampage across the 4,668 mile Russia-Kazakhstan border he had to increase the prices of basic goods in quick succession on the 16th, 24th and 30th of January before abandoning all restraints in early February.

The empty shelves in the shops were only one part of the problem. As the annual rate of inflation soared to 2,600 per cent, another grave difficulty emerged. There was no cash available to buy even the most overpriced of goods. This was because Russia's State Bank, Gosbank, was the monopoly supplier of all rouble bank notes, and its Moscow controllers were having acute rouble shortages of their own. Kazakhstan's cash flow was not high on their list of priorities. Despite personal calls from Nazarbayev to the Chairman of Gosbank and to President Yeltsin, Kazakhstan's money supply dried up. This was a catastrophe for a country in which cheques were rare, and credit cards non-existent. Because there was no cash, wages and pensions could not be paid. The commercial and financial life of the country ground to a halt. Thousands of businesses, large and small, ceased trading. Within months there was widespread anger among pensioners and workers. The government bore the heat of the public's outrage but had no power to produce remedies that might ease the situation.

Nazarbayev inwardly felt strong emotions at the plight of his people, but outwardly he kept a cool head. This was a combination that served him well as a communicator both within his small circle of advisers and to the population at large.

Listening carefully to advice had long been one of Nazarbayev's qualities as a politician. The problem for him just after independence was that he had no domestic advisers with any experience of free-market economics. His old guard of former Communist party officials were useless in this crisis. So instead, he turned to young academics who at least had studied various models of capitalism in theoretical form at their universities in Moscow. One of them was Serik Akhanov, 29 years old at the time of independence, who had been taught about the concept of free markets at the Moscow Institute for Economic and Fiscal Studies. Another even younger Russian-trained economist-mathematician was Umirzak Shukeyev. They and four or five other young Kazakhs were moulded by the President into his personal economic think tank. With outside guidance from the IMF and the World Bank, this group became Nazarbayev's crisis management team.

We worked two floors down from the President at his office in Almaty [recalled Akhanov]. Often we met him on a daily basis usually after 9 pm in the evenings. These were highly inter-reactive sessions with the President firing off questions on the briefs we had written for him. Sometimes there was an academic flavour to our discussions when he wanted to know the various options in answer to his favourite inquiry: "What should the role of the government be in a market economy?" But more often we were providing him with practical courses of action for dealing with what was going wrong in a particular government department or region. These were extremely stimulating sessions for which we had to prepare hard because the President was so fully engaged in the dialogue with us.

Nazarbayev's style of management was to use his bright young men as a filter for both the conceptual and the practical plans for pulling Kazakhstan out of the quagmire into which it had been plunged by the collapse of the Russian economy. The informality of these "learning on the job" sessions formed the preparatory process for the meetings of the Supreme Economic Council of senior ministers and officials. The President chaired this council, and allowed his "Young Turks" to be outspoken in their criticisms of government departments thought to be underperforming.

He gave us a free hand to speak out frankly [recalled Shukeyev], particularly on matters such as cutting the government's spending. But at the end of the day we knew we were talking theoretically, while only the President had the experience to know what could be delivered politically.

The burden of delivering politically fell largely on Nazarbayev's shoulders. Once he had been convinced by his youthful advisers that their revolutionary new policies such as supply-side economics, privatisation, expenditure cuts and free markets were the right strategy, he made energetic efforts to sell these ideas to the country. The great plus of his campaign was that he was emotionally committed to the new policy, so he spoke with a fervour that enabled him to communicate with even his most reluctant listeners. The great minus was that he had almost nothing to offer to workers who were not getting their wages, pensioners who were not receiving their pensions, and a general public who could not understand why they were suffering from such a severe crisis.

There were three factors that saved the day for Nazarbayev. The first was that the size and speed of the country's economic disasters brought out the survival instincts in the population. The President knew his people and correctly calculated that their national qualities of personal stoicism would see them through the dark winter of post-Soviet misery. However, he also calculated that their acceptance of the situation was partly dependent on the second factor in the crisis – his own ability to explain what was happening in what he euphemistically called "the period of transition". Nazarbayev therefore devoted a huge proportion of his time to engaging with the public in every imaginable form, from village meetings to nationwide television broadcasts. One of the most permanent witnesses of this communication offensive was the Presidential press secretary, Igor Romanov.

I travelled with Nazarbayev all around the country [recalled Romanov]. The best quality in him was that he was never afraid to go out and talk to people. Sometimes he would be travelling through an *aul* [village] and see elderly men and women holding up placards saying "We want our pensions". He would stop his car, get out, invite the demonstrators to come off the cold streets, go inside a room with them and explain why their pensions could not be paid for the time being. When there was a strike in the Karaganda coalfield, he went underground down the mine shaft. There he spoke to the men who had not had their wages, answering their questions for eight hours but without making easy progress. In the end, they went back to work. Besides these face-to-face meetings he was always communicating through the media. Once a month he held a live press conference on TV. It had no time limit, so he did not come off the air until the last question had been asked.

By such intense communication methods, Nazarbayev bought time. He was also helped by the third factor in the drama – the understanding of the Kazakhstani people that they were not alone in their sufferings. The dominance of the Moscow media (virtually all the newspapers, radio stations and TV channels were in the Russian language) meant that the economic troubles of the entire former Soviet Union were equally well reported. It was part of that same Soviet heritage that the Head of State was not the first target in the firing line of criticism for the disintegration of living standards. Helped by that tradition, Nazarbayev managed to keep himself above the perceived failures of ministers in his government. Many of them were dismissed by him for incompetence. Others did a fair job but had to act as lightning conductors for the President, deflecting the public anger onto themselves. The country's first Prime Minister, Sergei Tereschenko, was an example of this.

Of course I knew what was making people so furious [he has recalled]. It was my number one headache, which would wake me up in the middle of the night and keep me worrying all day long. The question which bothered me so much was simply "how are we going to pay the man in the street's salary?"

* * *

The reason why there was no answer to this question to be found inside Kazakhstan was that senior Russian government officials were behaving with outright contempt towards Nazarbayev's requests for fair treatment. All that Moscow had to do was to release the cash which was owed to Kazakhstan's people, companies and the government itself for routine business such as trade deals.

The officials responsible for Russia's economy started making their own priorities and holding back the cash assignments to Kazakhstan [recalled Nazarbayev]. There were a group of so-called reformers there like Gaidar, Shokhin, Fedorov, Shakhrai and others who spoke quite openly about it being to Russia's advantage to rid itself of the burden of "subsidised Kazakhstan", and us inevitably ending up crawling back on their terms without any political guarantees or independence. Getting us to "crawl back on our knees" was regarded as one of the ways of reinstating the Soviet Union.

Nazarbayev could not easily change this overtly political agenda coming out of Moscow, even though he somehow managed to maintain an amicable personal relationship with Boris Yeltsin. Unfortunately, Yeltsin's Presidential effectiveness was being steadily reduced by his personal alcoholism. An illustration of this came early in 1993 when Nazarbayev flew into Moscow for a Heads of State summit meeting, only to be told that Yeltsin could not meet him because he was "drying out" at his private dacha in Barvikha. Eventually it was arranged that Nazarbayev should be flown there by helicopter, although the Kremlin aide seeing him off said, "For God's sake don't give our President any vodka while you are there".

When Nazarbayev arrived at Barvikha on a cold winter's morning he found Yeltsin all alone, wrapped up in his greatcoat, fishing through a hole in the ice at a pond in the grounds of his dacha. Feeling sorry of this pathetically lonely figure, Nazarbayev found another rod and went out into the cold to sit beside his host. As the two leaders fished in wintry isolation through the same hole in the ice, the uppermost priority in the mind of Yeltsin was not the agenda for the Russia–Kazakhstan summit, but the chances of persuading Nazarbayev to help him find some vodka. In search of his forbidden alcohol, Yeltsin suggested that they should take a walk to Nazarbayev's guest house next door because it was certain that his visitor would have been provided there with a VIP's refrigerator stocked with food and drink. Realising what might be happening, Yeltsin's medical minders sprinted after their boss. This Keystone Cops-style chase ended in the farcical scene of the minders reaching the hospitality fridge just seconds before the two Presidents. As Yeltsin saw the alcohol he craved being snatched away from him, he flew into a terrifying rage. He was eventually calmed down when a member of Nazarbayev's entourage produced some Kazakh vodka from a suitcase. The episode ended in a convivial evening, but it demonstrated that Russia's President was a long way from being in charge of his own government.

In their efforts to stabilise Kazakhstan's economy and secure adequate supplies of roubles, Nazarbayev and his Prime Minister, Sergei Tereschenko, had to endure constant frustrations and erratic responses from Moscow.

Russia's economic policy was utterly unpredictable at this time [recalled Nazarbayev]. Confronted by huge cash supply difficulties, we were forced to make special trips to Moscow to "extricate" cash to pay people's wages, not to mention the economy's overall needs. These trips went on all through the summer and autumn of 1992.

These words convey less than a full picture of the betrayals, blackmail, bribe-demanding and bullying that the leaders of Kazakhstan had to endure from senior officials in Moscow, as the struggle continued for economic survival. The reality was that Kazakhstan was having to pay for its own cash to be released from Gosbank, the Moscow central bank which controlled all supplies of roubles. This continuing crisis and the exorbitant costs of "extricating" even the most inadequate flow of cash soon made Nazarbayev and his economic team give serious consideration to introducing Kazakhstan's own currency.

A later chapter will give a full account of how Nazarbayev was forced to leave the rouble zone, and how he introduced the new currency of the Tenge. It was a story of high drama triggered by ruthless Russian betrayal. But to understand why various key figures in Moscow behaved so badly in this matter and in the whole saga of Kazakhstan's struggle for economic survival, it is necessary to understand the problem of ethnic tensions in the country, particularly the Russian–Kazakh frictions.

In the eyes of many Russians, Kazakhstan was not a nation state at all. This hostile view had its roots in the demographics of the new country. Historically, the Kazakh nomads had comprised 90 per cent of the population at the beginning of the 20th century. But by the 1980s, Kazakhs were only 29 per cent of the 17 million people living in Kazakhstan. They were fewer in number than the Russians, who made up the largest group of inhabitants at 34 per cent. Their fears of domination by the Kazakhs were shared by many in the wider ethnic mosaic which was made up of Germans, Ukrainians, Belarussians, Poles, Bulgars, Chechens, Koreans, Turks, Chinese, Crimean Tartars, Moldavians, Armenians and over 50 other nationalities. The leadership of the Soviet Union, which had deported many of these communities into the wide open spaces of Kazakhstan as a result of Stalin's political purges and Khrushchev's virgin lands policies, had suppressed their national identities. But now the iron hand of Communism had been lifted by Kazakhstan's independence, ancient fears and feudings between these ethnic groups reappeared. Handling their tensions was one of Nazarbayev's most difficult problems in the first years of Kazakhstan's nationhood.

It was a benefit to the culture and spirit of the new country that its first President had a long history of personal tolerance and respect for multi-ethnic diversity. This dated back to his childhood in a rural village full of ethnic groups; to his student days in Russian-speaking Ukraine; and to his labours as a steelworker in the heat of a blast furnace manned by many different nationalities at Karaganda Magnitka. Nazarbayev remembered with filial pride how popular his father Abish had been among the immigrant families of Chemolgan for his welcoming and cooperative attitude towards them. Like father, like son. Moreover, friendliness to foreigners was a Kazakh tradition. Nazarbayev was fond of quoting two of his heroes on this subject. One was the 18th century Kazakh poet and philosopher, Abai, whose advice on the good life included the statement: "The knowledge of the language and culture of another nation makes a man equal with those people ... if their hopes and worries are close to his heart then he can never stand aside from them."

Another sage cited by Nazarbayev was the Sufi poet, Khodza Akhmet Yassaui, who wrote:

> The prophet has this wish:
> When one day you meet a stranger
> Do not do him wrong
> God does not love people with cruel hearts.

These words are carved on Yassaui's tomb in the town of Turkestan in southern Kazakhstan. To this day, his mausoleum in the local mosque is a shrine venerated and much visited by Islamic pilgrims from across the world. Nazarbayev was not a devout Moslem, but as a politician he seized on these lines, using them to calm down the anxieties of those ethnic groups who feared for their religious rights in the new state.

Calming the fearful was an essential part of Nazarbayev's Presidency in the early years, not least because other voices were causing alarm among the ethnic Russians. Alexandr Solzhenitsyn, who had spent part of his Gulag incarceration at a Soviet prison camp in Kazakhstan, published a pamphlet calling for the northern regions of the country to be amalgamated with parts of Russia, Ukraine and Belarus in order to create a new Soviet Union. Solzhenitsyn's suggestion caused demonstrations in Almaty and other cities. Another prominent Russian polemicist, the right-wing politician Vladimir Zhirinovsky, also caused street protests in Almaty (coincidentally the city where he was born) with his fiery speeches demanding the annexation of what he called "the Russian lands" of Northern Kazakhstan within Russia's borders.

Equivalent voices of extremism were to be found on the Kazakh side of the nationalities argument. Some locally born Members of Parliament tried to create a constitution in which only native Kazakhs would enjoy full polit-ical rights. These nationalists proposed amending the constitution to exclude non-Kazakhs from the highest offices including the Presidency and the

Chairmanship of the Supreme Council of Ministers. Nazarbayev, whose first appointee to the cabinet as his Prime Minister was an ethnic Russian, Sergei Tereschenko, was horrified. "I had to decisively repulse such pseudo patriots", recalled the President. "Time and again I reminded these Parliamentarians that the constitution we were devising had to unite the people, not divide them on the basis of their nationality." Nazarbayev stuck to this firm line in private conversation as well as in his public statements. A few months after independence, his long-serving personal aide, Vladimir Ni, recommended a local man for a job on the President's staff, adding the rider, "He's an ethnic Korean". As Ni himself was an ethnic Korean, the comment was intended as a favourable endorsement of the job applicant. To his surprise, Nazarbayev rebuked him, saying "Stop your 'ethnic this' or 'ethnic that' thinking! Origins don't matter any more in Kazakhstan. We are one big family."

* * *

Whatever Nazarbayev's long-term hopes may have been for ethnic harmony within the family, in the short term some large national communities were divorcing themselves from it. Once it was clear that free movement was permitted from Kazakhstan, over 2 million Russians departed. The next largest category of leavers were 400,000 Germans. This mass exodus was a serious blow to Nazarbayev's quest for stability. Many of the Russians and Germans who voted against Kazakhstan with their feet were managers and technicians. Their loss caused a devastating gap in the agricultural, engineering, industrial and mining sectors of the economy. Nazarbayev was upset by this brain drain and by the fall in the country's population from 17.6 million to 15.2 million in the first three years after independence. He accused the leavers of "suffering from a kind of psychological stress ... they panicked and headed back to their own countries" . This was not the whole story. Many of those who uprooted themselves had long yearned to go home to their original motherlands. Others had been influenced by exaggerated stories of the enthusiastic welcomes they expected to receive from the communities to which they were returning. But the most influential factor driving the exodus was the perception that the prospects for Kazakhstan's economy were so poor. Nazarbayev himself tacitly acknowledged the scale of the problem when he commented, "This process was exacerbated by the economic and political chaos which were features of the early 1990s."

The political chaos was caused by the emerging confrontation between President and Parliament. Nazarbayev had not anticipated such a scenario. He expected that it would be a comparatively easy task to create a Basic Law which he hoped would "keep pace with the new realities and prospects, encapsulate the experience of previous generations and create confidence in a better future". This was easier said than done. In the immediate aftermath of independence the country's constitution was the obsolete 1978 constitution of the Soviet Republic of Kazakhstan. Written in Moscow during the Brezhnev era, it was wholly inappropriate as a legal framework for a new nation striving to be free, democratic and capitalistic. The contradictions between what had been enacted 13 years earlier at the height of Soviet power and what was going on in Kazakhstan in 1992–1993 were so enormous that parts of the old constitution were a farce. Chapter 6, for example, consisted of statutes defining the rights and powers of the Communist Party – which no longer existed. However, the most unworkable aspect of the 1978 constitution was that all power ultimately resided with the Parliament, which was still called "the Supreme Soviet". By contrast, the powers of the President, who was supposed to be the executive head of the government, were vague and ill-defined. His authority had been conferred only in broad political terms by a law known as "the Declaration of State Sovereignty" which had been passed in great haste and considerable imprecision by the Supreme Soviet in October 1990.

Nazarbayev had identified the creation of a new constitution as one of his highest priorities. He set up a Constitutional Commission, chaired by himself, with the mission of drafting the first constitution of Sovereign Kazakhstan. This was a 35-strong body consisting of Members of Parliament, ministers, judges, academics, lawyers and representatives of the former Communist Party and Communist Youth League. So inclusive was the membership of the Constitutional Commission and so broad was the spectrum of opinions represented on it that virtually nothing was achieved by the deliberations of this body. Nazarbayev became increasingly frustrated by the absence of progress. His own agenda for reform was stalled while the Commission failed to agree on even the outlines of a basic constitutional law. However, one matter which most members did consider to be of paramount importance was the continuation of the principle that ultimate power must reside with the Supreme Soviet or Parliament. As Nazarbayev commented, evidently in a mood of some exasperation:

The atmosphere was becoming tense … most members of the Commission considered their main objective was to preserve the old Communist structure of a vertical of power with the Supreme Soviet at the apex. They were not ready for an open dialogue and discussion of alternative propositions. It became clear that moving forward was going to get increasingly harder.

In fact, the Parliamentarians seemed to be moving backwards rather than forwards. This was partly because of who they were and how they had become members of the Supreme Soviet. In ethnic terms, the majority of the Parliamentarians were Russians. They had risen to their positions not by any recognisable democratic process but by communist cronyism. Most had been promoted through the ranks of workers' committees on collective farms or from the shop floor of industrial enterprises. What this meant was that Kazakhstan's legislators were an old guard of over-promoted farm labourers and manual workers stuck in the time warp of communist philosophy and practice. Many of them liked Nazarbayev personally, but could not comprehend what he was trying to do politically. So there was a reality gap between the President's reforms and the Parliamentarians' response to them. Often that gap was filled by legislative fantasies which had no bearing on what was happening in the real economy. For example, in 1993 the Parliament responded to the unemployment crisis in Kazakhstan's agricultural sector by voting through a law that gave full retirement pensions to tractor drivers and dairy workers at the age of 45. Even more expensive legislation was passed granting huge sums of compensation to farmers whose land had been ecologically damaged. As he watched this "vote-now-and-someone-will-pay-later" attitude becoming entrenched, Nazarbayev caustically commented: "The Supreme Soviet were working on the principle 'we publish the laws and allocate the money and it's up the government to carry them through if it wants to'."

This unrealistic populism of a Parliament exercising power without responsibility could not last. Yet throughout 1992 and early 1993, Nazarbayev clung to the hope that his skills as a communicator would knock sense into the heads of the Parliamentarians. So he threw himself into the fray by spending long hours of pleading with members of the Supreme Soviet to pass the constitutional changes that would create a basic law of rights for such matters as property ownership, parliamentary responsibilities, and presidential authority. Unfortunately, this was a task equivalent to teaching dinosaurs how to dance. The old guard simply could not get their minds round such concepts as the rule of law, individual ownership of land, a bicameral legislature, the power of a president to dissolve Parliament or the power of Parliament to impeach a president. One close observer of the long and exhausting dialogue between Nazarbayev and the Supreme Soviet in 1992–1993 was Baurzhan Mukhamedjanov, a 29-year-old professor of law at the Kazakh State University who had previously studied at the Moscow Institute of Law and Jurisprudence. Mukhamedjanov was one of a small group of youthful legal experts whom Nazarbayev used as his personal think tank on constitutional reforms. They were equivalent in importance to the team of "Young Turks" who had become his most important advisers on economic issues.

I accompanied the President to many meetings with representatives of the Supreme Soviet [recalled Mukhamedjanov]. Day after day I watched him explaining to the 360 Members of Parliament why Kazakhstan needed a new constitution. But these deputies would sit there with blank eyes. They did not understand half of what he was saying. And after the President had spoken, these old guard types would talk among themselves, saying things like "Why don't we just amend the old constitution?" "Why do we need to have foreign investment?" "Why should anyone be allowed to have private ownership of state land?" "Why should we ever need to impeach a President?" "Why does the Supreme Soviet need two chambers?" It was all very frustrating for the President.

Nazarbayev at first tried to conceal his frustrations in humour. He was good at cajoling the recalcitrant Parliamentarians with jokes and stories. But he could not move them away from their overcautious conservatism on constitutional reform even after spending a disproportionate amount of his time with them. "Sometimes I used to wryly joke that I spent my entire working day in the Supreme Soviet only to come home and deal with the country's even more pressing issues", Nazarbayev recalled.

The impasse between President and Parliament was temporarily resolved by a botched-up compromise. This was the creation of the 1993 Constitution. It was, in effect, a defeat for Nazarbayev because to get the law passed he had to drop most of his demands for property rights, equal language rights and many other of the changes for which he had been pressing.

There were three main reasons for Nazarbayev's retreat. The first was that his Presidential time and patience were in short supply when there were so many other pressing national problems to be attended to. The second was that he did not want to create a major split in Kazakhstan's public opinion at a time when other neighbouring countries were demonstrating that rows over basic law could lead to violence or even civil war. As Nazarbayev observed these regional upheavals, he became fond of telling a cautionary tale about a nomad family. The symbolic story, related in his own words, went as follows:

One day the old father of the nomad family died. His sons decided to share out his possessions equally among themselves. As they divided his sheep, camels, horses and furniture, each son was happy with his share. But suddenly they remembered their father's copper saucepan. Who was to have it? They could not divide it up and as no one was prepared to give in, they began to fight for it. After a long struggle, they finally decided to make peace. But by then they had lost everything. All their sheep, horses and camels had wandered away. The only thing left was the copper saucepan itself, but nobody needed it any more because they had nothing to cook in it.

Nazarbayev, always a vivid raconteur, enjoyed concluding this parable with the moral: "We won't make the same mistake in Kazakhstan." It was this philosophy that brought him to the third reason for backing away from a clash with the Supreme Soviet. He thought that a temporary or transitional constitution would be better than keeping the 1978 constitution in existence. He was probably right, although the minimalistic 1993 basic law proved so unsatisfactory that it merely postponed the constitutional crisis between a reforming President and an unreformed Parliament. Nazarbayev's next phase of troubles over the development of a working constitution are recorded in a later chapter.

One of the reasons why so much presidential effort was devoted to constitutional reform was Nazarbayev's determination to establish the legitimacy of Kazakhstan as a nation state. Despite his domestic frustrations over the constitution and the economy, he was simultaneously able to set off down the international road towards legitimacy by securing recognition for the country from foreign governments. However, this initiative was made unusually problematic because Kazakhstan had no experience whatever in the arena of international affairs.

Starting a foreign policy from scratch was another of Nazarbayev's major challenges, because there was no culture in Kazakhstan of having external relations with other countries. Diplomatic connections, membership of international organisations, agreements with overseas governments, treaties, even the human resources to staff a foreign ministry simply did not exist, for they had always been handled by the Soviet Union. In this vacuum of total inexperience, the country's first steps in foreign affairs were a one-man show. Nazarbayev's first diplomatic order after independence was given to his government's one and only official stationed outside Kazakhstan's borders. He was Kanat Saudabayev, a former minister of culture in the old Soviet Republic of Kazakhstan, who since 1990 had been based in Moscow as Nazarbayev's personal representative to Mikhail Gorbachev. On receiving a presidential order in late December 1991 instructing him to obtain diplomatic recognition for Kazakhstan from as many foreign governments as possible, Saudabayev had no idea how to carry out his task. What he did was to take advice from a friendly Kazakh working in the Soviet Ministry of Foreign Affairs. He was Kassym-Jomart Tokayev, who had been trained for a career in diplomacy at the Moscow State Institute of Foreign Relations after graduating from his school in Almaty. Having been intensively taught the Chinese language, Tokayev had been assigned to the Far Eastern division of the Soviet Foreign Ministry, doing long tours of duty at the embassy in Beijing during the 1980s. When he was approached by Saudabayev for help with Kazakhstan's recognition requests, Tokayev knew the ropes of professional diplomacy well enough to draft the appropriate applications to a number of overseas governments and to get them delivered to their embassies in Moscow. The response to these formal recognition requests was encouraging. Over 40 nations recognised independent Kazakhstan within the first six months of its existence, including all the leading EU and ASEAN countries. Membership of the UN was also granted. Nazarbayev was pleased by this response and made great efforts to welcome visiting foreign ministers and ambassadors to Almaty. However, his most active diplomacy was reserved for the big three countries on whose good will Kazakhstan was likely to be most dependent for its future security – China, Russia and the United States. The first country to recognize Kazakhstan's independence was Turkey which took this decision on 16th December 1991, the day independence was proclaimed. But Turkey had its own interest in doing so.

The Chinese were the most helpful of the major powers to the new Kazakhstan. When Kassym-Jomart Tokayev had delivered his recognition request notes around Moscow's diplomatic quarter in December 1991, it was the embassy of the People's Republic of China which gave him the most encouraging response. This was no doubt partly due to Beijing's *Schadenfreude* at the breakup of the Soviet Union. But it was also due to the Chinese leadership's positive attitude to Nazarbayev, which was mutual on both sides.

Nazarbayev had shown an unusual curiosity about China as early as his schoolboy years. While a teenage pupil in Kaskelen School, he had established a pen-pal relationship with a Beijing student. Although that soon petered out, Nazarbayev kept alive his interest in China by following, in newspaper and magazine reports, the tortuous paths of Sino-Soviet relations. By the mid-1980s, these were improving, so much so that in September 1985 a delegation of Soviet Union politicians made an official visit to Beijing – the first such mission for over a quarter of a century. Nazarbayev, as the 45-year-old recently appointed Prime Minister of the Soviet Republic of Kazakhstan, sought and obtained a place on that delegation. Although it was nominally headed by an elderly Moscow parliamentarian, Lev Tolkunov, it was Nazarbayev who assumed the role of leader and principal negotiator. His youth, dynamism and receptiveness to new ideas emerging in the discussions impressed his Chinese interlocutors. These good impressions were reinforced when Nazarbayev made his first official visit to Beijing in July 1991. The Chinese, like other watchers of events in Moscow, had begun to anticipate the breakup of the Soviet Union. So they gave Nazarbayev red-carpet treatment as a future political leader with whom they might soon have to do business in bilateral relations between China and Kazakhstan.

The dawning of those bilateral relations arrived sooner than anyone expected. As President of independent Kazakhstan, Nazarbayev immediately made negotiations with China one of his highest priorities. In February

1992, he sent his Prime Minister, Sergei Tereschenko, to Beijing. Kassym-Jomart Tokayev accompanied him as principal adviser and interpreter. Before the delegation set off, Nazarbayev had resolved Kazakhstan's position on the neuralgic issue of Taiwan by declaring it to be an integral part of the PRC. This paved the way for the President's good personal and political relations with the Chinese leaders. "I am prepared to meet them on a regular basis, perhaps once a year", he told Tokayev, whose skills as a Sinologist led to his appointment in 1992 as Deputy Foreign Minister. A few months later he was promoted to Foreign Minister.

Nazarbayev made his first Presidential visit to Beijing in October 1993, surprising his Chinese hosts by his willingness to make proposals aimed at solving the border disputes. These had caused severe historical troubles in the 17th and 18th centuries between the Kazakh nomads and the Qing dynasty of China. As recently as the 1960s, there had been bitter fighting and bloodshed between Soviet and Chinese troops in the border area of Zhalanash, less than 150 miles from Almaty. So it was remarkable that Nazarbayev was able to strike up such a good rapport on the issue with the leaders of China, particularly the PRC Chairman, Jiang Zemin. "We spoke the same language", was Nazarbayev's comment (meaning it metaphorically), after his first substantive negotiating session with his opposite number in Beijing. From that meeting onwards, the previously intractable Kazakhstan–China frontier problem was defused and steady progress was made towards delineating and agreeing the details of the 1,760 kilometre border.

No such steadiness was achieved during the early years after independence in Nazarbayev's relations with the leaders of Russia. Volatile is perhaps the kindest word to describe the attitude of Moscow's power brokers towards Kazakhstan in the 1991–1993 period, although a number of more pejorative adjectives such as overbearing, aggressive, deceitful and treacherous could be more appropriate for certain times and episodes. The only constancy was that throughout the roller-coaster ride of the turbulent bilateral relationship between the two countries, Nazarbayev somehow managed to maintain a cordial entente with Boris Yeltsin.

Cordiality did not spread much below the two Presidents during the ups and downs of the early Russian–Kazakhstan relationship. At the less senior levels of the Moscow hierarchy there was much blustering and bullying of "those peasants" or "those nomads", as the Kazakhs were derisively labelled. This attitude was personified by the first Russian Ambassador posted to Almaty – Boris Krasnikov. Described by one observer as "a typical old-guard Communist Party apparatchik", Krasnikov was singularly lacking in diplomatic finesse. "He used to tell me that one of these days Yeltsin will be toppled, there will be no special relationship with Nazarbayev, the Soviet Union will be restored and Kazakhstan will be put back in its place as a Soviet Republic", recalled Kassym-Jomart Tokayev, who as Foreign Minister had many such strange conversations with Russia's envoy in Almaty. However, none of them were quite so diplomatically bizarre as the exchange between Ambassador Krasnikov and the newly appointed Russian Prime Minister, Viktor Chernomyrdin on the occasion of his first official visit to Kazakhstan in December 1992. After the Russian leader's plane had landed at the airport, the first person to greet him on the ground was his own government's accredited representative. "I am the Russian Ambassador", began Boris Krasnikov. "Who?", said Prime Minister Chernomyrdin, feigning astonishment. "I am the Russian Ambassador", repeated Krasnikov. "What do you mean? Who the hell are you?", demanded Chernomyrdin, going on to fire a volley of expletives at the unfortunate envoy, which ended with the audible put-down: "If Kazakhstan thinks it's a foreign country independent of Russia, it had better think again."

It was to Nazarbayev's credit that he ignored these offensive noises of aggression from Chernomyrdin and other leading figures from Moscow, concentrating instead on matters of real substance. Some of them were resolved by the Kazakhstan–Russia treaty which the two Presidents signed in March 1992. Yeltsin had to overrule many objections to this treaty from his own officials, who did not like its clauses guaranteeing respect for the two countries' territorial integrity and promising no interference in each other's domestic affairs. However, the treaty was generalised rather than specific, so there were continuing issues about borders, citizenship rights, separatist movements and above all the rouble zone which rumbled on at varying levels of tension throughout the 1990s. Because Nazarbayev had such a good understanding of the Russian political mentality, and of the leading personalities in Moscow, he was a skilful navigator of Kazakhstan's ship of state through those dangerous waters. "He always knew that he had to stay on good terms with Russia", recalled Tokayev, "but in the early years those terms were heavily dependent on the relationship between Nazarbayev and Yeltsin".

There was one transcendent issue that had the potential to damage, if not destroy, Nazarbayev's efforts to have good relations with his powerful neighbours, Russia and China. It could also make or break his diplomatic overtures to Washington. In addition, the matter was fraught with domestic complications for it was sufficiently emotive, unlike the economic or constitutional troubles, to bring tens of thousands of Kazakhstanis onto the streets in public demonstrations. This issue, which brought Nazarbayev to the mountain top of decision-making on national and international security, was the toughest of his personal leadership tests during the birth pains after Kazakhstan's independence. The question he had to resolve was what to do about the massive arsenal of nuclear weapons that had long been secretly stationed and tested on his country's soil.

9

To Nuclear or Not to Nuclear

Resolving the big issues about Kazakhstan's nuclear future was one of Nazarbayev's most complicated problems during the period immediately after independence. The complexities arose largely because of a conflict between his human heart and his presidential head. Emotionally, Nazarbayev had long been committed to ending all nuclear tests and removing the nuclear weapons on Kazakhstan's territory. Politically, however, there were both domestic and international pressures in the opposite direction. In addition, the methodologies and technicalities of disarmament required an extremely careful decision-making process. So Nazarbayev had to restrain his instincts to indulge in the gesture politics of an immediate renunciation of nuclear weapons after becoming President. Instead, he embarked on a delicate diplomatic minuet with the world's major nuclear powers, designed to extract maximum advantage for Kazakhstan. How Nazarbayev handled the choreography of his nuclear negotiations is a story that reveals much about him as both a man and a statesman.

To understand Nazarbayev's attitude to nuclear tests and weapons it is important to go back to his youth, long before he embarked on a career in politics. When he was only nine years old, a schoolboy in the village of Chemolgan, the Soviet high command took the strategic decision to start using the region around Semipalatinsk in north-eastern Kazakhstan as its principal testing ground for nuclear weapons. The first atmospheric nuclear test on the Semipalatinsk site (a land area approximately the size of Wales) was conducted by the Soviet army in 1949. Within a few years of these early thermonuclear explosions, some of them 20 times greater than the Hiroshima bomb, stories spread across the Steppes about the horrific consequences for animal and human life. The Kazakhs, who made up 99 per cent of the population around Semipalatinsk, were appalled. Their national anger was aroused partly because it was the nomadic people of the region who suffered the worst effects of radiation such as stillbirths, deformities, cancers and mental illness; partly because the district around Semipalatinsk was venerated with an almost sacred status in Kazakh culture as the birthplace of the renowned poet Abai; and partly because the Kazakh tribes felt a natural if not mystical bond between man and land which was suddenly being violated by the perverted science of nuclear testing.

Nazarbayev first became aware of these emotions that were welling up in the Semipalatinsk community when he was a young man working as a steelmaker in Temirtau. He went on a picnic to Karkaralinsk, an idyllic rural area about 40 miles from the test site. The local families at the picnic described the frightening flashes they had seen in the sky and the terrifying quakes that had rocked their homes after mysterious explosions. But they were scared to talk about their experiences, let alone connect them to military experiments. For in the Soviet Union of the 1950–1990 period it was a criminal offence punishable by the death penalty for anyone to disclose information relating to the nuclear testing programme.

Despite the threat of capital punishment, young Kazakhs did talk among themselves about the outrages that were occurring around Semipalatinsk. In his early months as a steelworker at Karaganda Magnitka, Nazarbayev formed a lifelong friendship with a fellow metallurgy student, Tuleutai Suleymenov. He came from a family who lived at the foothills of Degelen, a mountain in the middle of the testing ground. When Suleymenov was 13, his father died of brain cancer; his elder sister died of leukaemia two years later; his second sister was mentally retarded; and his third sister suffered throughout her life from radiation sores on her forehead. The agonies of the Suleymenov family made a deep impact on Nazarbayev, who used them as a graphic example of the Semipalatinsk horror story when conducting international disarmament negotiations 30 years later.

Bringing up his own family in Karaganda, Nazarbayev had other experiences of the test explosions even though his home was over 200 miles from Semipalatinsk. As a father, he would see his daughters so terrified by the nuclear tremors that they rushed into his arms screaming "Papa, Papa – it's an earthquake!" Later he recalled: "Gradually we began to accept every new 'earthquake' as part of our Soviet reality."

The reality was that during the nuclear arms race of the Cold War, huge areas of Kazakhstan became the Soviet Union's weapons laboratory. Between 1949 and 1989, tests took place at the rate of one every three weeks. In those four decades, there were 752 explosions, 78 at ground level, 26 in the atmosphere and the remainder underground. The regularity and radioactivity of these tests had devastating consequences on the natural environment as well as on the health of the population.

Because of the ruthless imposition of military secrecy on the testing activities at Semipalatinsk, no one in Kazakhstan had a clear picture of the true nature and extent of the nuclear programme. "I was told nothing about it as a Prime Minister, and I am certain that my predecessor as First Secretary, Dinmukhamed Kunayev, was never briefed on it even when he was a member of the Soviet Politburo", recalled Nazarbayev. "These issues were regarded as matters of the greatest national security. They were known only to the highest military leadership."

Cracks in this wall of secrecy began to appear in the era of *glasnost*, particularly in the aftermath of the Chernobyl nuclear disaster of 1986 in the Ukraine. As a result of Chernobyl there were 47 deaths and over 4,000 cases of cancer caused by radiation. The long-term effects of the Semipalatinsk testing programme were "equal to at least two Chernobyls", according to Nazarbayev and the scientists who later advised him. Although he did not have the accurate statistics available to him at the time to know that the amount of radioactive material accumulated in the environment after the nuclear tests in Semipalatinsk was double the quantity expelled from the Chernobyl reactor, nevertheless Nazarbayev was shocked by the limited briefings on the Ukraine disaster he did receive as Prime Minister of another republic with nuclear installations. "When I found out what had been happening at Semipalatinsk, I cannot express in words my sense of outrage and my feelings of hatred for those who had conducted these nuclear tests in Kazakhstan with such total disregard for human safety", he has recalled.

Nazarbayev's indignation rose even higher when, a few months after Chernobyl, he was given an extraordinarily insensitive instruction to expand the land area of the Semipalatinsk testing site. This episode occurred in January 1987, when Nazarbayev was telephoned by a senior defence official in Moscow on behalf of the Soviet Council of Ministers. The official stated that it had been decided to build a new testing range for nuclear weapons in the Taldy-Kurgan region of eastern Kazakhstan. He added that the recently appointed First Secretary of the Soviet Republic of Kazakhstan, Gennady Kolbin, had given his agreement to the project. "So we now urgently need some land", continued Nazarbayev's caller. "Could you please organise for 10,000 to 12,000 hectares to be allocated. Also, be ready to receive a delegation of generals and specialists who will make the concrete preparations."

Nazarbayev was appalled. "Excuse me", he replied, "but do you actually have a concrete resolution of the Central Committee of the Soviet Communist Party and of the government. And have you consulted anyone at all in Taldy-Kurgan? And why am I, the leader of the government of Kazakhstan, only hearing about this now for the first time?"

"What does it matter", snapped the official, showing his fury that anyone might dare to question the demands of the Soviet military establishment.

"The project has been drawn up and the Central Committee has agreed. Simply sign the document when we send it to you and do as you are told!"

Nazarbayev also became angry. "I am sorry, but I am not going to sign such a document", he retorted. "What's more, I am going to formally ask for it to be reconsidered."

"You just try!", growled the voice from Moscow and hung up.

Nazarbayev called Gennady Kolbin, who was his immediate superior as Moscow's appointee to the post of First Secretary of the Kazakh Communist Party. However, since the unprecedented demonstrations against him in December 1986, Kolbin was in a position of considerable political vulnerability, and his relations with Nazarbayev were tense.

"Gennady Vasilyevich, I have just been informed that Moscow has decided to build a new nuclear test site in the republic, and that you gave your agreement. Is it true?", asked Nazarbayev.

"There was such a conversation", replied Kolbin, "but as I recall, it was not about building a new site, but rather extending an old one. Why are you interested anyway? Is there some problem?" Nazarbayev explained there was a huge problem. Already the Kazakh opposition to nuclear tests was becoming increasingly vocal and visible. The announcement of a new testing range would provoke great public hostility, particularly as hundreds of square kilometres of land in the region next to Almaty would have to be cleared of all villages, homes and agriculture. Kolbin did not argue with Nazarbayev's assessment but was clearly unwilling to make any effort to support his Prime Minister. "Why do you want to fight against these tests? The military will have both of us removed if we try to stop them", was the First Secretary's fearful response. Later in the conversation, he distanced himself even further from his subordinate's concerns by saying: "Well, if you are really opposed to the new site, you try and stop it then."

Realising that he was on his own, Nazarbayev began to lobby against the project in conversations with officials in the central military agencies, and with secretaries of the Communist Party Central Committee. He made no progress in changing their minds. In an unusual move, Nazarbayev then tried to talk to Gorbachev about the folly of creating a huge new nuclear testing ground in Kazakhstan. The Soviet leader was not willing to discuss the project, which was perhaps an indication that his remit as General Secretary did not extend to challenging the plans of the Soviet military.

In a mood of increasing desperation, Nazarbayev decided to deploy unconventional tactics. One of his oldest political allies in Kazakhstan was Seilbek Shaukhamanov, the regional leader of the Taldy-Kurgan *oblast*, where the proposed new test site would be located. Nazarbayev had a private meeting with Shaukhamanov to brief him on the military's plans and to give his regional subordinate some most unexpected instructions.

Seilbek, you can do whatever you want as long as you make sure that the rumour begins to go around that they are planning to build this test site [said the Prime Minister]. Also, in the next few days make sure that some kind of spontaneous mass meeting takes place to protest against this, it may just be enough to stop it.

Shaukhamanov became nervous at this novel suggestion that he should begin leaking military secrets and encouraging public demonstrations. "But you and I could both lose our jobs if we do this", he objected. "You will certainly lose your job if you do not do it", retorted Nazarbayev, "because I will sack you myself."

In the face of this pressure, Shaukhamanov obeyed orders. "He carried out his mission rather well", recalled Nazarbayev. In the next few days the news spread across Taldy-Kurgan that an enlarged nuclear test site was about to be built in the region. Public hostility intensified after Nazarbayev leaked secret statistics from the health ministry, revealing the extraordinarily high incidence of cancer cases in the Semipalatinsk area. Worried by the rising levels of public anger and defiant opposition, local KGB officers reported their concerns to their bosses in the high command of the state security system. From Almaty, Nazarbayev sent his own Prime Ministerial despatches to senior officials in different departments of the Soviet government, warning them that the protests were serious and might easily escalate to the level of the December 1986 disturbances. Eventually, Moscow got the message. The project was quietly cancelled.

Nazarbayev's cunning orchestration of the opposition to a new nuclear test site showed how far and how quickly he was moving from his previous incarnation as a loyal Communist Party leader. He was coming out of the closet as a Kazakh nationalist, although not overtly. Publicly, he was working as head of the republic's government in uneasy harness with First Secretary Gennady Kolbin. However, their personal relationship had become one of mutual dislike, which grew worse when Kolbin ordered a new investigation by the KGB of Nazarbayev's expenses.

Having survived a previous round of such surveillance under Kolbin's predecessor, Dinmukhamed Kunayev, not least because of the ultimate protection of Mikhail Gorbachev, Nazarbayev regarded the KGB's inquiries as disturbing but not destabilising. He was never confronted with questions about his expenses, let alone accused of or charged with any misconduct. But throughout 1987–1988, his personal movements and Prime Ministerial meetings were covertly scrutinised by KGB watchers and eavesdroppers.

I was aware of this activity [said Nazarbayev]. I had been given several warnings by my friends in Moscow, who said in effect "be careful!" But I regarded the allegations as malicious. All they did was to create tension between Kolbin and myself. When the two party bosses were at odds with one another it made the whole government shake.

Another part of Kazakhstan was also shaking as more underground nuclear tests were conducted by the Soviet military in the late 1980s. One particular underground explosion in February 1989 caused a serious leak of radiation, followed by public demonstrations in Almaty outside the House of Writers, led by the well-known poet, Olzhas Suleimenov. These troublesome manifestations of public feeling had first surfaced two years earlier with protests against the expansion of the polygon nuclear testing facilities in Taldy Kurgan in 1987. This was the beginning of the Nevada-Semei anti-nuclear movement, which drew massive support not only from its original core of authors and journalists but across the whole spectrum of Kazakhstani society. Nazarbayev, whose private sympathies and political antennae were well tuned to these protests, gave them considerable clandestine support. After Suleimenov lost his election to the USSR Supreme Soviet or Parliament in the Almaty constituency and was seriously embarrassed by the failure, Nazarbayev advised him to run for a vacant seat in a Semipalatinsk constituency making the Semipalatinsk polygon issue the top item of his election campaign. Nazarbayev also promised Suleimenov the support of the Semipalatinsk top officials. With this encouragement Olzhas Suleimenov did stand as a candidate for Supreme Soviet in the Semipalatinsk constituency. Thanks to Nazarbayev's influence behind the scenes, Suleimenov won both the nomination and the election, thus giving himself and his anti-nuclear views a powerful platform.

Nazarbayev came out into the open with his own views on nuclear testing when he made a speech at a plenary session in Moscow of the Supreme Soviet on 30th May 1989. In his capacity as a Member of Parliament or Deputy representing the Almatinsk-Illisk electoral district of Kazakhstan, Nazarbayev was called to speak in a general debate on domestic issues. It was utterly unprecedented for nuclear policy to be discussed in a public forum. But this was the era of openness. So, with the architect of *glasnost*, Mikhail Gorbachev, sitting a few feet away from the podium with his spectacle rims glinting in the arc lights, Nazarbayev seized his opportunity, causing gasps of surprise in his audience as he said:

I want to talk about the Semipalatinsk test site which has been in operation since 1949, and which began with explosions in the atmosphere. The population in the region since those times has quadrupled. But the military is trying to convince us that nuclear testing is practically beneficial for human health. We understand that it is a state necessity today, but there must be a real, profound analysis of the effects of atomic explosions on the environment. And the results must be told to the people.

These words were a long way from being a clarion call for nuclear disarmament or even for a cessation of nuclear testing. But in its context the speech was a brave initiative. Although not directly attacked for it in public, Nazarbayev soon found himself the subject of criticism and character assassination. Several Supreme Soviet deputies, some of them wearing their military uniforms, savaged the Kazakh leader with their hostile comments in the anterooms and corridors of the Parliament building. Nazarbayev was accused of "selling out" (although to whom was unclear), and of "washing dirty linen in public". The most serious line of attack was that he was "undermining the defence capability of the Soviet Union". However, the political reality of those volatile times was that the Soviet Union was undermining itself.

The battle between conservatives and reformers was gathering momentum in Moscow during the winter of 1989–1990, while in the republics there was a growing demand for greater autonomy. The conjunction of economic and political crises, exacerbated by bloody ethnic clashes, accelerated the slide towards chaos. "The most turbulent year was 1990, when it sometimes seemed as if the whole Union was ablaze", recalled Nazarbayev. He himself became a beneficiary of that turbulence when, as part of a more general decentralisation of power to the republics, he was elected by the Supreme Soviet to be the first President of Kazakhstan on 22nd April 1990. If Gorbachev and others responsible for Nazarbayev's elevation thought they were appointing a compliant leader who would govern the republic in accordance with the Soviet Union's highest priorities, they soon found they had made a big mistake. For, within a month of becoming President, Nazarbayev launched a political initiative that shook the military establishment of Moscow to the core of its nuclear being. This was an international conference held in Almaty in late May 1990 with the title "Electors of Peace Against Nuclear Arms". It brought together anti-nuclear campaigners from all parts of Kazakhstan and from 30 countries around the world. The climax of the conference was a peace march in Almaty followed by similar mass demonstrations in Semipalatinsk and Karaganda. The latter protest rally was supported by over 130,000 miners from the Karaganda coalfield.

People made impromptu speeches releasing the fear and silence that had accumulated over all those years when we just waited for atomic rain in our cities and villages [recalled Nazarbayev]. Suddenly it seemed that all of Kazakhstan and all of its people were caught up in a single goal – no to nuclear testing!

Even in the enfeebled state of the Soviet Union government there was the will for a fight back against the rising tide of Kazakhstani opposition to nuclear activities. Nazarbayev was summoned to Moscow for urgent meetings with Oleg Baklanov, the secretary of the Communist Party in charge of the military industrial complex, Nikolai Ryzhkov, the chairman of the USSR Cabinet of Ministers, and Mikhail Gorbachev, who had formally been appointed to the new office of President of the Soviet Union in March 1990. At one of these meetings, Gorbachev urged Nazarbayev: "Calm the people down. They'll listen to you. The country needs three to five years to get things in place. Then we'll shut down the test site."

Nazarbayev explained that such delays were impossible in the present state of Kazakhstani public opinion. He told the Kremlin leaders: "When you were doing these tests you should have built a system of support for the local population. At least you could have given them hospitals, a supply of uncontaminated drinking water, and proper protection against radioactive fallout."

"Let's do these things", said Gorbachev.

"But now it's too late", replied Nazarbayev. "The people can't be calmed down. The only solution is to shut the entire nuclear test site."

There were no signs from the military leaders of the Soviet Union that they were willing to accept "the only solution" recommended by the leader of Kazakhstan. In fact, as a slap in the face to Nazarbayev, it was announced in Moscow that three further nuclear tests would take place on the Semipalatinsk site in the autumn of 1991. However, a different kind of explosion, political in impact, put a stop to those plans. This was the attempted coup against Gorbachev on 19th–23rd August 1991. In its aftermath, Nazarbayev saw and seized his chance.

The failure of the coup completely transformed the situation [he has recalled]. With the central powers dramatically weakened, I now had the authority to end nuclear testing once and for all. On 29th August, I issued a Presidential decree forbidding further nuclear tests of any sort to be held on the territory of Kazakhstan.

The Soviet military had no option other than to capitulate to Nazarbayev's pre-emptive strike. On the same day as the Presidential decree was issued in Almaty, the new Soviet Defence Minister, Yergeny Shaposhnikov, announced that the three further explosions scheduled to take place in Semipalatinsk would be moved to the Arctic test site of Novaya Zemlya. It was the beginning of the end for Kazakhstan's 40-year-long nightmare of nuclear testing.

* * *

The wider nuclear story that Nazarbayev learned for the first time in 1991 was far from over. As the collapse of the Soviet Union moved towards its final stages in December of that year, one of the key questions on the minds of military and political leaders around the world was: What was going to happen to the nuclear weaponry of the dying superpower – particularly those parts of it which might no longer be under Moscow's control?

In secret briefings, authorised by Boris Yeltsin as the Russian President claiming to be the inheritor of the USSR's military power, Nazarbayev was first told in December 1991 about the full extent of the weapons of mass destruction stationed on Kazakhstan's territory. "The information I was given was new to me", he has recalled. "It had previously been a tightly held secret known only to the highest officers of the Red Army." The secret revelations staggered Nazarbayev. He learned that in terms of firepower, Kazakhstan was the custodian of over 1,200 nuclear warheads for intercontinental ballistic missiles (ICBMs). This arsenal consisted of 104 SS18 ICBMs, each equipped with 10 MIRV warheads (multiple independently targeted re-entry vehicles) with a range of around 12,000 kilometres. The missiles were stationed in 148 launch silos located across the country, with the largest concentrations in Akmolinsk, Kyzylorda and Semipalatinsk. They were under the control of the Soviet army's Strategic Rocket Command (RVSN), the highest military elite of the former USSR. In addition, Kazakhstan was the base of the Soviet's 79th Air Division, whose fleet of 40 Bear H6 and H16 aircraft were armed with long-range bombs and missiles. The totality of these forces and weapons gave Kazakhstan the fourth largest concentration of nuclear weapons in the world after the United States, Russia and the former Soviet bases in Ukraine. In comparison, the number of warheads controlled by Britain (296), France (512) and China (284) combined were smaller in number than those located in Kazakhstan. Nazarbayev now found himself President of a country that had suddenly inherited a formidable and terrifying assembly of nuclear weapons. When he inspected the bases and missile launch sites (particularly the Akmolinsk silos containing the huge SS18 ICBMs, known in the West as "Satans"), he was filled with foreboding:

There was something truly Satanic about the fierce array of ballistic missiles with separating nuclear warheads based on our territory [recalled Nazarbayev]. They were overwhelming just in their size. I always felt uncomfortable simply looking at the enormous body of "Satans" – 34 metres tall and three metres in diameter. By their very existence, these missiles aroused a feeling in me of dread and horror. I had a sense that they could turn against their owners at any moment with Satanic unpredictability.

*   *   *

As the chief "new owner" of Kazakhstan's nuclear weapons, Nazarbayev was not short of advice on what to do with them. His fellow countrymen, although united in their opposition to nuclear testing, were surprisingly divided on the right national policy for the weapons themselves. There were hawks who wanted to maintain a permanent nuclear strike force under Kazakhstani control as a deterrent to potential aggressors from violating the security of the country's borders. There were bargainers who advocated retaining the warheads for some years until they could be exchanged for security guarantees of Kazakhstan's sovereignty from the world's nuclear powers. And there were doves who demanded immediate, unilateral and total nuclear disarmament. As Nazarbayev listened to these discordant voices, he sometimes quoted an old Kazakh proverb: "Take you in? But you're a monster! Chase you away? But you're a treasure." It was his way of admitting that the issue of what to do with the country's nuclear weapons was a complex one which would best be resolved by careful negotiations and, if possible, with support from a national consensus. As Nazarbayev put it: "We had no choice but to embark on the difficult path of measuring conclusions and counter-arguments, doubts and fears, in a grand debate as we deliberated whether or not Kazakhstan would become a nuclear power."

This grand debate was not confined to Kazakhstani politicians and citizens. Even before independence there were powerful contributions to the advice Nazarbayev was receiving, by global leaders such as Margaret Thatcher, President George H. W. Bush and his Secretary of State, James A. Baker III. The US Secretary of State arrived for his first visit to Almaty on 11th December 1991, five days before Kazakhstan formally became an independent nation. Baker was accompanied by Robert Strauss, the American Ambassador in Moscow. Nazarbayev invited his guests back to his home for a family supper. It included the singing of Kazakh and American songs led by his daughter Dariga at the piano, followed by several vodka toasts to what Nazarbayev called "A US–Kazakh strategic alliance". Afterwards, he explained why such an alliance was needed. "If you travelled around my country you'd see Russian kids beating up Kazakh kids. That's how it was for me. It's not easy to live with them", he said, as he described the potential threat to Kazakhstan's borders from Russian expansionism.

James Baker, who found Nazarbayev "extremely intelligent and capable", was sympathetic to their fears. The US Secretary of State outlined what he called "The Five Principles" which America believed should govern the process of post-Soviet coexistence in the region. Those principles were respect for existing borders; respect for democracy and free elections; respect for minorities and human rights; respect for international law and obligations; and respect for self-determination consistent with democratic values. Nazarbayev was quick to realise that these concepts could help to protect his country against Russian nationalists. "However, he seemed less interested in the democratic elements in them", recalled Baker, who then gave his host a warning that upholding all five principles would be crucial not just for American political support but for American economic assistance.

At this point in the discussion, Nazarbayev suggested that his guests might enjoy moving to the *banya* or steam bath. Although this was a normal style of hospitality for Kazakhs, conducting diplomatic discussions in a sauna was a novelty for the Americans. Ambassador Strauss was startled when, as part of the sauna ritual, Nazarbayev picked up a bunch of birch twigs and began striking Baker on his bare back to open up the pores and increase the therapeutic value of the heat. The Ambassador came out of the steam bath joking to the Secret Service detail standing outside: "Get me the President of the United States on the phone! His Secretary of State is buck naked and he's being beaten by the President of Kazakhstan."

It emerged as the evening wore on that the US administration had been seriously worrying over the possibility that an independent Kazakhstan could turn into a rogue state exercising its own military control over the former Soviet Union's nuclear weapons. Nazarbayev poured cold water over these feverish fears while he performed the same task over the hot stones of the sauna. He reassured his American guests that Kazakhstan had no aspiration to join the military club of nuclear powers; that it was realistic about its inability to master the technicalities and pay the costs of maintaining the missiles stationed on its soil, and that he was a President with a long history of opposition to the presence of nuclear installations in his country. However, Nazarbayev also made it clear that he was not going to renounce possession of Kazakhstan's nuclear weapons without getting something in return. "I was initially after security guarantees", he has recalled. James Baker, who knew that it would be impossible for the United States to become the security guarantor of a former Soviet republic with a 3,500 mile border with Russia, tried to cool Nazarbayev from this demand with some tough talk. It ended with a stern warning that three American missiles were targeted at each one of the ICBMs stationed in Kazakhstan: "I am not frightened of that and anyway it is not the point", replied Nazarbayev. "We will decide everything on an equal basis. First of all, we need to know what Kazakhstan will get in return for dismantling these weapons."

Before America could turn these sauna conversations into a constructive agenda of disarmament, the rest of the world began beating a path to Nazarbayev's door in order to discuss the same issue. From January 1992 onwards, a steady stream of diplomatic envoys arrived in Almaty, sometimes at the rate of two a day.

All of them, even ministers from the smallest nations like Luxembourg and Malta, asked us the same question: "What are you going to do with your nuclear weapons!" [recalled

Nazarbayev's newly appointed Minister of Foreign Affairs, Tuleutai Suleymenov]. My standard reply to them was, "We are working on this issue in cooperation with our partners".

Suleymenov was a good choice for the post of Kazakhstan's first Foreign Minister. He had the personal confidence of the President, for they had been friends since the 1960s when they both worked at the Karaganda Magnitka steel plant. Suleymenov's subsequent career had taken him into the Soviet Union's Foreign Service where he was trusted as a safe pair of hands. One of his strongest qualifications for handling discussions with overseas delegations on disarmament was that he himself had been a victim of Kazakhstan's tragic nuclear history. It was the Suleymenov family story that had touched the heart of Nazarbayev when he was first told it by his friend in their steel mill days. The surviving son of this Semipalatinsk family, now Kazakhstan's Foreign Minister, would at Nazarbayev's prompting, describe the personal effects of the Soviet Union's testing programme to visiting foreign statesmen.

I would tell them about seeing the blinding explosions in the sky above our land and then watching the sinister mushroom-shaped clouds move towards us [recalled Suleymenov]. I described how these clouds dropped their thick flakes of grey ash, and how our animals would go crazy, with cows mooing and horses becoming hysterical. We were frightened, too, when we saw the immediate physical effects of the blast, like the pipes in our backyard being twisted out of their sockets. The long-term health tragedies were that my father and one of my sisters died young of cancer. My other two sisters had their lives ruined by the mental and physical effects of radiation fallout.

Nazarbayev insisted that visiting foreign ministers such as Britain's Douglas Hurd, Germany's Hans-Friedrich Genscher, France's Roland Dumas and America's James Baker should listen to Suleymenov's eyewitness account of the horrors of Semipalatinsk in order to understand the national revulsion in Kazakhstan against the country's nuclear past. Nazarbayev also insisted that Kazakhstan did not want a nuclear future. He was unimpressed by the domestic voices, the Kazakhstani equivalent of neocons, who wanted the country's young and untrained military forces to take control of the missiles as if they were a national independent nuclear deterrent. The President was equally contemptuous of the secret approaches he received from Arab envoys urging him to retain what they called "an Islamic bomb". One of these emissaries delivered a flowery letter from the Libyan leader, Muammar Ghadaffi, pleading with Nazarbayev to keep the nuclear arsenal in place "for the good of Islam". Another envoy, from an oil-rich state in the Middle East, offered to provide $US6 billion to Kazakhstan to defray the maintenance costs of its nuclear forces. Nazarbayev regarded such propositions as ridiculous. He wanted international recognition, respectability, investment and security. These objectives were incompatible with keeping the nuclear arsenal in place, a move which would have swiftly resulted in Kazakhstan's isolation as a pariah state. So, for reasons of political realism as well as moral idealism, Nazarbayev was determined to lead his country to nuclear disarmament.

The most effective partners in this disarmament strategy were the Russians and the Americans. Both superpowers were helpful, but it was the military leaders in Moscow who provided the lion's share of practical assistance in the early stages.

Once the Russians realised that we were serious about disarming, they were very forthcoming with information and support [recalled Suleymenov]. My opposite number, the Russian Foreign Minister, Andrei Kozyrev, was extremely helpful. At all levels our relations were good and in this matter we were far closer to the Russians than we were to the Americans. Even at a time when we were having great difficulties with Moscow over the rouble and over border questions, we stood shoulder to shoulder with the Russians in our cooperation on all nuclear issues.

One sign of the closeness of the cooperation was that when Nazarbayev flew to Washington in May 1992 for negotiations with the US government on nuclear issues, he stopped off en route for talks in Moscow with Boris Yeltsin. "This was not a mere matter of politeness", recalled Nazarbayev. "I needed to know his position as far as the weapons on our territory were concerned. The whereabouts of the missiles on the territories of our two republics was something which the two of us should decide together."

As he flew on to Washington, Nazarbayev had a new member of his official party, General Vasselevich, a key figure on the Russia General Staff and Deputy Commander of the four Soviet Union's Anti-Ballistic Missile Division. He was to act as the President of Kazakhstan's special adviser in the negotiations that lay ahead.

The Americans were becoming restless about Nazarbayev's position, calling him "the nuclear holdout" and suggesting in press briefings that he was reneging on his promises made in the sauna discussions six months earlier to turn his country into a non-nuclear state. This was an oversimplification. Nazarbayev was indeed playing hard to get, but tactically rather than strategically. His tactics were to offer what he called "A third way" towards full nuclear disarmament. In a letter to President George H. W. Bush in April 1992, he suggested that Kazakhstan should be designated as a "temporary nuclear power". He wanted to delay signing the Nuclear Non-Proliferation Treaty for as long as it needed for America and other nuclear powers to come up with security guarantees for Kazakhstan.

Nazarbayev's hesitations caused the US State Department's diplomatic minuet to accelerate to a quickstep, if not a gallop. James Baker organised urgent negotiations with the Russians, the Ukranians and the other leading nuclear nations. The result was that by the time Nazarbayev arrived in Washington, all the other key players had agreed to the terms of the treaty. Even so, on the first two days of Nazarbayev's visit, 17th–18th May, when he was staying in Blair House across the street from The White House, his appointment with President George H. W. Bush had to be postponed three times. This was because James Baker needed to make four visits to Blair House before finally completing the complex negotiations on Kazakhstan's nuclear status. "All the time the Russian General was sitting beside me, giving me advice and correcting any mistakes which I made", recalled Nazarbayev.

Eventually, after meetings with President Bush which included a family visit to his private quarters in The White House, Nazarbayev made a commitment to sign the Nuclear Non-Proliferation Treaty, the Strategic Arms Reduction Treaty, and to remove 120 Soviet SS18 nuclear missiles, with Russian cooperation, from Kazakhstan's territory. In return, Nazarbayev left Washington with an aid, trade and energy cooperation package; a $US10 billion investment in Kazakhstan's oilfields from the American company Chevron; and a promise that in accordance with the UN charter, the United States would take all possible measures if Kazakhstan came under threat from aggression. Although this last pledge was a long way short of the blanket security guarantees that Nazarbayev had been seeking, he came out of the negotiations with a good story to tell. An immediate consequence was the signing of the Lisbon protocol two days later. Under this agreement, Kazakhstan, Ukraine and Belarus promised (in cooperation with Russia and the United States) to relinquish all the nuclear weapons in their countries by the end of the decade. This was the endgame of the international worries and uncertainties about what would happen to the nuclear forces in the former republics of the Soviet Union. Nazarbayev had been the wiliest poker player in this game, which ended with most of the moral and military results he had wanted right from the beginning.

Although the principles of the disarmament settlement were finalised in Lisbon on 22nd May 1992, the practicalities and technicalities continued for many more months – with several scenes of drama being played out with Nazarbayev on centre stage. In November 1992, he hosted the visit to Almaty of a US Congressional delegation headed by Sam Nunn, the chairman of the Senate Armed Forces Committee, and Richard Lugar, a member of the Senate Foreign Relations Committee. Nazarbayev was seeking financial compensation and practical assistance for the physical movement of Kazakhstan's missiles out of their 40-metre silos. He also wanted to obtain payment for the value of the enriched uranium in the 1,200 warheads. After difficult negotiations in which Nazarbayev impressed his visitors by his mastery of complex detail, the Americans came up with the Nunn-Lugar programme, which assigned some $US800 million of Congressional funding for paying these costs in the three former Soviet republics, Kazakhstan, Ukraine and Belarus, which still held nuclear weapons.

The next important American visitor to Kazakhstan was Warren Christopher, the new Secretary of State in the Clinton administration. He came to Almaty in October 1993, bringing with him a $US140 million economic aid package and an agreement detailing how Kazakhstan should spend an additional $US85 million, its first tranche of the Nunn–Lugar programme, on dismantling its nuclear weapons. To Warren Christopher's dismay, Nazarbayev declined to sign this agreement. His refusal was preceded by three hours of talks in which the Secretary of State was given a geography lesson. Nazarbayev unfolded a large map in front of his visitor, pointing out how Kazakhstan was surrounded by Russia to the north, China to the east and Iran to the south. "This is why we need security guarantees", said the Kazakhstan President, promising that he would sign the agreement – but only at a meeting with President Clinton. Nazarbayev's delaying tactics were partly a bid for the political prestige of doing business at Presidential level, and partly due to an instinctive feeling that Christopher was a weak player within the Clinton administration. After prolonged but unsuccessful efforts to get Nazarbayev to change his mind, the US Secretary of State had to concede defeat and promise a future signing ceremony by both heads of state. "You're a tough cookie, Mr President", was Christopher's rueful remark at the end of the abortive negotiating session. *The New York Times* correspondent covering the visit began her report even more bluntly: "The President of Kazakhstan played politics with the United States today and won." *The New York Times* story said that Nazarbayev had held out for "a pomp-filled, face to face ceremony with President Clinton. No matter that the funds will be stalled until after the agreement is signed. The 53-year-old former engineer is eager to look like a first-rank leader both at home and abroad and he considers the photo opportunity more important."

Nazarbayev did get his White House photo opportunity in early 1994, but first he had to sign the disarmament agreement with Vice President Al Gore, who came to Kazakhstan in December 1993. After delays due to airport fog in Almaty, there was further brinkmanship as Nazarbayev had to break away from his meeting with the Vice President in order to quell a rebellion by a section of conservative-minded Kazakhstani legislators against their own government's nuclear policy. By coincidence, the delayed date of Gore's visit coincided with the Parliamentary debate to ratify the Nuclear Non-Prolif-eration Treaty. A group of hardliners almost managed to derail the talks with the US Vice President by their last-minute opposition to the treaty. In the end, having listened to a passionate speech from Nazarbayev, the deputies voted by a majority of 238 to 1 in favour of ratification. After this victory, Nazarbayev put on a celebration dinner for his American guests. In an extension of sauna diplomacy to dombra diplomacy, he entertained the Vice Presidential party with a melody of Kazakh folk songs, accompanied on the strings of his own instrument in a duet with his daughter Dariga. In response, Al and Tipper Gore sang "Jingle Bells". The festivities concluded with speeches and an official invitation for President Nazarbayev to visit President Clinton in Washington eight weeks later.

Nazarbayev's St Valentine's Day visit to the White House on 14th February 1994 took on the appropriate atmosphere of a political love-in. At a televised press conference after the Oval Office meeting, Clinton praised Kazakhstan's progress towards eliminating its nuclear weapons and for its accession to the Nuclear Non-Proliferation Treaty. Another bonus for Nazarbayev was Clinton's announcement of $US400 million in increased US aid, together with a double taxation agreement which was of great importance to the 70 US companies who were making investments in Kazakhstan.

Behind this Presidential sweetness and light lay a separate and at the time top-secret extension of US–Kazakhstan nuclear cooperation, code-named Operation Sapphire. It had started with an inventory, taken some months earlier, of all the remaining nuclear material stored on the territory of Kazakhstan over and above the nuclear warheads for the SS18 missiles.

This inventory produced two extraordinary discoveries, both of which appeared to have been "forgotten" by the Soviet Union. The first was a store of highly enriched uranium at Ulba Metallurgical Plant near the city of Ust-Kamenogorsk in eastern Kazakhstan. The second was an undetonated charge of radioactive plutonium buried in a deep shaft at Semipalatinsk. Both required the personal involvement of Nazarbayev.

The inventory taken by the nuclear weapons inspectorate with the help of Kazakhstani experts showed that in the nuclear waste-processing plant at Ulba there was a previously unknown storage depot containing 600 kilograms of highly enriched weapons-grade uranium. This was enough explosive material to make at least 20 nuclear warheads. Nazarbayev immediately reported the discovery to the military authorities responsible for nuclear matters in Moscow. He was amazed by their dismissive response, which was in effect to profess complete ignorance of this lethal store of uranium and to say, in effect, "It's all yours".

The Russians must have known all about this material [recalled Nazarbayev]. After all, the Soviet Union used to be one country, and all the records of nuclear stores must have been held in one place, presumably Moscow. At first I believed that these supplies of weapons-grade uranium were part of the soviet military's secret plans for a war against China in the 1960s. They built underground bases all over Eastern Kazakhstan for this purpose. But whatever the original objectives were, I eventually concluded that the military had simply lost the records and forgotten about the store of weapons-grade uranium at Ulba. They made it clear that it was all ours, and that we were free to dispose of it ourselves.

Knowing that Kazakhstan did not have the technical resources to carry out such a disposal of weapons-grade uranium, Nazarbayev sent a message through diplomatic channels to Washington. This resulted in an urgent visit to Almaty by the US Defense Secretary William J. Perry, who later claimed credit for preventing "what might have been history's biggest and most devastating case of loose nukes". This was more a case of loose talk by Perry, for there had never been any "nukes", and the uranium depot had always been held under strict security conditions. However, there were rumours, picked up by the eavesdroppers of the CIA and NSA, that an Iranian terrorist group had learned of the Ulba cache of weapons-grade uranium and were discussing among themselves how to get their hands on it. This fragment of intelligence, flimsy though it was, precipitated a mood of alarm among security analysts in Washington. In theory, their concern was justified because if just a few kilograms of this weapons-grade uranium had been acquired by terrorists, the consequences could have been devastating. To give one example: If Al Qaeda had used 1 per cent or 6 kilos of the Ulba uranium in its attack on the World Trade Center, then most of lower Manhattan would have been reduced to rubble.

In practice, however, there was no likelihood of any such potential catastrophe, because Defence Secretary Perry and President Nazarbayev cooperated so well and so swiftly. Under their joint orders, Operation Sapphire took on the speed and spine-tingling drama of a spy movie. Once the American experts were admitted to the Ulba Metallurgical Plant inside the former Soviet "closed city" of Ust-Kamenogorsk, they were able to trace the "forgotten" 600 kilos of uranium back to a Soviet Navy programme of the 1960s intended to create a revolutionary new type of reactor for nuclear submarines. The reactor was designed to produce nuclear fuel rods which would enable Soviet subs to dive deeper, stay submerged longer, and travel at a faster rate of knots than any submarine in the US Navy. The project became so costly that Soviet scientists nicknamed it "Goldfish", because it would have been cheaper to have the submarines made of gold. Eventually, the reactor failed, the Goldfish never went to sea, the programme had to be abandoned and the weapons-grade uranium was transferred into a thousand steel canisters stored in the vaults of Ulba; where it stayed, safe but forgotten, for over 20 years.

Nazarbayev was probably the first political leader since Leonid Brezhnev to learn about this project. There was no hesitation from the President of Kazakhstan in deciding what to do about this lethal store of 90 per cent enriched uranium. He sold it at the going rate for enriched uranium to the Americans (approximately US$90 million), and handed over the responsibility to them of moving it back to the USA. So, on a weekend of November 1994, a fleet of C5 transport aircraft arrived in Almaty. Using a cover story that they were members of the Atomic Energy Authority, 31 specialist US Navy personnel transferred the uranium to smaller nuclear canisters, loaded them aboard the C5s and flew the entire cargo back to a nuclear facility at Oak Ridge, Tennessee. Only after the last of the material arrived there did Secretary Perry announce the successful conclusion of Operation Sapphire at a Washington press conference on 25th November 1994. In a letter from the White House on that day, President Clinton told Nazarbayev: "You deserve the world's praise ... This important operation reflects an expansion of trust in the maturing partnership between our two countries."

Nazarbayev's wider nuclear diplomacy was winning him further praise in other capitals that mattered most to Kazakhstan's long-term national security. Ten days after Operation Sapphire had been concluded, he achieved a further success at an OSCE* summit meeting in Budapest when a diplomatic accord, "Memorandum on Nuclear Safeguards for Kazakhstan", was signed by Presidents Yeltsin, Clinton, and Prime Minister John Major of Britain. A Chinese version of a similar statement about security safeguards for non-nuclear states including Kazakhstan was announced in Beijing two months later in February 1995. The effect of these agreements gave Kazakhstan international acceptance as a non-nuclear state and a signatory to the Nuclear Non-Proliferation Treaty. It also provided potential protection from the international community against aggression or threats of aggression. "As President, I felt I had done what my country needed", was Nazarbayev's comment at the conclusion of these international conferences and announcements.

* * *

There was one last domestic surprise on the nuclear front, which needed careful handling by Nazarbayev before the saga of the Semipalatinsk testing ground could be ended. This was the discovery of an undetonated 0.4 kiloton charge of plutonium buried 130 metres underground in shaft no. 108-K. Nazarbayev called this hidden cache of radioactive explosive "the forgotten stepchild of the test site". It had been prepared for detonation by Soviet

* Organisation for Security and Cooperation in Europe.

scientists under conditions of great secrecy in May 1991 as part of a planned test known as Experiment FO-100-SZLR. However, the political upheavals in the Soviet Union during the summer of 1991, including the abortive coup against Gorbachev, had caused the test to be delayed. Then Nazarbayev's Presidential Decree of 29th August 1991, banning all nuclear tests in Kazakhstan, turned the postponement into a prohibition. Thereafter, Semipalatinsk was officially dead as a nuclear test site, but it unexpectedly had a secret life of its own through this undetonated plutonium charge buried in shaft no. 108-K.

Destroying this unexploded nuclear device deep underground was a highly complicated operation. Nazarbayev's first concern was whether it might explode spontaneously. He was not entirely convinced by the reassurances given to him by his experts, particularly when his principal adviser declared "There is no danger", and then added in the next breath that there was the potential for an explosion if underground drillings near the shaft took place.

After considering various options, including the removal of the device and its transportation to Russia, Nazarbayev decided that the safest method of disposal would be to destroy it in its underground shaft by chemicals. So, on 31st May 1995, 400 kilograms of chemical explosives eliminated "Object 108-K" – the 0.4 kiloton charge of radioactive plutonium. Nazarbayev regarded it as symbolic that the last nuclear device at the Semipalatinsk site was destroyed rather than exploded. "That non-nuclear explosion symbolised Kazakhstan becoming a nuclear-free territory", he declared.

*　*　*

Looking back over the record of Nazarbayev's attitudes and approaches to the nuclear challenges he had to face, it is possible to identify four main phases in his journey.

Phase one, which lasted for over 45 years, was the silent but worried period. Like most Kazakhs he was disturbed by the rumours and stories of personal suffering that trickled out from the people of Semipalatinsk. However, he had neither the knowledge nor the audacity to challenge the walls of Soviet secrecy and military power. But from 1986 onwards, the combination of *glasnost*, Chernobyl, and the ham-fisted Moscow proposal to enlarge the Semipalatinsk testing site kindled in Nazarbayev a fierce moral indignation. This characterised the second phase of his conversion to disarmament. It soon developed into a third phase which might be called waking up to, and then using the forces of, democracy. Initially, Nazarbayev had some concerns over the fervour of the Semei-Nevada nuclear disarmament movement. But because he agreed with it, and had the political agility to go with the flow of

147

it, he was able to harness the protests to his own agenda for autonomy. As Nazarbayev said of his historic Presidential Decree No. 408, issued on 29th August 1990, banning all nuclear testing at Semipalatinsk:

In those days we learned about democracy. It was one of the first independent steps of an independent Kazakhstan. We recognised and began correcting the mistakes of the totalitarian Soviet past. We set forth on a new democratic path. And the foundation of that path was laid in that historic decision for a non-nuclear Kazakhstan.

These simple words mask the complexity of the fourth phase of Nazarbayev's nuclear education, which was learning about the realities of international negotiations. At a time when his relations with Moscow were so fragile on economic and ethnic issues, it was wise of him to maintain such an effective channel of secret communication with the Soviet military on nuclear cooperation. For a short period Nazarbayev seems to have nurtured a naive and alternative belief that Kazakhstan's destiny lay in a new relationship with the United States. He did indeed develop such a relationship, but not at the expense of the deeper relationship with Russia. This learning curve took him through several Western excitements, such as sauna diplomacy with James Baker, meetings in the White House with President Clinton, an OSCE summit and Operation Sapphire. Yet these episodes were the icing on the cake whose real making, baking and eating had to be done in cooperation with Russia.

Nazarbayev emerged from the closure of Kazakhstan's tragic nuclear history with his reputation enhanced. At the earliest possible moment he had taken a brave stand against the moral evils of nuclear testing and weaponry. Recognising the nascent stirrings of democracy, he had understood the will of his people and their overwhelming desire for disarmament. To keep faith with this groundswell of public opinion, Nazarbayev's first major international action on becoming President was to ban all nuclear testing. After independence he had examined his options over the weaponry Kazakhstan had inherited, but he steadfastly resisted both the financial temptations of Islamic nuclear collaboration and the nationalistic calls for nuclear independence. Having set his course towards disarmament, he bargained sensibly with America, communicated clearly with China and did the business realistically with Russia. All his major calls of judgement throughout this saga were right. As a result he gained considerable respect on the international stage, which strengthened him as he continued to wrestle with constitutional and economic challenges on the home front.

10

New Currency – New Constitution – New Economy

Some crises take longer to resolve than others. Nursultan Nazarbayev had been swift to settle the nuclear issues that were dividing his fellow country-men and worrying the world. By contrast, Kazakhstan's economic and con-stitutional difficulties were more protracted. In the early phases of these sagas, Nazarbayev made errors of judgement. Eventually he took bold initiatives that solved most of the problems. However, his critics accused him of act-ing undemocratically, or even dictatorially, as he pressed ahead with his agenda of radical reform.

The rouble crisis was foreseeable yet surprisingly shocking to Nazarbayev when it happened. Within days of Kazakhstan becoming independent, he had grasped the exposed plight of its rouble currency whose supplies and exchange rates were at the mercy of Moscow's central bankers. So one of his first acts as President was to issue a top-secret decree authorising the prepara-tory work on introducing a new national currency. Only five other people were privy to this state secret, of whom the most important was the Chair-man of the Kazakhstan State Bank, Galym Bainazarov. He has recalled:

The President signed the decree and gave me the only copy to keep in my safe at the State Bank. I think he hoped that we would not have to implement it, but at the same time he had fears about what the Russians might be planning for the future of the rouble zone. So I was authorised to start planning for our own currency, which I did by buying new computers, making monetary calculations and even designing the banknotes.

These preparations were discussed at monthly meetings, chaired by Nazarbayev. One of the few light-hearted moments came when first draw-ings of the proposed banknotes were produced for inspection. They por-trayed the head of the President on the largest denomination note. Nazarbayev, whether out of modesty or a sense of self-protection at a time when infla-tion was over 2,000 per cent, declined to be immortalised in this way, saying: "It's only African Presidents who put their own faces on banknotes during their lifetimes."

Commissioning local artists to design a new national currency was one of the first decisions. Another step was finding the right name for it. Nazarbayev's choice was "the tenge", which had its roots in mediaeval Kazakh history, when *tanga* coins were in use on the Steppes. This name also had contemporary resonance because the Russian word for money, dengi had the same linguistic root as *tenge*. This combination of balancing the ancient and modern cultures of his society was characteristic of Nazarbayev.

A more substantive problem was how to produce the new currency. Kazakhstan had no suitable printing press. The Russian mint could not be commissioned because placing an order with it would have given away the secret. So, in the end two experienced British companies, Thomas De La Rue and Harrison and Sons, were awarded the contract. "The quality of their banknotes, the financial side of the contract and the confidentiality all lived up to our expectations", said Nazarbayev.

Although the first samples of the tenge were secretly delivered to Almaty in early 1993, Nazarbayev was full of confidence that the new currency would not have to be introduced for several more years. His expectations were based on undisputable facts of economic life in the rouble zone of the former Soviet Union. Whether Kazakhstani nationalists liked it or not, most of the country's trade was carried out with Russia and transacted in roubles. Nazarbayev was enough of a pragmatist to see clearly that the status quo was in the national self-interest in the short and medium term.

I wanted to make sure that we stayed part of the rouble zone [he has recalled]. There would undoubtedly be a price to pay in terms of loss of sovereignty, for it was clear that the Russians would insist in return on having some control over our budget deficit and money supply. Our central bank would be subordinate to the Russian one. However, such a price was worth paying if it meant that our factories would not lose ties with their traditional business partners, and our people's standard of living would not be hit so hard.

By 1993, many factories were collapsing into bankruptcy like a pack of cards, and the living standards of ordinary people were falling like a stone. So the optimism of the President looked like the triumph of hope over experience. Nevertheless, Nazarbayev persevered with his hopes of Kazakhstan remaining for some time in the rouble zone with considerable confidence. Why? "I had faith in my personal relations with the leaders of Russia of the day", was his own explanation. It was a revealing comment, not only because it turned out to be such a poor political judgement, but also because it highlighted a personal weakness in Nazarbayev. Throughout his career he tended to trust his close associates too easily. It was a rather surprising Achilles heel in a politician with a reputation for ruthlessness. Yet once he had established a personal rapport with a fellow politician or government official, Nazarbayev

Above left: With his mother, Aljan, whose storytelling and singing caught his childhood imagination.
Above right: Age 20 in the protective felt hat of a blast furnace worker at Temirtau steelworks. This photograph was published in editions of *Pravda* all over the Soviet Union in 1960.

Below left: On the back of this studio portrait which Nazarbayevsent to his future wife, Sara, during their courtship, he wrote "As a Memory to Save – Nursultan 1962".
Below right: Engagement photograph: Nursultan Nazarbayev and Sara Kunekayeva shortly before their wedding on 25th August 1962. They have been married for 46 years.

i

Above: Mikhail Gorbachev, a patron of Nazarbayev who he brought into the Politburo and in 1991 offered to make him Prime Minister of the Soviet Union. The offer was not accepted. A few months later the Soviet Union broke up. Kazakhstan was the last republic to leave the Union.

Below: Friends and fellow Presidents. Nazarbayev supported Yeltsin during the failed coup against Gorbachev in August 1991. Yeltsin supported Nazarbayev on many issues, notably the division of oil rights in the Caspian Sea.

Above: Margaret Thatcher recommended privatisation and free market economics to Nazarbayev when he was the Communist Party leader of Kazakhstan.

Below: Nazarbayev negotiated the nuclear disarmament of Soviet missiles in Kazakhstan with President George H. W. Bush and his Secretary of State, James A. Baker.

Above: Nazarbayev successfully lobbied George W. Bush to support Kazakhstan's chairmanship of the Organisation for Security and Cooperation in Europe (OSCE) from 2010.

Below: Family life at 10 Downing Street. Nazarbayev with Tony and Leo Blair.

All smiles with the powerful neighbours. Nazarbayev with President Putin of Russia and Chairman Jiang Zemin of China.

Above left: Action Men. Presidents Nazarbayev and Putin take time off for a day's skiing in Kazakhstan.
Above right: Astana's Pyramid – The Palace of Peace and Concord.

Below: Astana by night with Transport Tower in foreground.

Above: The House of Ministries flanked by Golden Cones.
Below: The Baiterek Tree of Life Monument.

Above: The Nur Astana Islamic Cultural Centre and Mosque.

Below: The Al Akorda Presidential Office.

was apt to rely too heavily and confide too freely in the individual concerned – until disappointment dawned, as it so often did in the early years of independence.

There were few unhappier examples in Nazarbayev's career of excessive trust followed by devastating disappointment than the story of his relationship with Viktor Chernomyrdin. He became Prime Minister of Russia in December 1992, after Yegor Gaidar had failed to win the necessary votes for his confirmation to that office from Parliament. Chernomyrdin's first Prime Ministerial visit outside Russia was to Kazakhstan. Three days after taking office, he flew to Almaty and discussed a number of troublesome bilateral issues with Nazarbayev. Top of their agenda was the currency question, particularly the acute rouble shortages that were throttling Kazakhstan's economy. Chernomyrdin gave assurances that the cash flow of roubles from Moscow would improve. He also promised that if Russia did introduce its own currency then Kazakhstan would remain in the new rouble zone.

These assurances were repeated when Nazarbayev and Chernomyrdin met again six weeks later, at the World Economic Forum in Davos, Switzerland, in January 1993. They had dinner together with their respective national delegations present. After the meal and many formal toasts of friendship, the President and the Prime Minister left the table to go for a walk on their own. As the two leaders strolled through the snowy streets of Davos, Chernomyrdin divulged an important secret. On 1st April Russia would be withdrawing its old rouble bank notes bearing the portrait of Lenin, and issuing new ones. However, this change would not affect Kazakhstan, said the Prime Minister. As Nazarbayev recalled the ensuing dialogue: "Don't worry, we will print money for Kazakhstan as well", promised Chernomyrdin.

"All right. But are you sure?", asked Nazarbayev.

"Sure."

"Can I trust you?"

"Yes."

Nazarbayev was not quite so gullible as these words suggest in cold print. Although he believed in his heart that the Russian leader would keep his promises, Nazarbayev also listened with his head to his young circle of economic advisers, who were reporting the rumours from Moscow that the Central Bank was planning the opposite course to the one pledged by Chernomyrdin in Davos. "We had a strong feeling that the Russians were playing a double game with us", recalled Daulet Sembayev, the first deputy Prime Minister of Kazakhstan, who was in charge of day-to-day management of the economy. "So we encouraged the President to develop a strategy of backing two horses."

The two-horse race was wrecked when Nazarbayev's Russian mount veered off the track. Chernomyrdin's promise of sending fresh supplies of new rouble banknotes to Kazakhstan on 1st April turned out to be an April Fool. No money arrived. The Central Bank of Russia had discontinued printing the old roubles some weeks earlier, so exacerbating Kazakhstan's crisis of being unable to pay wages and pensions. Meanwhile, new-issue roubles were being printed. However, they were exclusively for Russian use because Moscow's leaders had secretly decided to create a new national currency that excluded Kazakhstan. The first news Nazarbayev received of this decision came in a telephone call from Chernomyrdin on 30th June 1993. The Russian Prime Minister's message was presented as a take-it-or-leave-it fait accompli. Nazarbayev was shocked by the blow and by the betrayal. "I held the view then and still do that this was totally unfair", he has recalled. "We trusted Russia and our mutual neighbourly relations. This step came like a bolt from the blue for Kazakhstan."

The first person Nazarbayev telephoned after taking Chernomyrdin's call was Daulet Sembayev. "It's over now", said the President in a shocked voice. "The rouble zone is finished. Russia is introducing its own new currency as from tomorrow."

The next few weeks were an economic disaster for Kazakhstan. Despite all the deceit that had been practised on him, Nazarbayev continued to try and negotiate in good faith with Russia's leadership. In an attempt at damage limitation, he flew to Moscow for talks with President Boris Yeltsin in August, and signed an agreement with him that kept Kazakhstan in the new rouble zone. Despite more meetings in the same month with Chernomyrdin, the agreement was being steadily undermined. For, at the same time as the terms for getting the new roubles were being discussed, huge quantities of illegal old roubles were being dumped into Kazakhstan, not only by cross-border speculators but also from the eight military bases in the country which were still under Russian control. The worthless currency being flown into these bases was clearly part of an official operation by the government in Moscow. In a matter of weeks, the Kazakhstani public realised what was happening. The value of the old notes plunged, inflation soared, and economic instability bordering on panic spread across the country. On 7th October, Nazarbayev attempted to calm the situation by signing an agreement in Moscow, together with the representatives of Uzbekistan, Armenia, Tajikistan and Belarus, for the creation of a new rouble zone. It encompassed these four countries plus Kazakhstan and Russia. However, the Russian government drove a hard bargain for this deal. The negotiators insisted that their central bank in Moscow would control the money supply. They also demanded that the budgets, taxes, customs duties and interest rates of Kazakhstan and the other republics must be unified with those in Russia. This amounted to a major loss of sovereignty, but Nazarbayev decided to accept the terms of the deal because he wanted to gain time as there was less than a month before the introduction of Kazakhstan's own currency. So, he persuaded the Parliament of Kazakhstan to ratify the deal by a vote on 12th October 1993.

These economic developments were overtaken by far more dramatic events in Moscow, where Yeltsin was coming under intense pressure from popular unrest and parliamentary rebellion. In mid-October he quelled the uprising by a massive show of force, calling up tanks to shell the Russian White House or Parliament building. These events caused further political turmoil. Within the Russian government, a faction emerged which strongly opposed the new rouble-zone agreement. This opposition was not made known to Nazarbayev until 19th October, when Alexander Shokhin, the Deputy Prime Minister in charge of integrating the monetary systems of the six republics, flew to Almaty. Nazarbayev asked him whether the new rouble zone was still going ahead. "We can't do it", replied Shokhin. "We have separate interests now." Nazarbayev was shocked, realising that he had again been betrayed by the Russian leaders in whom he had trusted. "It was clear that the idea of keeping Kazakhstan in the rouble zone was dead", he has recalled. "The declarations and joint statements I had signed with Yeltsin and Chernomyrdin meant nothing. From the very beginning they had intended to push Kazakhstan out." In a later comment, made with the wisdom of hindsight, Nazarbayev reflected:

The lesson I was taught was that heads of state don't have friends. They have the interests of their country and people. An independent state has to rely on its own strengths and be prepared in advance for any difficulties that may occur.

Although Nazarbayev had been too naive in his dealings with Chernomyrdin and Yeltsin, at least there was a "Plan B" in place for the introduction of Kazakhstan's own national currency. The secret decree that had been signed in early 1992 authorising preparatory studies on the tenge was urgently upgraded into an official government commission responsible for introducing it. After looking at various possible interim solutions, this commission, chaired by Nazarbayev, decided to bring in the new currency in one fell swoop. This was a massive operation logistically, politically and economically. The logistics required the despatch of a fleet of specially chartered transport aircraft to London to pick up the newly printed banknotes, followed by a high speed distribution exercise across the country. "The operation was conducted in great secrecy under the control of the Committee on National Security", recalled Nazarbayev.

I made it clear that anyone who revealed the secret would be fired immediately and taken to court. Within the seemingly impossible period of one week, and with incredible energy, the banknotes were delivered not just to banks in every town and region but to the smallest village post offices as well.

After physical distribution came political communication. This was a job that could only be done by the President. As he prepared to make a national broadcast on the night of Friday 12th November, informing his people that they would have a new national currency on the following Monday morning, Nazarbayev made the uncharacteristic admission that he was feeling "extremely agitated". There were several reasons for his high level of anxiety. His greatest worry was that he had no idea how the public would react. He knew that the introduction of the tenge had been forced on Kazakhstan by Russian bullying and betrayal. But he could not admit this in a broadcast to a population whose second largest ethnic element (around 30 per cent) consisted of Russians. So he had to pretend that there had been no rift with Moscow and that the introduction of the new currency would not disturb Kazakhstan's economic and business links with its mighty neighbour. As the arrival of the tenge had been a well kept secret, even from the Yeltsin government which had no inkling that it was going to be brought in so quickly, Nazarbayev was second-guessing their reaction to it. In his broadcast he tried to steer a careful course between not offending the Russians while simultaneously appealing for Kazakh national pride in a historic measure to strengthen the country's sovereignty. It was a difficult balance to strike, but Nazarbayev's carefully chosen words seemed to result in a speech whose political judgements were acceptable to most parts of his audience.

The initial economic judgements made at the time of the introduction of the tenge were far less successful. Although the first practicalities went well, with a five-day transition period when both the new and old currencies were legal tender, there were some bad mistakes. The country's gold and foreign exchange reserves of 700 million dollars were inadequate to back the new currency. The initial exchange rate of the tenge was set far too high at 1:5 to the US dollar. It had to be devalued in a matter of days by 50 per cent. The President, with his customary agility in escaping bad news, managed to rise above the inevitable public criticism that followed these devaluations with their adverse consequences on savings, pensions and business enterprises. In his later accounts of these events, Nazarbayev attributed the errors of judgment to his Prime Minister. "The devaluation was a serious mistake by Sergei Tereschenko", said the President. "He should have resigned immediately afterwards rather than staying on in office, as he did, until October 1994." In other comments he blamed the Parliament for the fall in the tenge. These excuses were self-serving revisionism, particularly from a President who was rarely slow to require resignations from ministers who underperformed. The reality was that the key decisions on the tenge, including its exchange rate, were taken collectively by the entire economic team, with the President at its head. For his part, Tereschenko has acknowledged his role in the misjudgement but with the comment: "At the time of the introduction of the new currency we had become prisoners of our illusions. We all believed we could keep the rate at 1:5, but this turned out to be a romantic view." There is little doubt that at the time, Nazarbayev was part of the romantic tendency.

Although the new currency had a rough ride in its first few months, seen from the perspective of history the introduction of the tenge was an enduring achievement which built economic and political stability. Tactically, there were short-term problems. Strategically, it was a bold move which strengthened Kazakhstan's independence and sovereignty. The tenge eventually floated on the international markets at a level of approximately 70 to the dollar. At this rate Kazakhstan's exports and productivity began to grow. There was a comparable improvement in the country's gold and foreign currency reserves as well as in its balance of payments. So the tenge was an important element in changing the country's economic course from chaos to competitiveness.

Even more significant than the tenge's contribution to economic success was its impact on Kazakhstan's self-confidence as a nation. The break from the rouble zone was involuntary at the time, but the speed and decisiveness with which the new currency was introduced were to the credit of Nazarbayev, Tereschenko and other key players on the Currency Commission. Although neither the people nor the Parliament of Kazakhstan were psychologically ready for such a momentous development, once the banknotes were in circulation and the roller-coaster descent of devaluation had slowed to the more gentle pace of a float, there was widespread national pride in the creation of an independent national currency. It was a major step forward in establishing the country's sovereignty. Nazarbayev was right to say, "The tenge is part and parcel of our history, and a landmark of its time".

*   *   *

In the saga of the tenge, Nazarbayev's actions were an uneasy mixture of being reactive and proactive. Faced with his next major crisis, which centred on Parliament and the constitution, he was far bolder. This was partly because the drama was a domestic one. However, as with the tenge, it was a sequence of surprising events which presented him with the opportunity to act decisively.

The introduction of the new currency had exposed fundamental flaws in the 1993 constitution and in the Supreme Soviet as Kazakhstan's ultimate source of Parliamentary authority. Many of the old-guard deputies did not understand what they were being asked to vote for in the replacement of the rouble by the tenge. Still less did they grasp the need for passing urgent legislative measures to reform the sclerotic economy, which was under alarming pressures of inflation and currency speculation. Parliament and President found themselves increasingly at loggerheads. As Nazarbayev put it:

The Supreme Soviet proved incapable of passing laws. Extended and unproductive discussions took place at its sessions, with lengthy intervals between them. We were forever waiting for Parliament's rulings, and gained the impression that it was simply blocking the formation of a legislative base for economic reform ... the issue of supremacy was constantly being contested.

The President's frustrations were shared by a growing number of Parliamentarians. In December 1993, 200 of the Supreme Soviet's 360 deputies tendered their resignations. This self-dissolution, described by Nazarbayev as "one of the most dramatic events in independent Kazakhstan's history" was an extraordinary case of turkeys voting for Christmas. Why did they do it? One explanation is that they were running scared of events both inside and outside the country. Hyperinflation and a plummeting currency were two causes of fear. Far more alarming was the example of neighbouring Russia's clash between executive and legislature, which had ended in Yeltsin ordering the Kantemirov tank division to open fire on the Parliament building. There were comparable battles raging across the region, particularly in Georgia, Azerbaijan and Tajikistan. Perhaps it was not surprising that a majority of Kazakhstan's deputies wanted to back away from responsibility for such potential bloodshed in their country. So they voted themselves into extinction as a Parliament on 8th December 1993, handing back all their powers to the executive.

In the period December 1993 to March 1994, Nazarbayev ruled by Presidential decree. He introduced a programme of economic reforms and set a date for new elections. After intense negotiations, it was decided that the next Parliament should consist of a single chamber of 177 professional deputies. Unfortunately, their professionalism lasted for only a few weeks after the March election. By the time it was 12 months old the Parliament was back to its predecessors' bad habits of filibustering, thwarting the executive programme and feathering its own nest. Nazarbayev declared himself "deeply disappointed", after his budget had been obstructed by 13 weeks of inconclusive debates. He became sharply critical of the deputies for enacting only seven new laws during their first year, while at the same time voting themselves extra salaries and allowances that cost the public purse more than one billion tenge. Far more serious was the Parliament's reluctance to vote for the government's major reforms, which included equal language rights, equality under the rule of law, private ownership rights, and the privatisation of major industries.

Nazarbayev was rescued from his deepening gloom over his frustrations with the legislature by an unexpected development. It arose out of a local squabble in one constituency, where the unsuccessful candidate in the March 1994 poll alleged there had been violations of the electoral code. This candidate, Tatiana Kvyatovskya, took her allegations to the Central Election Commission, to the newspapers and to the courts. To the surprise of many observers, including the President himself, the Constitutional Court handed down a favourable judgment on Tatiana Kvyatovskya's case in March 1995. The courts ruling was that in her district, and in constituencies across the country, the method of counting votes introduced by the Central Election Commission entailed a large-scale violation of the constitutional principle of "one man one vote" which had distorted the election results.

After seeking further clarifications from the Constitutional Court, Nazarbayev decided that the judgment had rendered the electoral mandates of all the deputies unconstitutional. On that basis, he ordered the dissolution of Parliament. There was strong opposition to his action, particularly among the deputies themselves. Under the leadership of Olzhas Suleimenov, who was a well-known poet as well as a deputy, 70 out of the 177 members of parliament voted against disbanding. If they had been able to secure a few more votes, their stance could have triggered a serious constitutional crisis. Nazarbayev realised that his decision had been "one of the most difficult of his career" but he stood firm in the face of demonstrations, hunger strikes and other protests by the dissenting deputies. It soon appeared that public opinion was far more apathetic about the existence of the Parliament than the parliamentarians themselves. The deputies were unable to maintain momentum for their protests, which noticeably failed to gather popular support. Nazarbayev moved quickly once he saw that his critics' accusations against him of exercising the powers of a dictator were falling on deaf ears among the population as a whole. He called a referendum extending his term as President to six more years. The simple question asked of the voters was: "Are you in favour of extending the authority of the President, elected by the people, until December 2000?" This was in effect a request for a vote of confidence in himself. Facing down his critics, Nazarbayev opened his referendum campaign with the challenge:

We hear cries that there will be a dictatorship. Yes, dictatorship will come, but it will be a dictatorship of the constitution and of the rule of law. The danger of real dictatorship comes instead if chaos and anarchy are created under the guise of democratic slogans. Then the people will call for a firm hand.

Nazarbayev's demand to be given a firm hand offended his critics, but resonated with the wider public. Most Kazakhstanis were nervous of a power struggle between President and Parliament. They feared a re-run in Almaty of the bloody clashes in Moscow that had taken place a few months earlier. Instinctively, they preferred the decisive governance of a powerful strongman to indecisive stagnation under a weak Parliament. There was also a growing understanding, at popular if not parliamentary level, that reforms in the direction of privatisation and a free market were the only viable alternative for the economy. For these reasons the President's referendum caught a wave of support. When the poll was taken on 29th April 1995, Nazarbayev won it by an overwhelming majority, securing 95 per cent of the votes cast. Although in the eyes of critical observers the size of the landslide was too good to be true, their allegations of vote-rigging went unheeded. For there was little doubt that the majority of the electorate were firmly behind their President.

Nazarbayev had an appetite for exercising Presidential power, but he was too canny a politician to use his referendum victory as a springboard to overt dictatorship. He realised that such a perception of his leadership would make him a pariah in the eyes of the international media and the world's democracies. He also knew that he would forfeit the long-term support of his own people if they saw him as acting unlawfully or unconstitutionally. So he placed great emphasis on the fact that he was governing in accordance with a section of the 1993 constitution which allowed the *temporary* delegation of additional powers to the President of the Republic. Under that legal authority, Nazarbayev made the creation of a new constitution his highest priority.

A team of young law professors and constitutional lawyers had been formed by the President at the time of his unsuccessful attempt to draft a satisfactory constitution in 1993. It was suddenly revived at the time of the dissolution of Parliament in April 1995. The then Justice Minister and famous lawyer Nagashbai Shaikenov and two other talented members of the team, Baurzhan Mukhamedjanov and Constantin Kolpakov, were summoned to see Nazarbayev who told them: "I am giving you the job of drafting the new constitution of Kazakhstan. You are free from all other duties. Move into my official residence and work there on your own. Nobody will interrupt you on this great task."

These two young law professors, both in their early 30s, got to work. They were well grounded, for they had spent two years wrestling with the earlier attempts to write the failed 1993 constitution. Unfettered from the chains of having to make their work acceptable to the uncomprehending conservatives in the now-dissolved Supreme Soviet, the constitution drafting team went into overdrive.

We did not feel we were burdened by an historic mission [recalled Mukhamedjanov]. We were young lawyers bursting with creative ideas which we continuously debated and tested in our intense discussions with the President. He came to join us every day. He usually arrived around 8 pm, carrying copious notes in his handwriting. As we sat down to supper, he would say "Here are my ideas of what I think should be in this or that part of the new constitution, but I am not imposing them. I want you to tell me what you think after further study."

This atmosphere of academic give and take was witnessed by one of the unemployed deputies, Zagipa Balieva, now Minister of Justice, who happened to visit the President's Alatau residence on an evening when the constitution-making team were discussing whether the legislature should have one chamber or two.

I was amazed by both the informality and the intensity of the process [recalled Madame Balieva]. The President was sitting in the garden on this lovely May evening in an open neck shirt, looking at lots of papers with these two young men. He was engaging in the arguments for and against a second chamber with real passion, quoting from foreign countries' constitutions. I remember hearing cries like "You are wrong!" "Prove it to me!", as the debate went one way and then the other. Then there was a break when the President went out of the room and I heard one of the young advisors saying to the other, "We're supposed to be the constitutional lawyers, but he has mastered the arguments better than us".

From these and other eyewitness accounts of the constitution-making process, it is clear that Nazarbayev was deeply and personally involved in every aspect of the drafting. He took what he called a "two-week holiday" in the middle of the process, which he used to study the constitutions of over 20 nations, Asian and Western. Among the most influential sources were the French and Singaporean constitutions. But Nazarbayev was careful to tell his experts: "We don't want to copy anyone else's constitution. Our basic law must have our own Kazakhstani imprint, incorporating the past Kazakh traditions and a Kazakh mindset for the future we are setting our sights on."

After the President and his two young law professors hammered out the first draft of the new constitution, it was reviewed and extensively amended

159

by an Advisory Council of Experts, headed by the Minister of Justice, N. A. Shaikenov. This council included two leading political figures from France, Jacques Attali and Roland Dumas. Their influence was significant because the eventual constitution created a Gaullist-style Presidential Republic of Kazakhstan with the most important powers vested in the Head of State. However, there were more checks and balances on the President of Kazakhstan than exist in the French constitution on the President of France, a point frequently made by Nazarbayev in debates with his critics. However, there were some near-dictatorial prohibitions against organisations which attempted to violate the integrity of the Republic, incite racial, religious or tribal hatred or change the constitution by violent means. Nazarbayev insisted that the powers given to the Presidency by these clauses were essential in the age of international terrorism and religious extremism.

A detailed analysis of a nation's constitution is not appropriate for a biography. But both as an individual and as a President, Nazarbayev stamped his personal imprimatur on the 1995 constitution of Kazakhstan. It was very much his brainchild at every stage, from conceptualisation to ratification. Throughout the process he was receptive to legal ideas, sensitive to cultural pressures and practical in winning public support. Even so, the constitution was born largely out of his own experiences as a man of government. He knew what had failed in the old Soviet models. He was disappointed in the tensions that had arisen between effective government and Parliamentary debate under the flawed 1993 Constitution. He preferred the constitutional arrangements he could see working better in other countries. And the final document may well have reflected the creative tensions between his past as an autocrat who had ruled a republic of the former Soviet Union and his potential future as a democrat looking to the long-term horizons of international acceptance and global economic strength.

So, like all workable constitutions, the 1995 constitution of Kazakhstan was a compromise. It went through 18 "final" drafts before Nazarbayev and his experts were satisfied. Then it went out to nationwide consultation, a process which resulted in over 1,100 amendments and 55 of its 98 articles being changed. On 30th August 1995, a national referendum was held asking the question: "Do you accept the new Constitution of the Republic of Kazakhstan, whose draft was published in the press on 1st August?" The result of the ballot was that 89 per cent of those voting were in favour of the constitution. Some journalists at a press conference held the day after the referendum alleged that the size of the majority seemed suspiciously high, and asked if the poll had been controlled by government officials. Nazarbayev brushed these doubts aside, saying that the referendum had been watched by over 1,000 observers, many of them from foreign countries, and that no serious violations had been reported.

Nazarbayev's mood at the conclusion of the adoption of the constitution was one of elation. "I felt an immense sense of satisfaction", he has recalled. "Every politician has his hour of glory, and gains tremendous satisfaction from the fact that he has done his duty." While basking in this glory at the post-referendum press conference, Nazarbayev was asked what he had learned from his experiences in the first four years of independence, 1991–1995. The opening words of his answer were a throwback to his childhood as the son of Abish Nazarbayev, the skilful grower of apples on the family smallhold-ing in Chemolgan village:

You plant potatoes in spring and by autumn you've already got a crop to pick. But you need five or six years to get apples from a tree [said the President]. During the past few years nobody in all post-Soviet space has told us how you can do it all quickly. But we've managed the main thing – to keep calm in our homeland, the Republic of Kazakhstan. We haven't allowed bloodshed. We have begun running our own finances. We have begun running our own economy and we know which way to turn for a better life. During that time we have gained trust worldwide. Investments are now being made in Kazakhstan.

*　*　*

Nazarbayev's linkage between the creation of a constitution and the encour-agement of foreign investment was no coincidence. He was acutely aware that without the inflow of international money and management expertise, Kazakhstan's economy had a bleak future. But what foreign companies would invest in a former communist country that lacked a stable legal framework, not only for its own citizens but also for overseas investors? They needed to see legislation that guaranteed such matters as property ownership rights, the repatriation of profits, and the encouragement of a free-enter-prise culture in which overseas companies could flourish.

Nazarbayev seized his opportunity for providing an investor-friendly regime in Kazakhstan during the months of 1993–1995 when he was gov-erning the country largely by Presidential decree. This was a temporary but legal window, allowing him to act as a one-man executive and legislature combined while Parliament was dissolved. Using these formidable powers given to him by the constitution, Nazarbayev issued 141 Presidential law-enacting decrees in 12 months, most of them dealing with economic issues at the top of the foreign investors' agenda. Of these issues, privatisation was by far the most important.

Nazarbayev's enthusiasm for privatisation stemmed from his early meet-ings with Margaret Thatcher, who had pioneered the policy during her years as Britain's Prime Minister, 1979–1990. Kazakhstan's first experiment as a privatising government came in 1993, when the state-run Almaty Tobacco Factory was sold to the US company, Philip Morris, for US$100 million. Under its management as a state industry, this enterprise had come close to collapse, unable to pay its work force regular wages, to buy spare parts for its machines or to invest in new equipment. Under Philip Morris's ownership, a US$240 million investment brought in a new cigarette making plant, increased wages for the employees and made good profits for the company. It was regarded as a showpiece privatisation, pouring hard cash into the government's coffers at a time of severe revenue difficulties, and at the same time reviving a near-defunct industry for the benefit of both its employees and its customers. Seeing what he had learned in economic theory become successful as an industrial reality encouraged Nazarbayev to experiment far more boldly with privatisation. Over the next two years, he allowed foreign investors to buy 94 major state enterprises including steel mills, coal mines, gold mines, electricity companies, oil refineries and the national airline.

Inevitably, the disposal of these assets provoked criticism. But Nazarbayev refused to be deflected from his policy, dismissing the opposition as "Soviet-style xenophobia which viewed any foreign presence as tantamount to treason". Retrospectively, he admitted that mistakes were made in the rush to make the transition from a state enterprise to a free-enterprise economy. "The process of economic reform was not entirely free of erroneous measures, ill-considered decisions and social complications", he has recalled, "but given the acuteness of the crisis we were in, privatisation could not have been 'just' or 'unjust'. It can only be evaluated in terms of being effective or not."

There were two enormous challenges facing Nazarbayev in this process. The first was changing the mindset of the population from fear of private ownership to support for free-market capitalism. The second was avoiding the "bandit capitalism" of neighbouring Russia, in which vast state monopolies were handed over to a handful of wealthy oligarchs with no appreciable benefit for the general public.

In meeting the first challenge, Nazarbayev won his battles by not faltering on the advance to privatisation. For some time, his reforms were wildly unpopular. He had to deploy all his skills as a national communicator to persuade the public to change their ingrained suspicion of free enterprise led by foreign investors. This was a difficult task and for some of the time, with some of the people, Nazarbayev failed at it. But he was courageous in keeping up the political momentum for privatisation. As he explained his rationale: "There was no time to wait for absolutely everyone to be won over, and then introduce the reforms in an environment of total concord. If we had waited, there would simply have been nothing – no state or economy – left for us to reform."

Although he was a President in a hurry, Nazarbayev was always looking over his shoulder at Russia during his drive to privatisation. He was watching the Moscow oligarchs carefully, becoming increasingly certain that their power plays were wrong for Kazakhstan. Nazarbayev wanted to create a much broader class of proprietors who would benefit from the sell-off of national assets. He pursued this policy somewhat selectively. His critics complained that as a result of Presidential favouritism and cronyism a handful of Kazakhstanis, including relatives of Nazarbayev, did become enormously rich. This was fair comment, but it should also be said that the sudden new wealth of the country was far more evenly spread than in Russia, reaching across the regional and tribal boundaries of ancient Kazakh society. To achieve this, Nazarbayev invented a multi-layered approach to the state sell-off, using a variety of models with names like Initiative Privatisation, Voucher Privatisation, Small-scale Privatisation and Agro Privatisation. The overall effect of these schemes was that they brought about a sea change in attitudes to the private sector. Instead of fearing free enterprise, people began to understand its advantages as the shops filled up with new food products, as new service industries such as garages and car repair workshops flourished and as a new stratum of small and medium-sized business proprietors began to emerge. Nazarbayev's vision of a property and business- owning middle class was partly built on his roots in Kazakh culture where families, tribes and *dhuz* had to participate in the nomadic life on a basis of individual stewardship and equal opportunity. But he also took his vision from the modern western societies he visited on his foreign travels. After intense questioning of his hosts wherever he travelled in Europe, Asia and the Americas, Nazarbayev understood that the cohesive strength of middle-class property owners, entrepreneurs and business people made them a force for stability in their own countries. So he became determined to inculcate many of the same values and virtues into the society of Kazakhstan. This was a major turnaround of Nazarbayev's own mindset from Communism to Thatcherism in little more than one decade, but once he felt sure his new vision would work, he pressed ahead on his agenda with conviction and energy.

Nazarbayev's agenda, whose key ingredients were economic reform, constitutional reform, the new currency and privatisation, soon started to produce results. From the nightmare year of 1993, when inflation had reached 2,600 per cent, the reform package of expenditure cuts and reconstruction brought inflation down to 59 per cent by 1995 and to steadily falling levels thereafter. By 1996, Kazakhstan's GDP was growing again for the first time since the 1980s, and by the end of the 1990s over 90 per cent of the country's productive industry was in private ownership. Inevitably, there were to be further hitches and glitches in the country's economic progress, not least on account of the Asian recession of 1998–1999 and the global credit crunch of 2008–2009, although between these two crises Kazakhstan enjoyed nine years of double-digit growth.

This transition from the doldrums of Soviet failure to a strong and successful free-enterprise economy owed much to Nazarbayev's programme of reform in the 1990s. However, there were two other important ingredients in the leadership of the President that changed his country. The first was getting along with the neighbours. The second was developing Kazakhstan into an oil and mineral-rich nation.

11

Russia, the Caspian and China

Moscow, the oil-rich Caspian and Beijing. These were the political and economic power centres that could make or break Kazakhstan's future as a newly independent nation. In each of them, Nazarbayev had to play his cards differently. Sometime he was a bluffer, often he was a charmer, and even when he was holding the aces he needed to be a supple and sensitive negotiator. He could not afford to offend the two superpowers on his borders. But nor could he be seen to give way to their pressures on bilateral issues which were important to Kazakhstan's national interest. In the Caspian he had his fair share of problems with American oil companies and international pipeline consortia. Among his smaller neighbours, he had issues of political rivalry and personal jealousy. Yet for all the constraints and despite frequent mistakes in his choices of appointees and associates, Nazarbayev gradually emerged as the region's clear winner. For, by the end of the 20th century, Kazakhstan was well ahead of all other CIS countries such as Uzbekistan, Turkmenistan, Kyrgyzstan, Azerbaijan and Ukraine, looking much healthier than Yeltsin's Russia in terms of economic progress and political stability. How Nazarbayev handled the 1990's version of "the great game" in Central Asia is a complicated but fascinating story.

Boris Yeltsin's volatile government was always unpredictable over its lingering disputes with Kazakhstan. No sooner had the turbulence of the rouble–tenge currency upheavals calmed down than another contentious issue soured the atmosphere between the two countries. The new row was about the future of the Baikonur Cosmodrome. Located in central Kazakhstan, this legendary space-launch facility generated strong political emotions in both countries. When a vocal section of Kazakhstan's public opinion demanded Baikonur's closure, Moscow's leaders were affronted because the Cosmodrome was at the heart of their national power and prestige.

The Russians were right to be proud of Baikonur, the jewel in the crown of the Soviet Union's space exploration programme. It was originally built as the Red Army's first long-range ICBM missile base, then its role changed to being the launch site for a series of historic space adventures. These included the flight of the first man-made satellite, Sputnik One, in 1957; the first man-made orbital flight by Yuri Gagarin in 1961; the flight of the first woman in space, Valentina Tereshkova in 1963; and the later launches of the Soyuz, Proton and Tsyklon spacecraft. At the time, these successful achievements were ahead of the equivalent programmes in the United States, so they were a source of immense pride for the people and scientists of Russia, particularly those leading the Soviet space projects at Baikonur.

The name Baikonur in the Kazakh language means "wealthy brown land with many herbs". It is symbolic of the fertile swathe of steppe pasture some 120 miles east of the Aral Sea where the Soviets built their facility, originally called Leninsk. In addition to the base itself, which had a perimeter approximately 60 miles long by 50 miles wide, guarded by a division of the Red Army, the Soviets built an entire city at Baikonur populated by scientists, technicians and military personnel.

After Kazakhstan's independence, many nationalistic campaigners called for the Cosmodrome to be closed down. This was partly for environmental reasons. The Soviet disregard for Kazakhstan's natural environment had been appalling in every region. After the nuclear devastation around Semipalatinsk, the next worst ecological abominations were in central Kazakhstan, particularly the draining of the Aral Sea and the abuse of the rural areas close to military bases. So the protest movement against Baikonur was fuelled by environmental emotions and also by the powerful legal argument that the Cosmodrome, as a matter of geographical fact, should come under Kazakhstan's sovereignty. In contrast, the Russians argued that as they had built and managed Baikonur for over 40 years, creating there a unique facility of global and scientific excellence, the Cosmodrome should remain under their sovereignty and control.

The stalemate between these two positions caused intense frictions between Russia and Kazakhstan. Although the two countries had signed a treaty of friendship and cooperation in 1992, Baikonur was spoiling the mutual intention to have good relations. It was an issue on which both Presidents came under heavy pressure from interest groups and public opinion within their respective countries. So when Nazarbayev visited Moscow in March 1994, Baikonur was top of the agenda.

The negotiations between the two heads of state took many hours of talks in the Kremlin, and were illustrative of their different styles of leadership. At first it was Nazarbayev who impressed as master of the details. However, Yeltsin had done his homework too, particularly on the arguments about command and control. Nazarbayev enlarged this part of the negotiations beyond the scope of a dispute between two adjoining nation states by declaring that "in the future, Baikonur should belong not only to Kazakhstan and Russia but to the whole world and all mankind". This global vision evidently appealed to Yeltsin who, contrary to the recommendations of his advisers, responded "All right then, I am willing to recognise the juridical sovereignty of Kazakhstan over Baikonur provided we retain control of it – but we are not willing to pay any rent to Kazakhstan".

Thinking that his major concession on sovereignty had settled the issue, Yeltsin called out "Bring vodka now!" A waiter came in with two glasses, putting one in front of each President. "No, bring us four glasses. Two glasses for both of us are necessary to settle such a big decision", commanded Yeltsin. As the extra glasses arrived, Nazarbayev joined in the first round of toasts. With the atmosphere mellowing, he seized his opportunity to reopen the question of Russia paying rent for the facility.

"Why don't you want to pay us anything?", asked the Kazakh leader.

"Because we have already made such a huge concession on the sovereignty issue. That is enough", replied Yeltsin.

Nazarbayev pointed out that he too had made a major concession by agreeing that Baikonur should be manned and maintained by Russia.

"Kazakhstan will never accept that you should pay nothing for this", continued Nazarbayev. "Surely you can afford to pay us a symbolic rent? Russia is a huge country of great resources and financial strength."

This compliment to Russia's economic greatness shifted Yeltsin towards a further step of the negotiations.

"How much?", he asked.

"Just a symbolic figure. I suggest $250 million a year", replied Nazarbayev.

"I call that a very expensive figure, not a symbolic figure", said Yeltsin.

"Well then, how about a rent of $100 million a year?", asked Nazarbayev, adding as a half-joking aside, "with another $15 million a year thrown in to symbolise the friendship between us."

"All right – done", said Yeltsin, slapping the palm of his right hand down on the table and laughing about the increase of the $100 million figure by "15 per cent for friendship".

The speed and decisiveness of this deal between the two Presidents took their entourages by surprise. The Russian Foreign Minister, Andrei Kozyrev, ran from his place and began whispering objections into Yeltsin's ear.

"Sit down and shut up", snapped Yeltsin. "I am the President of Russia and I have made my decision."

Nazarbayev also had to listen to grumbles from members of his delegation about the loss of Kazakhstan's control over Baikonur. But he too ignored the objections. The two Presidents signed their agreement for a 20-year lease over Baikonur then and there, with the unexpected rental figure of $115 million a year being written into the text in Yeltsin's handwriting.

The Russian saying "made of the same dough" was applicable to Nazarbayev and Yeltsin. It goes some way to explaining their personal rapport, their rough and ready styles of communicating, and their ability to reach difficult but important agreements like the deal over Baikonur. Both men were outsiders who had come up the hard way in political life. Nurtured by their strong roots from humble origins, they were influenced more by inner instincts than by outer pressures. On this particular occasion, the horse trading, the humour and the four glasses of vodka were for show. The reality was that they both knew that an agreement over Baikonur was in the national interest of their countries, and infinitely preferable to prolonged confrontation. Although this deal was fiercely criticised, not least in the Russian Duma and in the Kazakhstan Parliament, the Baikonur agreement (even though it took five years for the first instalment of rent to be paid!) has stood the test of time well. The Russian space exploration programme has continued to flourish, while Kazakh scientists and astronauts have had a significant share in the research and in the piloting of spacecraft.

*   *   *

A far more difficult bilateral problem than Baikonur was the question: Who owns the oil around and under the Caspian Sea? Of all the issues with which Nazarbayev had to wrestle in the 1990s, none took so much of his time, involved more intricate complexities and ultimately produced greater rewards for Kazakhstan.

Nazarbayev had been the first of all the political leaders in Central Asia to recognise the enormous potential of the oil reserves in the Caspian. He never guessed that they would one day be assessed as approximately equal in size to the oil wealth of Iraq. But a combination of luck, opportunism, diplomacy and hard bargaining eventually enabled him to put Kazakhstan in pole position for the race whose prize was likely to become one of the world's greatest oil bonanzas of the 21st century.

The luck was originally bad luck; the accident of a fire and then a blow out at an early onshore Caspian oil drilling well known as T-35. The disaster happened in July 1985, a few months after Nazarbayev had been appointed as Prime Minister of the Soviet Republic of Kazakhstan. His inexperience, his youth (45) for such an office, and Kazakhstan's subservient status as a satellite of the Soviet Union meant that he was merely a bystander at this dramatic event, which was handled, or rather mishandled, by the oil ministry in Moscow.

But even as a spectator at what industry experts called "the fountain of the century", whose extraordinary pressure sent burning oil flames soaring 600 feet above the surface and took over a year to bring under control, Nazarbayev got the message that the Caspian region contained oil fields of far greater wealth and size than anyone had previously imagined.

Nazarbayev's understanding of the Caspian's potential was not shared beyond a small circle of geologists inside Moscow's oil ministry. By the time the political leaders of the Soviet Union began to grasp the magnitude of this new source of energy, they were so preoccupied with the breakup of the Communist empire that they had lost the will to take long-term decisions on other issues. Developing the oil fields of the Caspian became a low priority. Although President Gorbachev signed an agreement on behalf of the Soviet Union with the American oil company Chevron for the development of the Caspian's Tengiz field during his visit to the United States in 1990, the project became slowed down by labyrinthine negotiations between Chevron and the oil ministry in Moscow. By July 1991, when the Russian talks with the American oil company appeared to be deadlocked, Nazarbayev seized his moment. He persuaded Gorbachev to transfer the authority for the Tengiz negotiations away from the Soviet oil ministry to the Soviet Republic of Kazakhstan's Council of Ministers. This persuasion was not a delicate operation. "Kazakhstan will henceforth take control of the field", wrote Nazarbayev in an imperious letter to Gorbachev in July 1991. Ostensibly, the Soviet leader went along with this blatant grab for power on the grounds that Kazakhstan's negotiators would be able to extract better terms from Chevron. A more likely explanation was that Gorbachev had no option other than to yield to Nazarbayev, who had made his bid for control of the Caspian negotiations at a time of such extreme vulnerability for the leadership of the Soviet Union. By mid-July 1991, the Soviet President was engaged in extremely difficult talks with the divided leaders of the republics about a new Union Treaty. With the disagreements worsening, Gorbachev needed Nazarbayev's help to reconcile the differences. The help was given. But the covert quid pro quo was that Kazakhstan should take over the deal-making with Chevron. When Gorbachev accepted this, it was the culmination of a long campaign of Caspian opportunism by Nazarbayev. Over a year earlier, when he had met the leaders of Chevron in San Francisco, after listening to their complaints of delays and obstructions from the Soviet oil ministry, Nazarbayev said: "If you want to solve your problems quickly, then you should not bother trying to discuss things with Moscow at all. You should deal with us directly." He was speaking out of turn when he made this first attempt to outflank the oil ministry negotiators, but he got his way in the end.

Once it was known that Nazarbayev was the Soviet Union's point man on Tengiz, everyone wanted to talk directly to him. When President George H. W. Bush began a state visit to Moscow on 29th July 1991, he asked to meet the Kazakh President; who was promptly added to the official Soviet delegation by Gorbachev. Bush, himself an oil man, had played a pivotal role in the earlier rounds of US–Soviet talks on Tengiz, which had resulted in Chevron's involvement. So the American President was knowledgeable about the details of the field, but he found himself upstaged by Nazarbayev, who reeled off complex statistical and technical figures on the high sulphur content and transportation costs of Tengiz with such mastery that Bush asked him, "Are you an oil expert by training?"

"No, I'm a metallurgist", replied Nazarbayev. "But life has made me get to know all branches of the economy."

The answer was an uncharacteristic display of modesty, for Nazarbayev was building up a considerable expertise on all aspects of Caspian oil – legal, financial, technical and, above all, political. The political dimension came to the fore after the Soviet Union ceased to exist at the end of 1991. Until that time, there had been only two littoral states claiming rights over the oil riches under the Caspian – Iran and the USSR, which in reality meant Russia. Suddenly, these claimants extended to five – Iran, Russia, Azerbaijan, Turkmenistan and Kazakhstan. Until the rights of each member of this quintet of littoral countries were agreed and legally established, it would be difficult, if not impossible, for foreign oil companies to start new drilling and exploration work, or for foreign bankers and investors to finance the development of a Caspian oil and gas industry.

Kazakhstan had most to gain from a fair settlement of the Caspian, because it was the northern sector of this inland sea that was known to contain the largest oil fields. But Russia took up an obdurate negotiating position on them. For a year or two after the breakup of the Soviet Union, the oil ministry in Moscow refused to relinquish the legal ownership of the onshore fields around the Caspian, even though they clearly lay within Kazakhstan's borders. These claims had nothing to do with international law or geography, and everything to do with Chevron's latest drilling results from Tengiz. They suggested that it contained at least 250 million tonnes of extractable reserves of oil, making it the sixth largest field in the world. Furious at having "lost" such riches, the Russian oil lobby put great pressure on Boris Yeltsin to get him to persuade Kazakhstan to transfer Tengiz back to Russia. These strong-arm tactics caused Nazarbayev to have what he called "many disagreeable conversations with Yeltsin about this", but with no ground being given on such a legally absurd proposition. Eventually, this part of the Caspian argument was ended by humour. As Nazarbayev has recalled the episode:

At one meeting in Moscow, Yeltsin said to me, "Give Tengiz to Russia". I looked at him and, realising that he was not joking, replied: "Well, if Russia gives us Orenburg province. After all, Orenburg was once the capital of Kazakhstan." To which he retorted "Do you have territorial claims on Russia?" "Of course not", I replied. He burst out laughing and so did I.

By contrast, Russia's intransigence over the rights to the Caspian's off-shore oil was no laughing matter. Moscow's opening gambit was that the Caspian was not a sea, but an inland lake. Therefore the international law of the seabed did not apply to it at all. Secondly, the Russians argued that even if the Caspian was a sea, it was governed by a treaty signed in 1921 between Persia (Iran) and the then Russian Federation. This treaty gave the two sig-natories the right to operate as a Condominium in control of all the oil rights of the Caspian, which meant that they alone had the power to hand out concessions to other littoral states.

For six and a half years after the breakup of the Soviet Union, Russian negotiators clung to their legally untenable positions on "the lake" and "the condominium". "This was immensely frustrating", recalled Nurlan Kapparov, who was Kazakhstan's Vice-Minister for oil and energy in the late 1990s. "We did not make much headway until the problem was seen not as a foreign borders issue but as an oilfields issue." It took a long time before this reality was accepted. Almost every month between 1992 and 1998 there was a Caspian meeting of the five littoral countries, attended by their Deputy Foreign Ministers or other high officials.

Progress at these meetings was negligible [recalled Erlan Idrissov, who was Kazakhstan's rep-resentative at many of them]. We wasted years going round in circles with no hope of an agreement, and no chance of a drop of oil coming out of the Caspian while this deadlock lasted. It was only when President Nazarbayev stepped in and negotiated face to face with President Yeltsin that we found a solution.

The deadlock was "broken at a private dinner" in Zavidovo, Yeltin's hunt-ing lodge 100 miles east of Moscow, on the night of 5th July 1998. The atmospherics were somewhat similar to those that had characterised the break-through over Baikonur. Good personal chemistry and good vodka made their contribution to the cordiality of the evening. But it was the realisation that Russia would gain from a Caspian agreement as well as Kazakhstan that swung Yeltsin into a negotiating mood. Nazarbayev brought his host down to a detailed discussion of a seabed share-out by seizing a table napkin and drawing on it a sketch map of the northern Caspian. This napkin and the scribbles on it have been preserved for posterity in a museum in Astana. His-torians may have difficulty in deciphering the postprandial hieroglyphics of the two leaders, but their intentions at the time were clear. Nazarbayev was proposing that the oil and gas rights of the northern Caspian should be geographically divided along "a median line" on the seabed between the two countries. However, Yeltsin objected to the route of the line on the grounds that it ignored the Russian claim of ownership to a couple of small, uninhabited and often submerged islands called Zhestkyi and Ukatnyi. Nazarbayev obligingly offered to redraw the line so that Russia had a larger share of the Kurmangazy field, which was situated close to these islands. Yeltsin also had concerns about the Lukoil company's rights to two fields divided by the median line, Hvalynskoe and Centralnoe. Nazarbayev offered to put these fields into a 50–50 joint venture between Russian and Kazakhstani oil companies, and added: "We won't let American oil companies buy into our share of the joint venture. If Lukoil wants to increase its share, that's fine with us." This hydrocarbon version of horse-trading evidently appealed to Yeltsin who, at two o'clock in the morning, announced that a settlement had been reached.

The leaders' nocturnal accord was swiftly converted into an official announcement by Yeltsin's assistant, Sergei Prihod'ko, and Nazarbayev's chief of staff, Nurtai Abikayev. "From 2 am until 9 am, Prihod'ko and I used our notes and the drawings on the napkin to draft the text of a joint statement by the two Presidents", recalled Abikayev. "This was the declaration of intent to delineate the seabed borders of the Caspian in accordance with a median line modified by the two Presidents."

By the time the announcement of the Caspian accord was made, it was the morning of 6th July 1998 – Nazarbayev's 58th birthday. At a state banquet in his honour that evening, Nazarbayev was told by his host, President Yeltsin, that the agreement was a fine birthday present for himself as well as a generous gift to the Russian leadership. "A great son of a great nation is only capable of great deals", was the final line of this hyperbole.

The mutual flattery continued at this level after the dinner when Yeltsin spontaneously offered to escort his guest on a short tour of the Kremlin's historic interior halls. As the two Presidents entered the throne room of the Tsars, Yeltsin said, "Here is the seat where our Russian Sovereigns sat enthroned and ruled the country."

Nazarbayev replied: "Boris Nikolayevich, maybe you should occupy this throne and rule Russia from here and not from your office." Yeltsin, who often displayed both the eccentricities and the regalities of a Tsar, appeared to enjoy the suggestion for he laughed heartily at this tickling of his vanity. Eventually he replied: "No one has offered me that, not even my comrades in arms. But Russia is now a democratic country, so let this throne remain unoccupied."

Nazarbayev well understood that the Russian power structure was far more autocratic than democratic. That was why he became a master of the art of stroking Yeltsin's ego, achieving many good results for Kazakhstan by his skills at the lofty level of one-on-one presidential diplomacy. Of all the deals the two leaders struck together, the nocturnal agreement of 5th/6th July 1998 was the most important, because it ended the locust years of political and legal wrangling over the northern Caspian. The announcement made clear that Russia was renouncing its previously claimed concepts of the lake and the condominium. This meant that oil and gas companies were now able to proceed with their exploration plans, even though the final and slightly amended agreement on the median line was not formally signed until 2002 by President Putin.

The subsequent importance of the so-called "napkin" deal was that it unlocked riches for Kazakhstan which were to prove far greater than Nazarbayev had dreamed of at the time. The first manifestation of this bonanza came in May 2000, when oil was struck at Kashagan, a new offshore field in the Caspian located some 48 miles southeast of Atyrau. Excited by early reports on the magnitude of the discovery, Nazarbayev flew out to the drilling rig on 4th July. As he took part in a ceremony which began with the crew manager declaring, "Mr President, we present to you Kashagan", and ended with oil being smeared over the faces of the visitors, Nazarbayev was over the moon with elation. He was told that the new discovery was much greater than Tengiz, with recoverable reserves estimated at over 1.6 billion tonnes of high-quality crude. Returning from the rig to Atyrau airport, Nazarbayev announced to reporters: "I can tell you today that there is oil, big oil and it is good-quality oil. This is a great aid to our independence, to our future and our future prosperity. The hopes of the Kazakh people have been realised."

The optimism of these remarks, and Nazarbayev's later comparisons of Kazakhstan's reserves to those of Iraq, have largely been justified by subsequent events and discoveries. However, at the time, finding new oil and defining the legal ownership of the hydrocarbons under the seabed was only Part One of the Caspian drama. Part Two was the building of pipelines which would give Kazakhstan its own outlets to its customers without having to rely on the inadequate Russian pipeline system built in the Soviet era. Both stages involved strategic decisions and intense negotiations in which Nazarbayev was the key player, assisted in his role by an unusually colourful adviser, originally introduced to him by Chevron.

Chevron had already spent many months at the negotiating table with oil ministry officials from Moscow when the Soviet Union collapsed. The demise of Gorbachev (who had personally invited the American oil company to start the talks with his government) looked as though it would also mean the demise of Chevron's involvement of the Caspian. When the Chairman of Chevron, Kenneth Derr, watched at his California home the TV new bulletins from Almaty, announcing the closure of the Soviet era and the formation of the Commonwealth of Independent States, he said to his wife: "Well, I guess we can forget about our Soviet deal."

Derr's pessimism was misplaced. Independent but cash-starved Kazakhstan desperately needed both the revenue and the recognition that an agreement with a major US oil company could provide. So, early in 1992, Nazarbayev wrote to Derr suggesting that the negotiations should be resumed. They were, but on very different terms to those on which Chevron had been expecting to conclude a deal with the Soviet Union.

In his first few weeks as President of Independent Kazakhstan, Nazarbayev immersed himself in what he called "an in-depth study" of the deal that Chevron had offered. "At moments like these, a knowledge of the facts and details become a decisive element. I was well aware that the destiny of future Kazakhstan was being decided at the negotiating table", he has recalled.

As he studied the details of the previous round of negotiations, Nazarbayev was appalled by the inadequacy of the Soviet oil ministry's team who had been conducting the talks with the Americans. Having discovered that the Soviet delegation had contained neither a lawyer nor a qualified translator, and that all the documents and financial calculations for the proposed deal had been drawn up by Chevron, Nazarbayev immediately raised Kazakhstan's negotiating game. He selected his own international advisers – JP Morgan as investment bankers, and Slaughter and May as lawyers.

Within weeks there was stalemate between the negotiating teams. Chevron had agreed a split of the profits from Tengiz at 38 per cent for themselves and 62 per cent for the USSR. The Kazakhs revised their offered terms to 13 per cent of the profits going to Chevron and 87 per cent to Kazakhstan. The two sides were even further apart on the size of the area for exploration and development. Chevron wanted a minimum area of 23,000 square kilometres, the Kazakhs offered a maximum of 2,000 square kilometres. Even though he had greatly toughened Kazakhstan's negotiating position, Nazarbayev found himself under pressure from nationalist critics who accused him of selling off the country's precious natural resources to a foreign oil company. He grumbled to a visiting American reporter of "a campaign in the press ... saying this is the plunder of Kazakhstan".

Another pressure on Nazarbayev was the timing of the visit he was due to make to Washington DC in May 1992. The most important strategic item on the agenda was finding a solution to the problem of Kazakhstan's nuclear arsenal (see Chapter 9). But in economic terms, the announcement of a deal with Chevron came a close second and was very important for the Americans too. Nazarbayev tied together the signing of the deal on Tengiz with an agreement with the United States for security guarantees of Kazakhstan's territorial integrity in the event of a nuclear attack. After much brinkmanship, Nazarbayev won most of what he wanted. On the oil front, a document called "a foundation agreement" was signed on May 1992 at Blair House in Washington by President Nazarbayev and Chevron's Ken Derr. Although not a final contract, it set out most of the final terms of the deal. Those closest to the negotiations on the Kazakh side agreed that they were a great improvement on what the Soviets had been willing to sign. For example, the profit share was finalised at 80–20 in Kazakhstan's favour, and the exploration area was reduced to 4,000 square kilometres.

Looked at in retrospect, the joint venture announced in Washington was a great deal for both sides. Known as Tengizchevroil, or TCO, it has in the last 15 years produced over 120 million tonnes of oil, 5 billion cubic metres of gas, and revenues to Kazakhstan of over $20 billion.

These lucrative oil production and revenue figures would not have been possible without Nazarbayev's leadership of the planning, financing and building of the vital pipelines from the Caspian. At the time when he signed the foundation agreement with Chevron, production capacity was severely limited by shortage of pipeline space, most of which was under Russian control. Some officials in the oil ministry in Moscow resented the loss of the Tengiz field to Kazakhstan, so they took their revenge by making it as difficult as possible for Kazakhstan to export oil to western customers. Only 30,000 barrels a day of Tengiz crude were allowed to be exported via Samara, the key pipeline junction in Southern Russia. As for the 130,000 barrels per day of gas condensate that went direct to Russian refineries, Kazakhstan should have been receiving over $200 million a year in revenues. In fact, not one cent of these dues were ever paid because of blatant false accounting and corruption at the Russian end. Nazarbayev protested to Boris Yeltsin, but the Russian President gave the extraordinary reply that he could not exercise his authority over the big refineries in distant parts of his country and lacked the power to force them to pay their dues to Kazakhstan. It was one of the few negotiations with Yeltsin which ended in failure for Nazarbayev.

These and many other early frustrations over the development of Tengiz pointed to one obvious solution. A new pipeline had to be built from the field to the nearest Black Sea port, Novorossijsk, a distance of 935 miles. But the pipeline itself was the cause of intense difficulties and frustrations for Nazarbayev. The first Caspian Pipeline Consortium (CPC), founded in 1992 between the governments of Russia, Kazakhstan and Oman, failed to deliver the necessary financing, and quarrelled with Chevron. Personality clashes were at the heart of the stalemate. Nazarbayev became impatient with the disputes inside CPC. His sole priority was getting the Tengiz export line built. "The problem is that the money has to be invested", he said. "What difference is it to me if it is Americans, Omanis or Russians? The main thing is that oil comes out."

Because the oil was neither coming out nor flowing along the non-existent pipeline, Nazarbayev turned for advice to a colourful oil industry middle-man, James H. Giffen. In the long run, the Giffen connection was to bring much conflict and many negative headlines for Nazarbayev, but at the time of the initial CPC troubles his choice of Giffen was a good one, because his wheeler-dealing delivered a workable and profitable solution to Kazakhstan's oil transportation problem.

Nazarbayev first met Jim Giffen on a visit to the United States a year before the breakup of the Soviet Union. At that time, Giffen was representing Chevron, the leading oil company in the American Trade Consortium, a group of US corporations who were starting to do business with the Soviet Union. Giffen had created the consortium himself. He appeared to have excellent contacts in both the Kremlin and the White House, with access to anyone who mattered in US–Soviet trade deals, from President Gorbachev to President Bush. Although some of this influence-peddling was illusory, some was genuine. Chevron itself relied heavily on Giffen's advice, which included a recommendation to roll out the red carpet for the then-unknown Kazakh leader in September 1990 when he visited the company's headquarters in San Francisco. On this visit, Nazarbayev was visibly impressed, not least by Giffen's skills as a power-broker. However, the power centre where he operated most effectively was itself breaking up. A month after the collapse of the Soviet Union, Giffen was out of a job. Chevron fired him on the grounds that they no longer needed an intermediary with the now impotent oil ministry in Moscow. But Nazarbayev, always eager to listen to Western advisers in the early years of his Presidency, gave Giffen a new job as adviser to the Kazakhstan government on oil policy, particularly on the growing pipeline crisis.

Giffen broke the logjam on the Tengiz pipeline by bringing Mobil Oil into a closer relationship with Kazakhstan. Nazarbayev was primarily interested in getting the pipeline built with Mobil's money, but to achieve this he was willing to negotiate the sale of a large area of the exploration rights in his country's sector of the northern Caspian. In May 1995, he flew to the Bahamas for talks with Mobil. According to Giffen's account of these discussions,

Nazarbayev was dazzled by the plan for a second major US oil company to take a stake in Tengiz, especially one that was willing to pay a bonus of over $100 million to the Kazakh government just to open the door for the privilege of an exclusive negotiation with it.

"Do you really think we can get $100 million just for negotiating rights?", asked Nazarbayev.

"You bet. In fact, I'm gonna ask for $150 million. How do you like that?", replied Giffen.

"Go ahead", said the Kazakh President, who was over the moon with delight when the price was settled at $145 million. This was really big money for Kazakhstan in 1995.

The entry of Mobil changed the dynamics both of the pipeline and of the ownership of the Tengiz field. The Sultanate of Oman's commitment to the original Caspian Pipeline Consortium was waning, partly on account of the death in a car crash of the Omani Finance Minister, Qais Zawawi, who had been a strong supporter of CPC. So Nazarbayev developed a new game plan, flying to Moscow in November 1995 for talks with Boris Yeltsin, equipped with a red-covered briefing book prepared by Jim Giffen. This "Red Book", as it was called, put forward an alternative new scheme for financing the pipeline. Yeltsin liked it. The way the plan ended up, half the pipeline would be owned by the governments of Russia (23 per cent), Kazakhstan (20 per cent) and Oman (7 per cent). The other half would be owned by four oil and gas companies – Mobil, Chevron, British Gas and Agip of Italy, who would put up the entire $2.6 billion costs of building the 935-mile pipeline from Atyrau on the shores of the Caspian to the Black Sea port of Novorossijsk. The complexities of the various deals, trades and restructurings which brought about this eventual pipeline agreement were so opaque that the end result seemed almost inexplicable, even to the most seasoned of oil industry observers. As the *Wall Street Journal* reporter Steve LeVine summed up his account of the saga: "When the way was finally cleared to build the big Tengiz line, nobody could say with total confidence how it had happened. It was as if the warring parties had fathered an accidental pipeline."

What may have looked like an accident to the outside world was an intentional result for Nazarbayev. It had been intensely frustrating for him to be leading an landlocked nation that was oil-rich but pipeline poor. Once again, he had to use all his personal negotiating skills with Boris Yeltsin to overcome the Russian bureaucracy's obstruction to the CPC agreement. The deal was eventually done between the two Presidents at Yeltsin's hospital bed in Moscow in 1999. The ailing Russian leader was pressed by Nazarbayev for a final decision on the go-ahead for the CPC. After listening to the terms,

Yeltsin turned his head on his pillow and asked his two key advisers, Viktor Chernomyrdin and Boris Nemtsov: "Is this pipeline good for Russia?" Both aides replied in unison, "You bet". On the Kazakh side of the bed, Nazarbayev's oil minister, Nurlan Balgimbayev, whispered congratulations to his boss on "a great breakthrough". In the prevailing atmosphere of harmonious agreement, the paperwork on the deal was promptly signed by Yeltsin in his hospital room. Once again, the personal chemistry had delivered a good public result for both countries.

Kazakhstan did, however, have to pay a further price for solving the Caspian's oil and gas transportation problems. It came in the form of a further restructuring – this time of the ownership of the Tengiz field itself. Mobil Oil bought 25 per cent of Tengiz for $1.05 billion. That left the Kazakhstan Government with a 25 per cent stake, Chevron with 45 per cent, and a partnership of the Avio and Lukoil oil companies with 5 per cent. James Giffen was rewarded for bringing the Mobil deal to Kazakhstan with a personal commission of 5 per cent, which earned him $51 million. What happened to this commission and to other large sums of money connected to Giffen's wheelings and dealings in the Caspian continues to be the subject of court cases, media headlines, allegations, counter-allegations and murky controversy. At the time of writing, Giffen has been indicted by the US authorities on charges of fraud, money laundering and bribery of foreign government officials. He denies the charges and has produced the unusual defence that he was acting as a CIA agent inside Kazakhstan, authorised by the equivalent of an 00 licence to make millions and hide them away in Swiss bank accounts. Although he is in theory awaiting trial, Giffen's right to use his CIA agent defence has been upheld by a New York appeals court. This has led to speculation that the charges may be dropped.

In any event, Giffen himself had been dropped by the Kazakhstanis. In the light of his indictment by the US government, Kazakhstan decided in 2000 to deny Giffen any access to or involvement with the government and Nazarbayev. His exclusion took place soon after the appointment of the new Kazakhstani Prime Minister, Kassym-Jomart Tokayev. He arrived as a fresh adviser on the scene of the complex oil and pipeline negotiations in late 1999.

I noticed that whenever Jim Giffen was sitting on our side of the table in these discussions, the reactions of the American side was negative [recalled Tokayev], so I shared this observation with President Nazarbayev and he excluded Giffen from the negotiations. From then on, the President dealt with Chevron over the big decisions on his own, supported by his oil minister and his prime minister but without Jim Giffen – who at the time was very angry with me.

Although he was no longer connected to Giffen's swashbuckling methods of financial management and deal-making after the year 2000, Nazarbayev did become implicated in the American middleman's legal troubles. For the US prosecutors who indicted Giffen in 2003 backed up their charges with evidence that the defendant had arranged financial benefits for certain senior officials of the Kazakhstan government, including President Nazarbayev, by transferring substantial funds to their Swiss bank accounts. These unproven allegations, though well reported in the media, did not cause much of a stir within Kazakhstan. Domestic public opinion in the country seemed to take the view that if some of their political leaders did make hay while the sun was shining, that was acceptable because the results from the Caspian were so much in the interests of Kazakhstan. A more fundamental criticism of Nazarbayev's stewardship of the Caspian was that he sold some of the oil rights too cheaply to foreign companies. This is an easy assertion to make with the wisdom of hindsight, some 15 years after the original decisions, and in the light of a 900 per cent rise in the price of oil. From the perspective of history it might be argued that in the pioneering phase of the Caspian's development, few people were clear about the risks or clean over the rules. Nazarbayev's priorities were to get the oil out of the ground, flowing through the pipelines and earning revenue for Kazakhstan. Chevron had similar objectives for the benefit of their shareholders. For both sides it was a high-risk, high-reward partnership. It has succeeded far beyond expectations by creating 3,000 oil industry jobs for Kazakhstanis and by earning revenues for Chevron and Kazakhstan of approximately $US20 billion for each side by the end of 2008. Moreover, as will be shown in a later chapter, the best of Caspian oil and gas production is still to come.

* * *

While Kazakhstan's relations with Russia and all the offshoots into Caspian oil demarcation, pipelines and other bilateral issues continued to be Nazarbayev's primary preoccupation throughout the 1990s, he did not take his eye off the relationship with China. This improved steadily throughout the first decade of Kazakhstan's independence, partly on account of the harmonious (musical as well as political!) communications between the two national leaders, and partly because so much progress was made on potentially divisive issues such as borders, ethnic minorities and access to natural resources.

The personal chemistry between Nazarbayev and Jiang Zemin, Chairman of the People's Republic of China, was an important factor in the development of good Sino–Kazakh relations. One key ingredient in their rapport was a shared common language. Another was a reciprocal enjoyment of singing folk songs, playing musical instruments and discussing literature.

The common language in which both the Chairman of the PRC and the President of Kazakhstan were fluent was Russian. Jiang Zemin had acquired his fluency from working on the assembly line of a Soviet automobile factory in Gorky. "I lived among workers and learned my Russian from them", he told Nazarbayev, who could make a similar claim from his days in a Soviet steelworks. Dispensing with interpreters, the two leaders were able to drop diplomatic formalities and to discover that they had many personal and cultural tastes in common. A knowledge of Russian literature was one such interest. Another was music. Jiang Zemin loved to play the piano and the clarinet. Nazarbayev was good on the dombra. Both men had fine tenor voices and enjoyed singing romantic ballads and folk songs. Their talents came to the fore during Jiang Zemin's visit to Kazakhstan in July 1996, and again during Nazarbayev's visit to Beijing two years later. At the state banquet in Almaty they both performed, in Russian, a famous ballad, "Podmoskovnye Vechera" (Moscow Nights). Even more surprising was the two leaders' rendition in Beijing of a classic Kazakh folk song, "Dudarai". As Nazarbayev picked up his dombra and strummed his way through the first verse, Jiang Zemin amazed the banquet hall by taking the second microphone and joining in the chorus – but in Chinese! Singing in their respective languages, the President of Kazakhstan and the Chairman of the People's Republic of China completed the entire lyrics of "Dudarai". In Kazakh the words are all about a handsome young man from Kazakhstan whose curly hair wins the heart of a Russian girl. However, in Chinese the song is a more politically correct version with fewer romantic touches and no mention of nationalities. When this amazing duet finished, Nazarbayev wanted to know where and how Jiang Zemin had learned this national Kazakh song. The PRC Chairman replied that it was a Chinese composition known as "The White Rose". Evidently, the musicians in the two countries had been cooperating long before their politicians began to establish diplomatic relations.

The Kazakhstan–China summit meetings were of course political not musical events, although Nazarbayev's ability to create an atmosphere of personal goodwill suffusing the business agenda was almost as important with Jiang Zemin as it had been with Yeltsin. One example of the effects of Nazarbayev's charm offensive was noticed by Kazakhstan's former Ambassador to Beijing – Kuanish Sultanov.

In the middle of the sing-song at the Almaty dinner, I heard a very happy PRC Chairman saying to our President, "Nursultan, I believe you have raised the correct issues with us today".

180

This was a significant signal from the leader of China because, during the substantial negotiations earlier in the morning, Nazarbayev's priority had been to settle the border problems between the two countries, particularly in two contested areas. The disputed issues were solved shortly afterwards in a deal which gave 53 per cent of the contested regions to Kazakhstan and 47 per cent to China. The agreement was subsequently ratified by both national Parliaments. For Nazarbayev, this was an important breakthrough. Beijing had never before agreed a frontier with any of the Soviet Republics on its borders. Some Mandarin maps were even showing large regions of Kazakhstan, including Lake Balkash, as Chinese territory. The urgency of settling the disputed areas seemed real to both leaders. As Jiang Zemin said with unusual candour to Nazarbayev: "We must settle these border issues now, while we are both in charge. One day in the future a new generation may come to lead China who I am not sure will be so eager to reach an agreement." With such a warning ringing in his ears, Nazarbayev needed no urging to achieve an accord. As a result of the deal he signed with Jiang Zemin, Kazakhstan and China now have judicially approved a ratified border for the first time in their history. After centuries of wars, invasions, skirmishes and border clashes in the disputed areas, this was a major historical achievement.

One of the reasons why the border issue was solved had its roots in the ethnic minority problems faced in Western China and Eastern Kazakhstan. For Beijing, there was the potential of Tibetan-type troubles in the border areas. China had a large population of over a million Kazakhs in Xinjiang province. Kazakhstan had around 140,000 Chinese Uigurs living within its borders. Both ethnic groups were sources of tension. Nazarbayev secured an agreement from Jiang Zemin that the Chinese authorities would not create any obstacles to Chinese citizens of Kazakh origin wishing to emigrate to their homeland of Kazakhstan. There was also an understanding that Uigur separatist movements would not be allowed to operate in Kazakhstan. Both governments saw considerable benefits in full cooperation on these ethnic minority issues, which had never before been discussed at the highest political levels.

The final mutual benefit that flowed from the good personal and political relations Nazarbayev so assiduously cultivated with the Beijing leadership was cooperation on oil policy. This was the most impressive development in a burgeoning two-way trade relationship, which rose from virtually zero in 1991 to over $14 billion of exports and imports by 2008. Long before it was fashionable to recognise the PRC as an industrial giant, Nazarbayev had shown a prescient awareness of his neighbour's mighty economic potential. "Not all the leaders of Central Asian states have fully realised that China is now a world power – but you have", said Jiang Zemin to Nazarbayev in 1997. Two years later, the two friends signed a treaty called "A strategic partnership for the 21st century". This partnership between Kazakhstan and China was strengthened by Jiang Zemin's successor, Hu Jintao, who in his first meetings with Nazarbayev on a visit to Astana talked candidly about China's future energy demands, and emphasised the priority his country attached to obtaining uninterrupted oil supplies from Kazakhstan. To this end, Nazarbayev signed an agreement to build an arterial oil pipeline between Atasu in Kazakhstan and Alashankou on the Chinese border. Five million tonnes of oil exports a year are now flowing along this pipeline, which will be extended into a 3,000-kilometre pipeline linking China to the Caspian by 2010. It is a visionary scheme which has only become possible because of the political foundations laid by Nazarbayev and Jiang Zemin when building the relationship between Kazakhstan and China in the 1990s.

Although his priority was to establish good relations with his two superpower neighbours, Nazarbayev did not neglect personal diplomacy with other states in the Central Asia region, particularly Uzbekistan, Kyrgyzstan, Tajikistan and Turkmenistan. Among those who understand the complex nature of the tensions, jealousies and rivalries among "the Stans", Nazarbayev is given credit for being a moderating influence in solving the endless disputes over borders, transport routes, trade tariffs, terrorist threats, drug trafficking, religious extremism and wider security issues. It would take another book to chronicle Nazarbayev's dealings with his fellow regional leaders and their often erratic regimes. In the latter category, the most troublesome player in the area is undoubtedly President Karimov of Uzbekistan. His record of misgovernment, violation of human rights, political extremism and economic failure has been second to none in Central Asia. As the normally cautious former Kazakhstani Prime Minister Kassym-Jomart Tokayev bluntly declares:

I must openly say that President Karimov is often a thoroughly nasty person, and a most unreliable neighbour. Much of his behaviour is driven by the jealousy he feels towards President Nazarbayev, who always treats Karimov with respect because he is the older man by three years. But this age difference does not hide the difference between the economic chaos and political instability of Karimov's Uzbekistan and the opposite conditions of success and stability which exist in Kazakhstan.

It is not just special pleading by a loyal senior government official of Kazakhstan that highlights the better conditions that exist at home in comparison to the troubles in the smaller neighbouring countries. Every economic statistic or political indicator points to the same conclusion. But whether the leaders of the "Stans" cooperate with each other in harmony or fight like ferrets in a sack, their antics must look like small change to Nazarbayev, who has moved into a bigger economic league thanks to the oil wealth of the Caspian, and into a safer political environment thanks to his accommodating foreign and trade policy towards Russia and China.

Yet because Kazakhstan's population of 15.5 million is so much smaller than China's 1.1 billion and Russia's 150 million, there will always be anxieties about the potential for future tensions arising out of the imbalances in these two relationships. At present, Nazarbayev appears to have been as successful as any Kazakhstani President could hope to be in creating a climate of mutual respect and goodwill between his country and his mega-neighbours. However, there are lurking problems still needing a solution, such as Kazakhstan's water rights to important rivers sourced on the other sides of the Russian and Chinese borders. There are also fears of economic colonisation, particularly by China, whose state enterprises regularly offer to develop projects in Kazakhstan on financial terms which are unmatchable elsewhere in the world. In the Kazakh language there is a saying about the Chinese which closely approximates to Virgil's famous line in the *Aeneid*: "I fear the Greeks even when they bear gifts." The thought must not be far removed from President Nazarbayev's mind when he takes decisions about how much of his country's economy should be developed for the benefit of China, and at what speed.

If the problem of the first decade in the 21st century for Kazakhstan has largely been about managing success, this is greatly preferable to the nation's problem in the last decade of the 20th century, which was how to avoid failure. The tightrope which Nazarbayev had to walk between these two political destinations was more perilous than most of his countrymen realised. Whether it was developing the Caspian, managing Moscow or building bridges with China, Kazakhstan needed a strong pilot. It had one in Nazarbayev, but he had to draw on his full reserves of strength at the turn of the millennium in order to navigate through Asia's great financial crisis of 1999–2000.

12

Entering the 21st Century
Part I – The Domestic President

1. DEVALUATION, RECOVERY AND GROWTH

Nazarbayev often calls himself "an economic President". This is a true but oversimplified job description. The leader of a country so strategically located and so rich in natural resources dependent on international prices cannot afford to focus exclusively on in-country economic affairs. However important Nazarbayev's domestic reforms may have been, the early years of the 21st century have shown that regional and global forces can make a massively unpredictable impact on Kazakhstan's progress. This has been true of both the Asian stock market crisis of 1998 and the world economic crisis from 2008 onwards.

Towards the end of the 1990s, Nazarbayev's reputation as an economic innovator seemed well established. He had weathered the storms that battered Kazakhstan's fragile economy in the years immediately after independence. His free-market reforms were succeeding; his privatisation programme was gathering momentum; GDP was growing steadily; and Caspian oil was becoming a major factor in strengthening business and foreign investor confidence. But suddenly, like a thunderbolt from what appeared to be a cloudless blue sky, came South East Asia's financial crisis of 1998.

The sudden collapse of currencies and stock markets among the "Asian Tiger" economies of Malaysia, South Korea, The Philippines and Thailand had severe repercussions for Kazakhstan. The plunge in regional business activities caused a slump in exports and oil prices. Caspian crude fell to $9 a barrel, which made the Tengiz and Kashagan fields temporarily uneconomic. Simultaneously, a rouble crisis, debt problems and political instability in Moscow during the final phase of Boris Yeltsin's Presidency sent the Russian economy into a downward spiral of chaos.

The timing of these troubles in other countries was very bad for us [recalled Nurlan Balgimbayev, who had been promoted by Nazarbayev from Oil Minister to Prime Minister in 1997]. We had just started to lift up our heads as a nation, and then these blows kept hitting

185

us from Russia and Asia. But no matter how bad the crises became at home, the President stuck to his program of economic reform. They were tough years in 1998–1999, but he saw them through.

Many Kazakhstanis were using harsher adjectives than "tough" to describe the precipitous decline in their living standards. The Asian stock market crash created a downturn which was severe, although not as devastating as the crisis years of 1992–1994 in the economy. Nevertheless, a return to those bad old days of shortages and hardships dealt a severe blow to the nation's self-confidence. Once again, the shelves in food shops were empty. Workers were laid off from their jobs in large numbers. Construction sites shut down. Pensions could not be paid. Soup kitchens had to be opened by the Red Cross to feed the starving in several cities. Electricity supplies failed so frequently that some families had to burn their own furniture to keep warm in the winter.

It was a very bad time [recalled Kassym-Jomart Tokayev, who took over from Balgimbayev as Prime Minister from 1999–2001]. The national budget had to be cut three times in this period. There was a lot of suffering, particularly among older people, although we did pay back their pension arrears in the end. Inevitably, the government was quite unpopular because of the expenditure cuts and the feeling that we were back again in a crisis.

Nazarbayev described the turbulence as "a sort of endurance test for our young country and its financial system". His toughest test came over the issue of whether to devalue the tenge. At the beginning of the crisis, the National Bank, under the chairmanship of Grigory Marchenko, held to the view that devaluation was wrong. In support of that policy, the Bank had to make frequent interventions in the foreign exchange markets and lost over $600 million of its gold and dollar reserves. Nazarbayev appointed a new National Bank Chairman, K. Damitov, who initially favoured devaluation.

I invited him over and we spent a long time discussing the pros and cons [recalled Nazarbayev]. Only in April 1999, once the financial situation in Russia had stabilised and devaluation expectations had died down in the country, did we proceed with the introduction of a free floating tenge exchange rate.

Although there were plenty of critics who felt that the President's policy of the floating tenge had taken too long to introduce, once the decision had been implemented the benefits to the economy quickly became apparent. Within months of devaluation, growth resumed, exports picked up, and the balance of payments deficit was reversed. "As a result of the measures taken, we were able to keep the negative impact of the world financial crisis to a minimum and maintain macroeconomic stability", claimed Nazarbayev. His assertion was broadly justified. Of all the regional economies adversely affected by the Russian and South East Asian crises, Kazakhstan showed the earliest and strongest recovery. Much helped by the strengthening price of oil, the country's GDP grew by 8 per cent in 2000; 13.1 per cent in 2001; and recorded double-digit growth for the next seven years. These achievements were consolidated by what Nazarbayev called his 2030 Plan, a long-term economic strategy to make Kazakhstan a globally competitive nation with free markets, low taxation, reduced government expenditure, widespread private ownership of land, high investment and a prosperous middle class. When the strategy was going well, Nazarbayev was quick to claim credit for his management of the economy. When there were periods of stagnation or disruption, he was skilful in playing the part of the "Teflon President", to whom political opprobrium did not stick. As ministers took the heat of public criticism, the head of state rose coolly above it. For example, when the Asian financial crisis was at its peak, Nazarbayev managed to disassociate himself from his entire government, saying in a speech to Parliament and the nation on 30th September 1998, "No one in Kazakhstan, including myself, is satisfied with the performance of our government.... We find that every day the operation of government is too slow, too bureaucratic, too confused and lacking responsibility."

This professed detachment from his government explains why Nazarbayev was sometimes ruthless in his hiring and firing of ministers. He was constantly reshuffling his cabinet, running through four different Prime Ministers in as many years between 1997 and 2001. Nazarbayev's iron grip on political appointments enhanced his image as a "strongman", to use one of the politer epithets that were beginning to be applied to him by western journalists. Some of them preferred to label him as a "dictator", "autocrat", or "authoritarian ruler". These epithets worried Nazarbayev. Once Kazakhstan's economy was firmly set on a course of stability and growth, he turned his mind to improving the image of his country as a free and democratic society. The results were not without merit, yet they fell short of finding favour with his international critics.

2. FREE ELECTIONS OR FIXED ELECTIONS?

Nazarbayev often speaks the language of democracy when describing Kazakhstan's elections and political institutions. But his words have not, so far, been sufficiently convincing to give him the reputation of leading a credible democratic system. That is the opinion of most international observers and commentators who have witnessed the country's first three elections in the 21st century. Yet many of these same observers acknowledge that progress has been made by Kazakhstan towards electoral democracy. They also accept that the President himself has widespread popular support, even if the size of the majorities for himself and his party look suspect. So the picture of elections in Kazakhstan is a mixture of confusing words and images, some favourable, some unfavourable. Does this mean that Nazarbayev's democratic glass is half empty or half full?

It is hardly surprising that any politician who spent the first 51 years of his life immersed in the totalitarian system of the Soviet Union should move cautiously before introducing full-scale Western democratic practices into a country located in what many of its citizens call "former Soviet space". Kazakhstan is politically as well as economically conditioned by sharing some 5,500 miles of its borders with Vladimir Putin's Russia and Hu Jintao's China. Yet by the standards of his region, Nazarbayev is a democratic innovator. Unlike Putin, he accepts international observers from the OSCE at his country's elections, receiving both compliments and criticisms in their reports. But when he promises to remedy the system's failings in future electoral contests, Nazarbayev has to keep an eye over his shoulder on his domestic public opinion with its conservative traditions which flow from Khanates, Dzhus and tribes that characterise both the ancient roots and modern power structure of Kazakh society. The complexities of these structures are little understood in the West. The older generation of Kazakhstanis are unschooled in the concept of adversarial opposition, and unenthusiastic about lectures from foreigners about the need to import more of it into their country at a fast pace. For these reasons, the view of the men of the steppes about the speed of progress towards democracy seems to be at variance with the voices of the media in Washington or London, who expect the political processes of their societies to be imported perfectly and immediately. The three most recent elections in Kazakhstan need to be seen from both perspectives.

The 2004 Parliamentary elections for the 77-seat Majlis, or lower house of Parliament, resulted in only one candidate being elected from an opposition party. He refused to take his seat in protest against election irregularities, that included a ban on two leading opposition figures from standing as parliamentary candidates due to convictions (for slander and corruption), which were widely seen as politically motivated. However, 12 parties contested the election, all of them getting a chance to put their cases to the electorate in seven television debates, and through media outlets which were not harassed or shut down as had happened in the 1999 Parliamentary elections. So the OSCE observers reported that there had been improvements over past elections, while concluding that "serious shortcomings remain, and the election process fell short of international standards".

In 2005, Nazarbayev was re-elected for another 7-year term as President. He received 91 per cent of the vote. His main opponent, Zharmahan Tuyakbai, won 6.6 per cent. The *Economist* commented, "The election showed that few people were willing to risk their material gains, even for the sake of greater democracy, freedom of the press and a crackdown on widespread corruption, which were all promised by Tuyakbai", and also noted "Mr Nazarbayev is genuinely popular".

That popularity was boosted by the most frequently shown TV commercial in the Presidential election. It showed a number of Kazakhstani businessmen declaring "We entrepreneurs have made our choice", as they lined up to shake Nazarbayev's hand, delivering sycophantic sound bites in praise of the country's economic success. As with all campaign commercials, the format looked artificial. Yet the voters bought the message that Nazarbayev deserved the credit for his country's prosperity. Another factor working in his favour was the turmoil in neighbouring Uzbekistan and Kyrgystan, which may well have made the Kazakhstani electorate grateful for their stable leadership. So, in spite of continuing OSCE reservations about the process of the Presidential election in 2005, there was no serious argument over the validity of the result, even though the authenticity of the figures remained open to question.

The third election of 2007, held under a new proportional representation system, created a Kazakhstan Parliament in which the opposition had no seats at all. The President's party, Nur Otan (Fatherland of Light), won 88 per cent of the vote. The only two opposition parties to trouble the scorers, ANSDP and *Ak Zhol*, took respectively 4.6 per cent and 3.3 per cent of the votes cast. They did not win any seats because the threshold for taking a seat at all in the new parliament had been set by the rules of the PR system at 7 per cent. Inevitably, there were complaints from the disappointed opposition parties about this outcome. Some critics protested that the 7 per cent threshold figure had been set arbitrarily and artificially high. Others alleged that in some districts the vote had been rigged, possibly by local officials from the provincial *akim's* department, who did not want their own areas to lag behind in popular support for the President's party. One specific voting irregularity was highlighted in an interview for this biography by Alikhan Baimenov, the Chairman of the opposition Ak Zohl party. "In the village of Karsakbai where I was born, there were five times more voters than there were people registered to vote", he complained, "so no one really knows what the actual turnout was." Shades of the Cook County, Illinois precinct voting anomalies in the US Presidential election of 1960, or the South Florida counts in 2001! But in all these cases it is far from certain that the alleged

189

irregularities (even if they had been upheld by some impartial electoral tribunal) would have affected the end result of the election.

As for the OSCE 1,000 foreign observers, they gave Nazarbayev some credit for improving the electoral process. Their 2007 report praised the calm atmosphere at the polls, the increased level of media access for opposition parties, and the transparency of the Central Election Commission as the supervising body. However, at 40 per cent of the polling stations the vote count was orally assessed as "bad" or "very bad", a conclusion that rather took the shine off the claimed 88 per cent figure of support for the President's party, although no specific violations of election law were documented. Yet once again, there was no real doubt about the end result. Moreover, OSCE statements such as "a noticeable improvement over previous elections", and "the state authorities demonstrated a willingness to conduct a more democratic election process" were indications that Kazakhstan's democracy, although still flawed, was moving in the right direction. The most fulsome tribute to the improvements came from the leader of the British team of independent observers, Lord Cecil Parkinson, a former Cabinet Minister in Margaret Thatcher's government. Speaking of the 2005 election, he said: "At this election, Kazakhstan has taken a major step forward in becoming a full democracy."

In May 2007, the Parliament voted for Nazarbayev to have the right to stand for re-election to the presidency for a third term when his current term expires in 2012. This innovation was greeted positively by most EU governments and by the US. However, the Western media, taking their lead from the opposition media in Kazakhstan, widely reported that Nazarbayev had arranged to become "President for life".

Comparisons between Nazarbayev and the world's only claimed "President for life", "Papa Doc" Duvalier of Haiti, were unjustified. For the Kazakhstani Parliament had not changed the constitution or ended presidential term limits which, under normal circumstances, remain at two five-year periods of office. Perhaps some westernised Kazakhs were nearer the mark when they claimed the arrangement as "our equivalent of the Franklin D. Roosevelt third-term amendment passed by the US Congress in 1944". For, in the face of the gathering storm that was soon being called the world credit crunch, the Kazakh legislature voted to strengthen the stability of their young nation by granting Nazarbayev the unique status of being able to stand for a third term of office. He has not said whether or not he will exercise this option. Personal health and political circumstances are likely to decide whether or not he retires from the presidency (perhaps into some role equivalent to Singapore's Lee Kuan Yew's honorific ministerial rank) when his present term expires in 2012, when he will be 72.

On the domestic political scene there is no successor or serious opponent yet in sight. For the time being, Nazarbayev remains master of the game in Kazakhstani politics, with all the power and support he needs to remain in office until the time, and probably the successor, of his choosing. As for democracy, although there has not yet been a fully free and fair election in Kazakhstan, the 56 nationals of the OSCE apparently think sufficiently well of Nazarbayev's good intentions in this direction to have offered him and his country the OSCE chairmanship in 2010. Time will tell whether the President's performance in this area will live up to his promises. So far, the only troublesome opposition has come from a disaffected ex-member of his family.

3. TROUBLE IN THE FAMILY

One of the images which Nazarbayev cultivates is that of a happy family man. In private, and on special public occasions, he enjoys his patriarchal role as husband, father, grandfather and great-grandfather. Like most Kazakhs, he reveres his ancestors. He takes pleasure in being photographed with the rising generation of children who are his descendants. But there have been cracks in this façade caused by the predictable rivalries of life in a Presidential household. Until recently, such tensions were hidden from the world. But, between 2001 and 2007, a spectacular drama played out as Nazarbayev's eldest son-in-law launched an internecine onslaught of misbehaviour consisting of actions that were soon dubbed "Rakhatgate". This eponymous saga included corruption, coup plotting, kidnappings and the murder of political opponents. It ended with the high court of Kazakhstan sentencing Aliyev (but in his absence abroad) to 20 years' imprisonment. Although the story had many episodes, its two most salient features were that Aliyev had committed serious crimes and that Nazarbayev had been caused major embarrassment.

The son-in-law whose status within the Nazarbayev family has fallen from golden boy to black sheep to convicted criminal in exile is Rakhat Aliyev. Born in 1962 as the scion of a well-connected Kazakh family whose members had held Ministerial portfolios in the Soviet era, Aliyev married the President's eldest daughter, Dariga, in 1982. A combination of political ambition, personal ruthlessness and dynastic nepotism propelled the rising son-in-law into some of the most powerful positions in Kazakhstan during the 1990s.

At various stages in his early years of power, Aliyev was head of the tax police, and a key figure on the Committee for National Security (KNB), where he was in charge of counter-terrorism in the period after 9/11. He was also active in media businesses. With his wife Dariga, he acquired 50 per cent of

Kazakhstan's main television channel, Khabar; the other 50 per cent was owned by the state. He also controlled another private TV channel, KTK, and the popular Karavan newspaper. Aliyev earned himself a reputation for ruthless behaviour in these various roles, making many enemies and acquiring great wealth.

Of all the bad things that this man did, the worst was that he told many people that he had talked to me about his dealings and received my authority for them [recalled Nazarbayev]. Unfortunately, none of them ever checked with me. So great harm was done. For me, it was a very unhappy and unpleasant episode, made much worse because he was my son-in-law.

In 2001, Aliyev was suddenly removed from all his official duties amidst claims that he had been plotting a coup, with the help of the security services, against his father-in-law. No evidence of this alleged coup has been made public. Perhaps a more likely explanation of Aliyev's fall from grace is that his controversial dealings in security matters, tax investigations, business deals and politics had made him too troublesome a figure to keep at the centre of power. Nazarbayev's solution to the problem was to exile Aliyev to Vienna, appointing him as Kazakhstan's Ambassador to Austria.

After four years in Austria, Rakhat Aliyev was brought back to Kazakhstan and made first deputy minister of foreign affairs. However, his restoration was soon accompanied by further controversy. In February 2006, three months after Presidential elections, a senior opposition politician, who had been a strong critic of Nazarbayev, Altynbek Sarsenbayev, was brutally murdered. He had also been an outspoken critic of Aliyev for his persecution of insubordinates when he held high positions in the KNB security service. Another former member of this service alleged that Rakhat Aliyev had been involved in Sarsenbayev's killing. Aliyev successfully sued the KNB officer for libel. His wife, Dariga, published a sensational newspaper article claiming that the murder of Sarsenbayev had been an orchestrated conspiracy by people at the heart of the government to discredit her husband and family. It is widely believed that Nazarbayev was angered by what one commentator called "This airing of dirty laundry". One consequence of these goings-on was that Mr and Mrs Rakhat Aliyev had their wings clipped. The Asar political party founded by Dariga was suddenly merged with the President's party, Nur Otan, thus neutralising one part of the Aliyev's power base. It was also announced that the state share in the Khabar television channel would be increased from 50 per cent to 100 per cent.

Meanwhile, Rakhat Aliyev was expanding his other business operations, allegedly using brutal methods. After acquiring a controlling stake in Kazakhstan's eighth largest banking group, Nurbank, in January 2007, Aliyev (according to the High Court's findings) masterminded the kidnapping of its chief executive, Abilmazhen Gilimov, and his deputies, Zholdas Timraliyev and Aibar Khassenov. The bankers were tricked into getting into a car, which drove them to a *banya* (bath house) outside Almaty. According to witness statements, Aliyev held them as his prisoners for 11 days, tortured them, and forced them into signing over a prized city centre building into his ownership.

I can do anything I want in this country [said Aliyev]. Now we'll put a stamp in your passport saying that you crossed the border and that you are flying to Kiev, and we'll bury you here. And then let the police and your relatives look for you for the rest of their lives – they will never find you.

Gilimov and Timraliyev eventually managed to escape from Aliyev's captivity. Timraliyev and Khassenov disappeared and have never been found. But Gilimov gave a statement to the police and then went public with the story of his abduction. Opposition politicians and newspapers began campaigning for a formal investigation of Aliyev's role in the kidnapping. Nazarbayev instructed the Procurator-General's Office to commence an inquiry into the allegations. On learning about this investigation, Aliyev disappeared and eventually surfaced in Austria where he resumed the role of ambassador.

In June 2007, it was announced that Rakhat Aliyev had been dismissed from his post because he faced charges of violent kidnapping, money laundering and fraud at Nurbank. An international arrest warrant was issued against him, and a formal request for his extradition was made to the Austrian authorities. A Vienna court refused the application on the grounds that Aliyev could not be guaranteed a fair trial in Kazakhstan. Opposition and Kazakh authorities claim that Aliyev bribed or "oiled" his way in Austria.

After winning the extradition case, Rakhat Aliyev launched a counterattack. He claimed that the charges against him were false. They had been fabricated, he said, because he had recently met with his father-in-law to express concern about the lack of democratic development in Kazakhstan. According to Rakhat's account of this meeting, he had told Nazarbayev that he intended to run for president in 2012, the date of the next election when Nazarbayev's final term of office ended. At the time of this conversation, Kazakhstan's parliament was discussing lifting the constitution's term limit in order to allow Nazarbayev to run again. "I told him that this change amounted to the establishment of a monarchy in Kazakhstan, and several times I tried to talk him out of this", claimed Aliyev.

Public opinion in Kazakhstan was underwhelmed by Rakhat Aliyev's sudden concern for an improvement in the country's democratic development. "Complete nonsense" was how one of the opposition party leaders, Oraz

Zhandosov, described it. Many others had the same reaction, not least because it was well remembered that Aliyev had written an effusive newspaper article in 2006 calling for the establishment of a monarchy in Kazakhstan. Nazarbayev himself described his son-in-law's claims as "total lies". A group of business leaders attacked Aliyev, saying: "Many of us have experienced his methods of doing business, and using law-enforcement agencies to apply political pressure for his own ends." This was a thinly veiled reference to Aliyev's acquisition of huge wealth, allegedly by violent extortion.

Despite the lack of support for Aliyev, there was speculation in the international media that the row between father-in-law and son-in-law could be the beginning of the end for Nazarbayev, because so much political turmoil would be caused by it. This speculation intensified when the constitutional amendment was passed by Parliament, allowing Nazarbayev to stand for a third term. However, it was notable that the US State Department welcomed this news, as did several other commentators from diplomatic or domestic sources. Far from causing turmoil, Aliyev seemed isolated in his fears about "the establishment of a monarchy" in Astana.

The next move in the saga came in July 2007, when Dariga Nazarbayeva divorced Rakhat Aliyev. The divorce papers were allegedly slipped under the door of Aliyev's home in Vienna during the night, leading him to complain that he had been divorced by stealth and that his signature had been forged. The ending of the marriage put a stop to the gossip that Dariga was still supporting her husband and planning to open up a political rift with her father. Further legal moves continued in the Kazakhstan courts against Aliyev. His principal assets were sequestrated by the state, or awarded to his ex-wife. A military tribunal found him guilty of planning a violent *coup d'état*, disclosing state secrets and abusing power as a government official. The highest civilian court convicted him of a number of criminal charges, including the kidnapping of the two Nurbank executives. In absentia, he was sentenced to 20 years in jail.

In retaliation for these legal blows, Rakhat Aliyev issued many threats to expose Nazarbayev. He claimed to have written a memoir, *The Godfather in Law*, which contained allegations of corruption and cronyism against the President. Although the book has not yet been published, much of its contents have appeared on the web, but with little impact in either Kazakhstan or the rest of the world. Its most sensational claim did, however, make headlines when, in November 2007, Rakhat Aliyev publicly accused Nazarbayev of ordering the murder of Altynbek Sarsenbaev, the senior opposition figure. According to Aliyev, "The order for the elimination of Altynbek Sarsenbaev was given from the territory of Austria when President Nazarbayev was on holiday in Klagenfurt, Austria in February 2006".

There are good reasons for treating this allegation with scepticism. The cold-blooded murder of Sarsenbaev together with his bodyguard and driver was indeed a terrible crime, but the killer was caught, tried and sentenced for it. A member of the Presidential family was linked to the murder, but he was Aliyev, not Nazarbayev. Aliyev denied his alleged involvement but, according to opposition leader Oraz Zhandosov, a motive existed. For Altynbek Sarsenbaev, a former ambassador to Moscow, had been the whistleblower who revealed the evidence showing that Aliyev had been planning a coup against Nazarbayev with the help of disaffected members of the security services.

These tangled tales are unlikely to be unravelled, disproved or corroborated, given the secretive ways of the inner circles of Kazakhstan's élite. All that can be said so far is that Nazarbayev has been damaged by Aliyev. Yet the end result of this clash between two alpha males inside the presidential family is that the father-in-law appears to be the clear winner. The son-in-law may still be a loose cannon, but he has little or no support in Kazakhstan. He is a nuisance but not a threat. His reputation as an intimidating thug who allegedly often resorted to violent threats or actions has left him with few friends and many enemies. His ex-wife, Dariga, has now rejoined the family fold and is conspicuously loyal to her father. Whatever Rakhat Aliyev does or does not do from behind the walls of his comfortable residence-in-exile in Austria, he seems unlikely to influence the course of events in Kazakhstan. Although there remains a damaging trail of unanswered questions about political murders and financial kidnappings, the main result of "Rakhatgate" is that President Nazarbayev will surely be far more cautious in future about letting political succession become a family business.

4. EDUCATION, INNOVATION AND TOMORROW'S LEADERS

Whatever his troubles of succession or non-succession within his own family, Nazarbayev has devoted a great deal of thought, action and government expenditure to the future general leaders of Kazakhstan in succeeding generations. His efforts have been focused on giving an increasingly high priority to education. In budgetary terms he has presided, since 2000, over a seven-fold increase in government spending on schools and universities which amounts to 4 per cent of GDP. Every Kazakhstani child now gets 12 years of primary and secondary education. As a result, the nation has a 99 per cent literacy rate and claims to rank 14th in the world league tables of country-to-country educational ratings.

Despite these statistics, education in Kazakhstan is widely regarded as a neglected and less than successful area of government activity. With the notable exception of the Bolashak programme (of which more later), the country's educational institutions inherited from Soviet days are inadequate for a nation which aspires to be in the top 50 of the world's most competitive economies by 2030. More than a quarter of the state schools are in a crumbling state of disrepair. Teachers' skills and morale are low. Exam results are suspect because too many grades are awarded as a result of undercover bribes from parents.

At university level, there are no institutions offering degree courses that are internationally recognised. In Almaty there are one or two technical colleges whose graduates achieve acceptable standards at particular disciplines, but these establishments owe more to their past roots in the Soviet system than to the educational policies of independent Kazakhstan.

Nazarbayev is acutely aware of the deficiencies in his country's schools and universities. Having been fortunate in his own education from dedicated teachers in the village schools of Chemolgan and Kaskelen in the 1940s and 1950s, he is keenly interested in raising professional standards in contemporary Kazakhstan. "A teacher doesn't lead you by the hand on the road to knowledge, he simply points the way", is one of the President's most cited aphorisms. Another is a quotation from his favourite Kazakh poet, Abai: "If you want to be rich, learn a trade", adding the comment "His words perfectly sum up my modern education strategy."

The trades young Kazakhstanis will need to master if they are to compete in the modern world lie, according to Nazarbayev, in the fields of scientific and technological excellence. "Kazakhstan needs educational establishments of a new type right now", says Nazarbayev. "These should be élite universities – powerful, educational, scientific, research and production complexes closely linked with industry." Putting his government's money where his mouth is, the President has given generous backing to several recently founded institutions such as the Kazakhstan Institution of Management and Economic Prognosis (KIMEP); the Gumilev Eurasian University and the Kazakhstan-British Technical University. The project which is dearest to Nazarbayev's heart is the new National University which he is developing in Astana. He is determined that it will one day offer degrees whose academic excellence will be on a par with what the international community's finest institutions attain. However, that day may take some time to dawn.

Because he saw early in his Presidency that Kazakhstan's higher education institutions had no ability, for the foreseeable future, to meet the demand for world-class university degrees from the rising generation of students,

Nazarbayev embarked on one innovative programme which has been re-soundingly successful – Bolashak (literal translation: "The Future").

Under the Bolashak programme, 3,000 young Kazakhstanis a year are awarded scholarships which enable them to study for degrees at international universities. 500 of these Bolashak students go to the UK, 1,000 to the USA, and the rest are scattered around 32 different countries. The universities they attend range from the world's best-known higher education institutions such as Oxford, Cambridge, Harvard, MIT, the Sorbonne and Moscow Central, to a wide spectrum of international colleges specialising in technical and scientific qualifications.

The Bolashak initiative was Nazarbayev's brainchild and he maintains a close personal involvement in it. He launched it in 1994 with a class of 180 students. At a time when the government coffers were almost empty and desperately short of foreign currency, it was a bold decision to take on an annual spending commitment which soon rose to over $10 million; exporting the best and brightest young scholars in the country to overseas universities, paying every cent of their tuition fees, travel expenses and living costs for the next four years. But Nazarbayev was adamant that his initiative should go ahead, comparing Bolashak to "planting our seed corn". Kazakhstan has certainly reaped a good harvest from the programme, both in the public and private sectors.

Any international visitor to the upper echelons of business or government in today's Kazakhstan soon becomes aware of Bolashak graduates and postgraduates. They are a high-profile meritocracy of new-breed movers and shakers. Their work ethic, ambition, attitudes and outward-looking approach are quite different to those who were raised entirely in the old Soviet-shaped domestic educational system. Many of them are now rising if not risen stars in banks, big companies, government departments or entrepreneurial businesses which they themselves have started. "We are this country's equivalent of Rhodes scholars", said one proud young Stanford graduate, now a partner in an international law firm in Almaty.

This self-conscious élite is developing into a powerful network within the country. Its mystique as a magic circle of tomorrow's leaders is deliberately fostered by Nazarbayev. He sees them regularly at Bolashak receptions, takes a well-informed interest in their progress, encourages them and often gives them fast-track promotion within his government.

A Bolashak scholarship, for which the competition is fierce, places every successful candidate under a contractual obligation to come back and work in Kazakhstan for a five-year period after graduating abroad. Since the employment opportunities are so good, most of the scholars are happy to do this.

And for all the legends of dizzying ascents to pinnacles of power and wealth by returning Bolashakians, the vast majority of scholars in the programme get their jobs in more predictable areas such as engineering, medicine, mining, veterinary science, art and design. One of the many Bolashak students met by this author was 22-year-old Danik Beshymbaev from Astana. He was half-way through his four-year degree course in aerospace engineering at the Wentworth Institute of Technology in Boston.

I get all my tuition fees and accommodation expenses paid by the programme [he said]. Then, on top of that I am given a living expenses allowance of $1,700 a month, and an air ticket back home once a year. The package costs the government around $50,000 for all my costs, so I am fantastically grateful to get this opportunity. With my aerospace engineering degree I may work for one of the air transport companies. Or I may stay on in the US and get an MBA at somewhere like MIT. Then I would try to found my own aerospace company.

Such confidence is typical of Bolashak's young men and women. The programme is clearly successful, particularly if it results in a culture and work ethic step change for the students, as well as giving them an international education. If there is a weakness, it lies in the schools from which the scholars are selected. Too many of them are stuck in a time warp of second-rateness. And therein lies a troublesome new problem. A significant percentage of Kazakhstan's rural Islamic madrasas (schools) which were built along with rural mosques were receiving generous funding from wealthy donors. It is a development that worries Nazarbayev.

It has become a fashionable trend among businessmen over recent years to erect mosques and madrasas in their home villages [he says]. The problem is that once they are built, it is often not clear who should be teaching our young people there, or what syllabus they should be following. We need a law to straighten out these issues.

This comment by the President introduces a challenging subject on which he has strong views – religion.

5. RELIGION – A THREAT OR AN OPPORTUNITY?

Nazarbayev is not a religious man by upbringing or inclination. He is hostile to extremism from any faith or denominational group. For both personal and political reasons, he champions religious tolerance, interfaith dialogue and secular government. However, he is troubled by undercurrents of Islamic pressures from various parts of his region. Occasionally, he also has to deal with difficulties created by other faiths whose representatives (for example, the Jehovah's Witnesses) have caused sectarian pressures within Kazakhstan. So Nazarbayev is vigilant in his determination to keep all forms of religious fanaticism from taking root in his country. His policy-making speeches on

198

this subject are exemplary, but there have been criticisms of the way the policies are being implemented in practice.

In one of his regular annual addresses to the people of Kazakhstan, Nazarbayev said, in 2005:

All of the world's religions have left their mark on Kazakhstan soil, which explains why we are strangers to intolerance and religious fanaticism. This spiritual tradition, this openness to the word of God in any form is one of the most important foundations of interfaith accord in Kazakhstan. We are known throughout the world for our tolerance, interethnic and interfaith accord and dialogue.

Like many Kazakhs, Nazarbayev calls himself a Muslim, but his real spirituality is shaped by the steppes and the traditions of his nomadic ancestors. They worshipped as their principal deity *Tengri* – the god of the sky. When imams from Iran and Arabia first tried to import Islam to Central Asia in the 10th century, they found it pointless to build mosques in Kazakhstan because the peripatetic nomads were always moving their flocks around, and had no fixed abodes or places of worship. The net result was that Kazakhstan's Muslims were at best semi-detached followers of the Prophet. Their lukewarm religion was further diluted by Paganism, Shamanism, Zoroastrianism and Buddhism, which all had their followers in various parts of the country.

Under the Soviet empire this dilution continued, when atheism was the order of the day. Nevertheless, some of Stalin's 3 million deportees from his purges – who included ethnic Russians, Ukrainians, Poles, Chechnyans, Jews, Kurds, Armenians, Tartars, Balkans and Germans – managed to continue practising their faiths after settling in Kazakhstan. Nazarbayev was well aware of this throughout his own multi-ethnic boyhood in the village of Chemolgan. So he grew up with an attitude of "live and let live" towards religions. This laid-back universalism from his childhood has stayed with him into his Presidency.

What may have changed in the early years of the 21st century is that Nazarbayev's early laissez-faire approach to faith has mutated into an almost militant emphasis on religious tolerance. He has come round to this approach partly because he likes to proclaim a clear strategy for every aspect of life in Kazakhstan and partly because he discerns a potential long-term threat to his country's political stability from fundamentalist Islam.

Left to themselves, the Kazakh people are about as "Islamic" as most members of the Church of England are "Christian". The problem is that the Kazakhs are not being left to themselves. Mosques are now being built all over the country in ever-increasing numbers, from the gold-domed extravaganza in

Astana (a gift from the ubiquitous Emir of Qatar) to much simpler Islamic structures in small towns and *auls* (villages) in rural areas. Madrasas are following Mosques. Preachers, often financed by Saudi or Iranian money, are vigorously promoting their various Shia, Sunni or Wahabi interpretations of the Koran. In the wake of the preachers, strange sects are springing up, such as the Islamist group Hizb ut Tahir. Thirty of its members were arrested in Karaganda in 2007, charged with attempting to overthrow the government by setting up an Islamic caliphate. Similar subversive activities are alleged to have been detected among militant groups exported to the Almaty area from the mosques of Uzbekistan.

Some Kazakhstani Members of Parliament became so worried by these alleged plots that in April 2008 they introduced sweeping amendments to the basic law of religion. These required the registration of religious groups under more restrictive procedures; placed limitations on the activities of small sects; required local government permits for preachers, and prohibited all financial contributions from foreigners and anonymous donors. The United States government, through its ambassador to the OSCE, protested against these parliamentary amendments on the grounds that they could "seriously threaten the protection of religious freedom in Kazakhstan".

Nazarbayev, who has placed a high premium on keeping the approval of OSCE in the months approaching his country's chairmanship of this international body, referred the amendments to Kazakhstan's Constitutional Council, a watchdog organisation which oversees the compliance of legislation with the Constitution. In February 2009, the Council ruled that the amendments did violate the Constitution's guarantees of "the inalienable right to exercise freely one's religion, or to not exercise freely any religion at all". This ruling put an end to the controversy, and resulted in the Council's decision being warmly welcomed in statements issued by various international human rights and faith organisations. Nazarbayev evidently found the issue a difficult one to handle in the face of conflicting pressures, but he ended up getting the result he wanted. He is personally committed to religious freedom and secular government in Kazakhstan. One of the most public ways he has found to emphasise the religious tolerance he believes should be at the heart of his country is his creation of a symbolic monument in Astana, known as The Pyramid.

The Pyramid, whose official title is the Palace of Harmony and Concord, is a 93-metre high triangular edifice towering over the left-bank section of the national capital. Designed by the British architect Norman Foster, at a cost of approximately $80 million, the summit of the Pyramid contains a large circular conference room which Nazarbayev calls "the world centre for interconfessional dialogue". What he means by this is that the Pyramid has twice hosted a well-publicised gathering of global religious leaders – in 2003 and 2006. A third similar event will take place in 2009. Some cynics say that these assemblies of senior clerics from Islam, Christianity, Buddhism, Judaism, Hinduism, Taoism and other faiths result only in vague but vacuous out-pourings of spiritual hot air. More optimistic observers argue that the symbolism of peaceful coexistence between religions is important in a country where over 40 faiths and 3,000 religious establishments are apparently flourishing. Most of the newer spiritual buildings are Muslim mosques, but there are also several hundred older Orthodox, Protestant and Catholic churches. A recent survey by the US embassy in Astana reported that less than half the population (47 per cent) regards itself as Muslim, compared with 46 per cent who claim to be Christian.[1] However, the number of those who observe their faith by regular mosque or church attendance is far smaller. It should also be noted that a large number of other religions are practised at shrines, temples and holy places around the country. It says something about the general atmosphere of tolerance that Kazakhstan is the only Muslim country in the world where over 15 new synagogues have opened in the past decade. In them, the nation's 40,000 Jews worship without any Islamic pressure or harassment.

Nazarbayev likes to point out that the new diversity and vibrancy of religious groups in his country has been achieved after inheriting a long legacy of militant Soviet atheism. Before Kazakhstan became independent in 1991, not a single word was officially allowed to be spoken in favour of religious freedom or spiritual faith. So progress has indeed been achieved in the past 18 years, although the way ahead may be more difficult than the President's public declarations suggest. In a private conversation with one foreign visitor in 2008, Nazarbayev said "Religious freedom here is real in the sense that preachers can preach whatever they like, provided they say nothing that is intolerant of other faiths. That's where we draw the line." However, the line-drawing may be an increasingly demanding exercise as the polarisation of faiths intensifies in the 21st century. Do Nazarbayev's liberal policies on religion open the door to a greater long-term threat from Islamic fundamentalists? Or do they herald a brave new world of religious tolerance in a Eurasian country with a Muslim majority? The jury is still out.

1. Kazakhstan's official statistics on religion say that 70 per cent of the population are Muslim.

6. CONFLICTING PRESSURES

Economy first and then politics. Our statehood and nationhood will become stronger through the economic growth and economic well-being of the population rather than through hasty democratic transformations.

The last three words of this comment by Nazarbayev reflect his ambivalence about the pace of his country's progress towards democracy. Along with many other Kazakhs, he respects the ideals of this goal but has been made anxious about it by the early failures of the democratic experiment in Yeltsin's Russia. A second cause of his ambivalence has been a degree of cynicism over what he sees as the blatant commercialism of US and European leaders, when they lobby for contracts in Kazakhstan in almost the same breath as they advocate democratic reform. In the context of recent events in the former Soviet Union and in Central Asia, Nazarbayev today argues that there should be less pressure for the cause of introducing full democracy into Kazakhstan, on the grounds that the local and national complexities of this issue are not well understood. How sound are his arguments?

In Central Asia, there are plenty of pressures against democracy. The governments of Russia and China have no enthusiasm for a full and fair electoral process being developed by a large neighbour on their borders. In the volatile "Stans" who also have frontiers with Kazakhstan, notably the dictatorships of Uzbekistan, Kyrgyzstan and Turkmenistan, there are fears that premature experiments with democracy would lead to the installation of fundamentalist Islamic regimes. These regional forces are little appreciated by journalists and politicians in Western capitals. As Nazarbayev puts it:

Few people in the US, the EU or the OSCE have taken the trouble to learn what is really going on in Central Asia. They do not appreciate the challenges of culture and history in our area. They do not understand that it takes time to overcome the burdens of the Soviet mentality with its illiberal politics and state planned economy. Over and over again I have tried to explain this in Washington and European capitals.

Washington and London's political leaders have disturbed Nazarbayev by their linkage between the interests of multinational corporations and democratic pressures. "Let us recall the direct interest of George H. W. Bush in Chevron's involvement in Kazakhstan", he says, "or Dick Cheney's in ConocoPhillips and Halliburton in securing big contracts here. Or direct requests by Tony Blair to support BP and BG Group."

Although there should be no complaint about a Western leader who lobbies for export deals by Western companies, the alleged blurring of the lines between political reforms and corporate contracts have caused some resentment in the Kazakh leadership. Where these lines should and do merge is in the quest for national stability. Nazarbayev believes that the strong centralised authority given to the President under Kazakhstan's constitution has been essential in steering his country through the difficult early years after independence. The historical record appears to justify this claim. Unlike any other state in the region, Kazakhstan has avoided bloodshed and turmoil in its reasonably steady journey to economic and political stability. New challenges may well lie ahead in the environment of recession created by the global credit crisis. But compared to Russia, where the early experiment with democracy unleashed economic failure, inter-ethnic discord and a reversal of the very freedoms that democracy was meant to create, Nazarbayev's more cautious approach has resulted in a peaceful equilibrium of quietly improving political conditions. He deserves credit for this achievement.

On electoral reform, it is now guaranteed that future parliaments of Kazakhstan will have two-party representation even if one of them does not achieve the 7 per cent threshold figure. Voting irregularities of the past should be reduced, hopefully eliminated, by recent changes to 18 articles in the Law of Elections. These changes, based on ODIHR[2] recommendations, make it easier to register political parties, to regulate fair voting and to have greater oversight of elections by international observers.

In addition to these electoral changes passed by Parliament in 2008, there have also been significant media reforms along lines suggested by the OSCE office of Freedom of the Media. The new legislation lifts restrictions on electronic media, including the restrictions on internet sites. This has resulted in an increase in political blogging in Kazakhstan, some of it highly critical of the government. Although this facility and a small but vociferous number of opposition newspapers gives the country a welcome dimension of press freedom, the major TV channels remain largely under government control.

Nazarbayev likes to deny that the above improvements in his country's electoral and media laws have anything to do with outside pressures. However, the reality is that Kazakhstan is constantly being influenced by other countries and international bodies. The actions of the domestic President are inevitably affected by the reactions of the international President. Nazarbayev's dual role needs to be examined from both perspectives.

2. ODIHR = Office for Democratic Institutions and Human Rights.

13

Entering the 21st Century
Part II – The International President

1. BALANCING AND BORAT

Nazarbayev is a careful balancer and an enthusiastic joiner of international organisations in his foreign policy. This has been a sensible leadership policy for a new and vulnerable nation born out the collapse of the former Soviet Union. Although such a cautious approach might look obvious, no other comparable state in Central Asia has taken the same route. The increasingly erratic behaviour by the volatile border country of Uzbekistan, Turkmenistan and Kyrgyzstan has earned them the reputation of international pariahs. By contrast with his neighbours, Nazarbayev has made Kazakhstan a nation state which is respected, although not universally applauded, as a responsible member of the international community.

Nazarbayev first earned his spurs as a cooperative international leader in the early 1990s, when he voluntarily renounced Kazakhstan's stewardship of the world's fourth largest nuclear arsenal (see Chapter 9). Working closely with the United States under the Nunn–Lugar Cooperative Threat Reduction Program, Kazakhstan has fully rid itself of nuclear weapons and their infrastructure. It has continued to be an active participant in global non-proliferation processes.

Nazarbayev has gained status both regionally and globally by being a willing partner in a wide range of international organisations. In addition to its full membership of the UN and all its offshoots, Kazakhstan has been elected as the chair of the Organization for Security and Cooperation in Europe (OSCE) and the Organization of Islamic Conference (OIC). It is also a founder member of the Shanghai Cooperation Organisation (SCO); a partner in Operation Enduring Freedom, the international coalition in Afghanistan; and the host country for several high-sounding conferences of foreign leaders such as "Common World Progress through Diversity" (Astana, 2008) and "Congress of World and Traditional Religions" (Astana, 2003, 2006 and 2009).

These internationalist activities have won, within the diplomatic community, some respect for Kazakhstan's usefulness as a secular Eurasian country with a Muslim majority which tries hard to bridge the understanding gap between Islam and the West. Nevertheless, to the wider public of the world, complete ignorance of Kazakhstan was an almost universal characteristic, at least until 2006. In that year, this knowledge vacuum was filled by a Hollywood comedian who created an eccentric character who became a global icon. His name was Borat.

Borat tested Nazarbayev's sense of humour. But at a reasonably early stage in the progress of this satirical movie, he managed to see the funny side of it. "This film was created by a comedian, so let's laugh at it ... any publicity is good publicity", he joked at a Downing Street press conference alongside Prime Minister Tony Blair in November 2006. It was a neat way of deflecting the efforts of journalists to turn a caricature into a controversy. Yet, when Sacha Baron Cohen's parody first became a box office hit, the reactions of the Kazakh government were not so benign.

Young countries tend not to have well developed reflexes of tolerance towards aspersions on their national image. So it was no surprise that *Borat: Cultural Learnings of America for Make Benefit Glorious Nation of Kazakhstan* should have been given a mixed reception at home. "Utterly unacceptable, being a concoction of bad taste and ill manners, which is completely incompatible with ethics and civilised behaviour", was the foreign ministry's denunciation of the spoof charade in which Cohen's fictional alter ego, Kazakh TV host Borat Sagdiyev, tours and shocks America with the boorish crudity of his sexism, racism and anti-Semitism.

In another mark of official disapproval, the country's website regulators suspended the domain name www.borat.kz, saying they were preventing the British comic "from bad-mouthing our country". Cohen responded by opening another website on which he announced: "Since the 2003 Tulyakev Reforms, Kazakhstan is as civilised as any other country in the world. Women can now travel inside of bus. Homosexuals no longer have to wear blue hats. And age of consent has been raised to eight years old."

Far from enjoying the joke, some Kazakhs became even more indignant, among them one of the nation's most liberal voices, Zharmakhan Tuyakbai, leader of the opposition party, National Social Democrats. Apparently outraged by Cohen's claims that Kazakhs are addicted to rape, incest and Jew-baiting, Tuyakbai condemned the comedian for his offensive humour, saying: "If it happened in a country where rules are more strict than ours, there would have been a government decree to destroy Borat ... If I see him, I will hit him in the face."

Amidst many such expressions of outrage and official threats of legal action against the producers of the movie, 20th Century Fox, it took an intervention from the President's daughter to lower the temperature of domestic public opinion. In an interview with an Almaty newspaper, Dariga Nazarbayeva criticised the censorship of Sacha Baron Cohen's website. "We should not be afraid of humour, and we shouldn't try to control everything", she said, adding that the original satire had hurt the image of Kazakhstan much less than the suppression of the jokes on the web. "Its closure was covered by all global news agencies", she noted.

As *Borat* was on global release by October 2006, the intemperate reactions inside Kazakhstan were manna from heaven to the movie's publicists. An added boost to their efforts was the timing of Nazarbayev's official visits to Washington and London, which coincided with the US and British premieres of the film. "*Borat* sparks White House crisis talks", announced one newspaper headline over a report that Nazarbayev had protested to President George W. Bush about Hollywood's misrepresentation of Kazakhstan. The story was invented, but the fictional controversy did wonders for ticket sales. By the time Nazarbayev reached London to more tabloid headlines such as "Kazakh President arrives for three-day visit amid *Borat* storm", official denials of diplomatic tensions became necessary. Nazarbayev handled the problem with a light touch, asking the Downing Street press corps, "Maybe the journalist himself, Borat Sagdiyev, is here representing Kazakhstan? I would very much like to speak to him if he is."

Once it became clear that the visiting President had a sense of humour about *Borat*, the so-called "diplomatic row" evaporated. Journalists began writing articles pointing out that the movie was a travesty of modern Kazakhstan, from its skyscrapers to its synagogues. The Israeli Ambassador weighed in with the comment: "If you want to look for anti-Semitism in the world, it is not hard to find. But this is one of the only places in the world where it does not exist." Other non-existent notions of Kazakhstan were the movie's portrayals of its people drinking horse urine, buying wives for 15 gallons of insecticide, defecating in living rooms and throwing Jews down wells. These absurdities were more of a mockery of American gullibility than Kazakh bigotry. The only people who were really made to look ridiculous were those geographically challenged citizens of middle America duped on camera by Borat's comic antics.

Nazarbayev, like many Kazakhs, saw the Western movie-going public's enjoyment of *Borat* with an ambiguous mixture of bemusement and amusement. But, although he may well have been privately upset by the parody (which he claims never to have seen), he was probably smart enough to realise that the ridicule might have an upside. For an unknown new nation in Central Asia, to be lampooned was not as bad as being ignored. The problem offered an opportunity, which was to set out the real story of contemporary Kazakhstan. For better or worse, *Borat* created an international curiosity to learn the facts behind the fiction. Instinctively, Nazarbayev felt he should make a response to that curiosity. So, after showing that he too could laugh at the lunacies of *Borat*, his next move was to give new thought to the presentation of his own and his country's international image.

2. HIS FACE TO THE WORLD – IMAGES AND REALITIES

Nazarbayev cares about his international image. Rightly so, for he, not Borat, is Kazakhstan's face to the outside world. Yet, beyond his own region he is not a well-known figure. However, there is a growing recognition that the journalistic stereotypes of the 20th century such as "Ex-communist dictator", or "Moscow-trained autocrat" may be yesterday's clichés. Nazarbayev's constant curiosity and search for new solutions gives him many of the qualities of a political chameleon. His outward image of supremacy masks an inner willingness to deal in subtleties and surprises. As he and his country become increasingly significant international players, more questions will be asked about this long-serving President of the world's ninth largest and eleventh richest (in oil and gas) nation state. So what does Nazarbayev stand for on the global stage? In what direction is he leading his country as the 21st century unfolds?

A useful starting point in the search for answers to such questions is the phrase "Multi-vector diplomacy". The term was invented by Nazarbayev to describe his foreign policy balancing act, which seeks to position Kazakhstan as an even-handed ally of Russia, China, the European Union and the United States. But to paraphrase George Orwell: all allies are equal but some allies are more equal than others. Moreover, the perceptions of Kazakhstan and its President can be very different from the standpoints of Moscow, Beijing, Brussels or Washington DC. So the various vectors in Nazarbayev's multi-vector diplomacy deserve separate analysis.

A few days after he was elected as the new President of Russia in May 2008, Dimitri Medvedev made his first official overseas visit – to Kazakhstan. "Astana did not become the first foreign capital I have visited as President of Russia by chance", declared Medvedev at a joint press conference with Nazarbayev. "Russia values the genuinely and mutually advantageous relations with Kazakhstan, our strategic partner." In response, Nazarbayev referred to his country's "uniquely close friendship" with Russia, and added "I do not think there are such close fraternal relations as there are between Kazakhstan and Russia elsewhere in the world." Even after allowing for the exaggerated courtesies that characterise communiqués at the end of bilateral summits, the words and the evidence suggest that both Presidents (as well as Medvedev's predecessor, Vladimir Putin) have entered a phase of exceptionally warm cooperation.

The era of Putin has helped Kazakhstan to shed it's former inferiority complex about its northern neighbour. There are no longer any serious frictions over old areas of difficulty such as territorial claims, the status of ethnic Russians, borders, or the boundaries of oilfields. The former President (now Prime Minister) of the Russian Federation held over 40 cordial meetings with Nazarbayev in the last eight years, and their agreements on matters such as borders, tariffs, terrorism, gas prices, Caspian oil, CIS diplomacy and joint ventures between national companies have been self-evidently beneficial to both countries. "Soon I will settle here in Astana", joked Putin, on a recent visit to Kazakhstan's capital. The humour underlined what everyone knew to be true, that the two leaders and their respective countries have been moving steadily closer together with fewer and fewer of the old hang-ups about Russian dominance or Kazakh subservience. Although mutual mistrust will never be totally absent from the deeper levels of this bilateral relationship, the two countries are now genuinely good neighbours and good friends.

Not all international observers are pleased by the new warmth in Astana–Moscow relations. In the final months of the Bush administration, there were signs that Washington was becoming increasingly critical of Kazakhstan's record of democratic elections, human rights and restrictions on the media. Some Kazakh foreign policy advisers saw this as a concerted effort by the State Department to prevent Nazarbayev from moving closer to Putin's Russia and developing what was feared to be a similarly autocratic style of government. The cooperation of the two countries in energy policy also troubled Washington. Whatever the explanation, there was a cooling of the diplomatic atmosphere from the days when Nazarbayev was praised by successive US Presidents for his statesmanlike handling of the nuclear issue, and for his steadfast cooperation with the West against international terrorism in the aftermath of 9/11.

One of the clearest indications of the changing attitudes of the Washington establishment towards Nazarbayev came at the US–Kazakhstan summit in 2006. Kazakhstan was bidding for the OSCE Chairmanship. The State Department opposed its bid. When Nazarbayev raised this problem with George W. Bush, the American President's first and evidently baffled reaction was to ask his Secretary of State:

Condi, are we still a member of this organisation? [When that had been sorted out, a better-prompted Bush advised his visitor:] Think whether you need this chairmanship. The OSCE is an organisation discussing, condemning or accusing someone on a daily basis. It won't bring any good. They will be carefully examining your accomplishments and drawbacks through a magnifying glass, comparing Kazakhstan with other countries. So think once again whether you really need this organisation.

Nazarbayev stood his ground, pointing out that virtually all the other 56 OSCE member nations supported Kazakhstan as their future chair. Thanks to the support of leading EU nations such as Germany, he won the argument. The OSCE chairmanship is going to Kazakhstan as from 2010. Although this is an important leap forward for Nazarbayev in his quest for greater acceptance by the international community, nevertheless there were further warnings from the Bush administration that more progress is needed by the Kazakh leader on internal reforms. The US State Department has stepped up its private and public criticism of Kazakhstan's record on democracy and human rights in a manner that is obviously embarrassing to Nazarbayev.

The initial phase of the State Department's campaign started in a series of Washington briefings dating from April 2008. Senior officials directly challenged Kazakhstan's forthcoming chairmanship of the OSCE in pejorative language. "It is ironic that this democracy-building organisation, which is known for its monitoring of elections around the world, would be led by a country which is dubious at best", the officials stated. They then attacked Kazakhstan's media restraints, corruption allegations, lack of judicial independence and failings in past elections. Concurrently, US diplomats at the OSCE, led by Ambassador Julie Finley, were instructed to intensify their criticism of Kazakhstan's infringements of OSCE human rights and democratisation procedures. Ambassador Finley subsequently filed a series of "Statements of Concern" and "Statements of Protest" about religious freedoms, media freedoms and human rights in Kazakhstan. Nazarbayev, who found these criticisms a disagreeable surprise, was nevertheless responsive to them. He made changes in electoral and media law, and avoided Parliamentary proposals which might have restricted religious freedom (see Chapter 12). These actions in early 2009 pleased some of Kazakhstan's critics on the human rights front. There have even been private and public hints that Nazarbayev may be considering early elections run in accordance with OSCE rules. "Since chairing the OSCE lies ahead for Kazakhstan, and we intend to fulfil our obligations to the organisation, I do not rule out early parliamentary elections in the fall of 2009", said Presidential adviser Yermukhamet Yertysbayev in an interview with *Liter* newspaper. As the only reason for such elections would be a desire to strengthen his credentials as a good democrat in the eyes of the West, Nazarbayev's apparent receptiveness to the idea, which may earn him brownie points in Washington but will bring him no credit in Beijing or Moscow, is another example of the careful tightrope walk he continues to tread between the competing powers and pressures around him.

Multi-vector diplomacy runs in parallel with multi-vector economic management. Nazarbayev has often said that he gives building a strong economy for his country a higher priority than introducing new constitutional or political reforms. His critics argue that this is just an excuse for foot-dragging on progress towards full democracy. His supporters reply that their President is a practical leader with a long-term strategy for Kazakhstan's growth, designed to make it a modern and competitive state high in the top 50 of the world's successful economic powers by 2030. As greater democratic freedom and rising economic prosperity are complementary rather than contradictory goals, there is no good reason why Kazakhstan should not achieve both. But, given the tensions between Nazarbayev's Russia-leaning political caution and his American-led enthusiasm for free-market experimentation, an analysis of the President's overall vision may give the clearest signposts to his own and his country's future.

3. A VISION FOR GLOBAL COMPETITIVENESS

Nazarbayev is both a hands-on President immersing himself deeply in the day-to-day details of government and a strategic President who has dreams and visions for his country's long-term future. The latter side of his political persona is coming more into prominence as he approaches two milestones: his 70th birthday in July 2010 and the 20th anniversary of Kazakhstan's independence in December 2011. As he says, "The period of putting out the fires is over. It is now time for us to stop and imagine what our country is going to be like in 20 and 30 years time."

Events have an unfortunate habit of interrupting visions. Few would have predicted that the global banking crisis of 2008 could cause a slump in Kazakhstan's construction industry and a halving of the country's nine-year record of double-digit growth. The unforeseen military dramas between Russia and Georgia in 2008 also sent shock waves around the region. Nazarbayev's refusal to criticise either of the warring parties, making the vacuous comment that the trouble was due to "lack of adequate regional institutions", demonstrated how delicately he feels Kazakhstan needs to tread in Russia's back yard. No doubt he hopes that his carefully nurtured relationships with Putin and Medvedev will be strong enough to keep Kazakhstan immune from

211

similar troubles. But, given that economic volatility and regional instability will always be factors in calculations about Kazakhstan's progress, how realistic are Nazarbayev's plans for the next generation of his countrymen?

Kazakhstan is rich, and destined to become richer. All today's official estimates of its already huge oil, gas and mineral reserves are understatements. To give one example: Kazakhstan's three major oilfields in the Caspian-Tengiz (7 billion barrels); Karachaganak (8 billion barrels) and Kashagan (at least 10 billion barrels) are likely to be producing far more than their present projected output of 3 million barrels a day by 2015. These hydrocarbon deposits are almost as large as those in Iraq or the Gulf States. Over the next decade, they are expected to result in output of around 5–6 million barrels a day. There are credible private forecasts of comparably staggering size of Kazakhstan's future production of natural gas, uranium, copper, iron ore, grain and other vital commodities. A modern visitor might echo the comment of the Queen of Sheba when she saw the wealth of King Solomon: "Behold the half was not told me."

Although Nazarbayev does not dissent from the higher-end forecasts of his country's wealth, he had a sceptical attitude to the notion that Kazakhstan can live off its oil and gas reserves. "We must not sink our citizens and our economy's competitiveness in oil dollars", he says. "We must live and work as though we do not have any oil." To this end, he is aiming to position Kazakhstan as a nation of scientific and technological excellence. He talks enthusiastically of emulating the Finland example. By this, he means implementing the methods that transformed this small-population country, which until recently had no firm scientific base or advanced industry, into one of the world's most competitive and effective modern economies. The hallmarks of the Finnish "innovation miracle" were the highest standards of education, the competitive principle in the allocation of science funding, and a forward-looking national infrastructure linking the state, science and business together.

To show that such thoughts are not a mere pipe dream, Nazarbayev is expanding his Bolashak educational programme, opening new universities and information technology parks, and setting up a national centre for nanotechnology. As part of this strategy he established a Fund for Future Generations, usually known as The National Fund. This is a form of sovereign wealth fund that will act as a treasury for surplus oil resources. By mid-2008, it had accumulated approximately $27 billion dollars. Nazarbayev said in his speeches that The National Fund would be used partly as a reserve fund for the state to use as a stabiliser of the economy in periods of downturn, and partly as an investment fund for the benefit of future generations, particularly in the high technology and scientific sectors.

212

Whatever is achieved in the field of long-term investments for the benefit of the next generations of Kazakhstanis, the present belongs to the oil and gas industry, the mining industry and to the foreign investors who are developing them. In these vital areas Nazarbayev has thought through his vision, which includes two interesting innovations. He has encouraged leading Kazakhstani companies to list their shares on the world's stock markets. He has maintained a close dialogue with foreign investors, both individually and collectively through the mechanism he has set up of the Foreign Investors Council.

Two of Kazakhstan's biggest companies, Kazakhmys (copper mining) and KazMunaiGaz (oil and natural gas production), pioneered the listing of their shares by IPO on the London Stock Exchange in 2005–2006. These huge placings, which immediately raised the profile of Kazakhstan throughout the global financial community, were approved and encouraged by Nazarbayev. He gave his blessing to this initiative partly in order to carry his domestic free-market philosophy onto the international stage of world stock markets, and partly in order to introduce full accounting transparency into Kazakhstan. In the country's early years of free enterprise, the financial statements of many local companies were opaque – to use a polite word. The IPOs introduced the disciplines and standards of public company accounts verified by inter-national firms of accountants. This was a step change for the Kazakhstani business community, which soon had to follow the trail blazed by the big IPO companies. According to the chairman of Kazakhmys, Vladimir Kim, his own company would not have gone down the IPO road without the direct encouragement of Nazarbayev:

The President gave us his personal and political support at all stages [recalled Chairman Kim]. At least 80 per cent of my staff did not feel comfortable with the IPO process, but President Nazarbayev said to me: "Go and get access to the money of big international share-holders. This will bring transparency, confidence, and new technology, not just to Kazakhmys but to the benefit of all Kazakhstan."

These words, although applied to the listing of Kazakhstani companies on international stock markets, are a fair summary of Nazarbayev's overall vision for his country's economy. But in 2008–2009 the world, including Kazakhstan, was blown off course by global events and crises which shattered the confidence of the foreign investors on which the country's prosperity so heavily depended. Among other effects, the slump in world oil and commod-ity prices caused a slowdown in the development of the Kashagan oil field, and caused the IPO companies Kazakhmys and KazMunai Gaz to lose over three-quarters of their market value on the stock exchange. How Nazarbayev responded to the interruption of his vision, particularly in relation to foreign investment, is an important part of his story.

4. FOREIGN INVESTMENT

Nazarbayev has long been keenly aware of the priorities required by foreign investors. In the early days of bringing in business pioneers to Kazakhstan such as Philip Morris and Chevron, he negotiated the terms of their agreement with his government personally. He still stays close to the country's largest overseas investors by one-on-one meetings and through the mechanism of the Foreign Investors Council (FIC). This is a body which Nazarbayev chairs at its twice-a-year meetings, which are held in various strategic locations around Kazakhstan, with a businesslike agenda and specific policy goals. One of the most recent biannual meetings of FIC was held in Atyrau, the oil capital of the Caspian region in June 2008. It was attended by over 70 chairmen, CEOs or their equivalents from global corporations including Arcelor-Mittal, Mitsubishi, J. P. Morgan, BG Group, Chevron, Deutsche Bank, Lukoil, Exxon, Philip Morris, ABN Amro Bank, Ernst-Young and many others. The agenda was focused on the development of a more efficient power generation industry for Kazakhstan. With most of his cabinet in attendance, Nazarbayev listened for several hours to a discussion of detailed issues, ranging from the practical technicalities of modernising the country's electricity grid to the financial provision for capital grants and tax incentives for the companies investing in the new power-generating infrastructure. Although some of the speeches in the plenary session veered towards the ritualistic, much of the dialogue was effective. It is hard to think of any other modern state in which the President gets down to such a level of practical cooperation with foreign investors. In the margins of the public sessions, Nazarbayev had private bilateral meetings with overseas corporate leaders such as Lakshmi Mittal of Arcelor Mittal, Lord Renwick of J. P. Morgan, Vagit Alekperov of Lukoil, Bill O'Reilly of Chevron, Leonard Blavatnik of Access Industries and Sir Richard Evans, the former supremo of BAE Systems.

Dick Evans is today the overseas executive who has more influence on Nazarbayev than any other non-Kazakhstani national. This relationship between the President and the Chairman and Chief Executive of BAE began in the mid-1990s, when Evans was asked if he could sort out the problems of Kazakhstan Airlines, the then national carrier, which was burdened with debt and operated inefficiently. Nazarbayev's request was for the creation of a new international airline, which would achieve the highest Western standards of engineering, safety and management in full compliance with international regulatory requirements. Evans took on this challenge, created Air Astana as a 50-50 joint venture between BAE and the Kazakhstan Ministry of Transport, and succeeded in delivering exactly what Nazarbayev wanted.

We were not popular. We had to overcome many local vested interests and change just about everything from aircraft to pilot training to senior management [recalled Evans]. We ran Air Astana exactly as if it was a UK or European airline. It became admired throughout the region and accepted internationally. It is now a successful and profitable airline, but we could never have done it without the personal support and intervention of the President.

In the restructuring of Kazkhstan's major industries in the 1990s, Air Astana was a trailblazer of unprecedented commercial achievement. There were not many other companies on that same trail from the ranks of former Soviet corporate structures in Kazakhstan. Nazarbayev was quick to realise that the principles of governance, transparency, management information, account-ing and profitability which had been applied to the national airline needed to be applied to other national industries. Someone who came to the same conclusion was the energetic Minister of Transport who had worked closely with Evans over the creation of Air Astana. He was Karim Massimov, a rising star in Kazakhstani politics, soon afterwards appointed Prime Minister. Massimov and Nazarbayev were already talking about setting up a mega state holding company, that would own and manage the "Big Five" industries which at that time were under the control of government departments – the railways, the post office, the national grid, telecommunications, and the oil and gas companies. The plan to create a state holding company on these lines had been recommended in a report by McKinsey. But who in Kazakhstan possessed the strategic vision or the managerial ability to run such a Leviathan?

Since there were no local candidates for the job, Nazarbayev had to search internationally. He had already built up a relationship of trust with Dick Evans over Air Astana. So the President offered the chairmanship of the state holding company to the BAE chief. But Evans was initially hesitant about taking it on because of the intractability of the political problems that would come with the territory.

"I told President Nazarbayev that if I was going to do the job properly, many people would lose their jobs and many local interests would be upset", he has recalled.

The President responded to Evans by giving him a clear mandate: "My brief to you is simple", he said. "You can do whatever you need to do, but you must always put the interests of Kazakhstan first and foremost. If you do this, I will always support you."

On that basis, Evans accepted the Chairmanship of Samruk, the state holding company named after the mythical Kazakh bird which lays golden eggs. There was indeed great value within the portfolio of industries which Evans and his team began to manage, but persuading them to lay eggs was a formidable challenge.

We were aiming for value creation, but first we had to devise a strategy and then set up management information systems which would give us the basic data on which our strategy would be developed [recalled Evans]. This work was in progress when we were hit by the global banking and credit crisis of 2008.

Nazarbayev's response to the crisis was to merge the Samruk state holding company with Kazyna, the Sustainable Development Fund, a separate umbrella fund established earlier along with Samruk to properly manage and govern the sizable assets of a half dozen key development institutions founded in 2003–2004 in such areas as investments in non-extractive sectors, R&D and innovations, export promotion, market research. This gave the combined fund Samruk-Kazyna an enormous asset base difficult to value but worth at least $25 billion. Of this, $5 billion was pumped into the banking sector to improve liquidity and another $5 billion into the property and construction sector. Further support was given to the SME (small and medium sized enterprise) sector, particularly in manufacturing and agriculture. Help was also given to pensioners, state employees and more than 20,000 stranded property owners who had invested their savings in apartments that had never been built. This massive rescue operation was the Kazakh equivalent of the bail-out plans introduced by governments all over the world in the autumn of 2008.

But it took all Nazarbayev's skills of political leadership and communication to sell the rescue plan to the people of Kazakhstan.

5. STEERING THROUGH INTERNATIONAL TURBULENCE

Nazarbayev is often at his best in a crisis. Looking back over the turning points in his career, such as the power struggle with Kunayev; the Jeltoqsan drama of December 1986; the rejection of the Moscow coup in August 1991; the collapse of the economy in 1992–1993; the nuclear disarmament of Kazakhstan between 1990 and 1995, and the Asian financial crisis of the late 1990s, it becomes clear that bold decision-taking combined with articulate speech-making are the hallmarks of his approach. His talent is to instil his doubtful or worried listeners with a new confidence to follow his lead. These qualities came to the fore during the 2008 global credit crunch both in the run-up to the crisis and when it hit Kazakhstan hardest in the winter of 2008–2009. Here are two snapshots of a President under pressure as the international turbulence started and deepened.

When the banks of the world and Kazakhstan first began to send out danger signals of toxic debts and mortgage failures, Nazarbayev went out on a limb to try and maintain business confidence with both foreign investors and domestic consumers. This author travelled with the President on one of his early confidence-building trips to the Caspian oil capital of Atyrau in June 2008. In the space of a 24-hour visit to the city, most of it focused on one of the biannual meetings of the Foreign Investors Council, Nazarbayev also found time to inaugurate a new road bridge over the Ural River; to watch a race in the region's first Olympic swimming pool; to host a banquet for foreign investors; to open a Marriott hotel; to perform the production-starting ceremony at a huge new petrochemical plant on the Caspian, and to give numerous TV and radio interviews at all these events.

Nazarbayev's skills as a crowd-pleasing politician were much on display throughout this hectic programme in Kazakhstan's most western region which stands astride the borders of Europe and Asia. Approaching the Ural River that divides the two continents, Nazarbayev took on the demeanour of a US Presidential candidate in mid-campaign. He worked his way along the surging lines of spectators, shaking their hands, pressing the flesh and delivering stirring speeches full of rousing sound bites on peace and prosperity. Halting his motorcade far ahead of the ribbon he was due to cut on the bridge, the President seemed to be emotionally moved by the warmth of the welcome he was getting from some 5,000 well-wishers. The loudest cheers came from a contingent of Atyrau State University students in yellow T-shirts, who kept leaping in the air like bouncing trampolinists to wave their Kazakhstan flags at their President with a near-hysterical enthusiasm more usually shown to pop stars than politicians. Nazarbayev made a point of greeting several groups of hard-hat construction workers. "You built this bridge too quickly", he joked. "Now I've got to pay for it."

At the opening ceremony, Nazarbayev took on the dignified role of a head of state, sonorously reciting statistics about the numbers of highways and bridges that had been built in the region, as he reminded his audience that some 15 years ago this oil-booming metropolis of skyscrapers and 250,000 residents had been a small port of fishermen and agricultural workers. Sharing his vision for the future, Nazarbayev spoke of the huge potential of the Caspian and then gave an international perspective as he told the crowd: "Our achievements are being recognised around the world. So is our political stability. That is why we have been invited to become chairman of the OSCE in 2010."

It did not seem likely that this youthful assembly of muscular hard hats and teenage students would know what the OSCE was. But Nazarbayev radiated such confidence in his histrionic presentation that his listeners cheered him to the skies. "What he promises he delivers. That's why he's popular here", said one local resident. That seemed to be the spirit of the Atyrauans; optimistic and happy to turn out on the streets for a glimpse of their leader.

What Nazarbayev had certainly helped to deliver was the latest progress on the oilfields of the Caspian. Flying on the Presidential helicopter, a Russian-built Sikorsky M18, to the Tengiz field some 50 miles south of the city, the magnitude of the oil and gas production in the region became clearly visible. Nazarbayev's official role was to inaugurate a new petrochemical plant which would cleanse the sour gas coming out of the field before the oil was pipelined to the Black Sea and western markets. He was also marking the 15th anniversary of the Kazakhstan-Chevron joint-venture development of Tengiz. So, before he turned the wheel that opened the flow of oil, Nazarbayev again reeled off a cascade of statistics of which the most impressive were that Kazakhstan had so far received $20 billion in revenues from this one field; that Caspian oil production should double in the next seven years, and that 80 per cent of Chevron's workforce are now Kazakhstanis. As if to highlight this localisation of the oil and gas industry, Nazarbayev started an impromptu interviewing session over his microphone with several young men and women in the crowd of Chevron employees, asking them to describe their jobs, the technologies they operated and their hopes for the future. Their pride in their work, and their optimism about their lives spoke well for the rising generation of Kazakhstan.

Later in the schedule, the President put on another display of optimism in an upbeat speech he gave to the Foreign Investors Council. After feasting his guests on mountainous platefuls of Beluga caviare, which came straight from the roes of freshly caught Caspian sturgeon laid out like corpses for dissection on nearby serving tables, Nazarbayev toasted the major new projects which some of the foreign business leaders were bringing to his country. He sounded excited as he described the new Arcelor Mittal investment which would expand production at the Karaganda Steel plant from 6 to 10 million tonnes a year; as he outlined the second phase of oil production at Tengiz; and as he announced that a new petrochemical facility and an oil and gas pipeline would be built on the Caspian towards the new Kazakh oil port of Kuryk. At a time when many western economies were falling into recession, Nazarbayev's message was that Kazakhstan was bucking the trend and maintaining fast growth. It was not an occasion for mentioning difficulties such as the paralysis of many banks in the country because of their excessive loans to property developers. Nazarbayev the political visionary and investment salesman was in the ascendant on this Caspian tour, enjoying a role he would be playing even more enthusiastically in a few weeks time, on the 10th anniversary of his national capital. "See you in Astana", he said to several of his principal guests at the end of the 18th biannual meeting of the Foreign Investors Council. It was an invitation to quite a party, described in detail in the next chapter.

Nazarbayev's über-confidence on the Atyrau tour, and at the 10th anniversary celebrations of Astana, was not based on false propaganda or wishful thinking. He was right to believe that Kazakhstan has better prospects than any other country in its region, and most other countries in the world, for coming through a recession in relatively good shape. However, he seems to underestimate the scale and ferocity of the global economic storm.

Kazakhstan had more than its fair share of greedy businessmen, over-borrowed property developers, and reckless bankers who crashed to self-destruction in the winter of 2008–2009. But, in his rescue plan Nazarbayev put the interests of ordinary people first by making it the government's priority to protect pensioners, state employees, small property owners and bank depositors. It was clear that he had learned important lessons from Kazakhstan's far more devastating economic crisis of 1992–1993, when none of these groups was adequately sheltered.

In October 2008, Nazarbayev gave an hour-long TV interview, broadcast on all channels in Kazakhstan, explaining the global financial crisis and doing his best to assure his audience that the nation would weather the storm. "Despite the crisis that has affected our country, the economy continues to work in normal mode", he said, emphasising that Kazakhstan's gold and currency reserves plus the assets in the National Fund stood at a combined total of over $51 billion. For a population of 15 million people this is a sizeable reserve from which to find resources for a national bail-out.

The President's reassurance exercise, which has so far consisted of rescue package measures costing 10 per cent of the national GDP, had a favourable impact on Kazakhstan's business community. Confidence stabilised as Nazarbayev made it clear that he had given his government the resources and the powers to navigate through the crisis.

It's time you banged your fist on the table and started working abnormally [he told Prime Minister Karim Massimov and the cabinet on 13th October 2008, adding that the government has] carte blanche to carry out a programme to stabilise the economy and financial system as well as wide powers to make unorthodox decisions.

Almost six months after Nazarbayev's first major announcements of crisis measures to steer through the worsening global storm, the author visited Astana and interviewed both the Prime Minister and the President. Both were in sombre mood, emphasising that the crisis had not originated in Kazakhstan; that the emergency measures of tenge devaluation and deploying huge resources from the National Fund were working; and that major new initiatives were about to be announced. Prime Minister Massimov emphasised that his boss the President had given the government the instruction: "It is better to make a decision than to be afraid to make a mistake."

Nazarbayev unveiled some of his biggest decisions to deal with the crisis five days after his final interview for this biography, when he delivered his annual state of the nation address on 6th March 2009. He could not be accused of lack of boldness. His announcements included 350,000 new jobs mainly for workers on infrastructure projects such as motorways, agricultural irrigation schemes, sewage works, water reservoirs, meat-processing plants, schools, hospitals and general utilities. The most grandiose of these plans was the creation of a 3,000-mile Western Europe to Western China motor-rail transit corridor.

There will be 5,000 people working there this year and up to 50,000 workers will be employed on it in 2010–2012 [declared Nazarbayev]. This is going to be an artery that will turn Kazakhstan into a transit corridor between Europe and Asia.

As the President's mega-project list rolled onwards and upwards in his address, covering new gas pipelines, power stations, hydroelectric plants and vast agricultural developments, some listeners in his audience must surely have silently asked themselves: "Can he really deliver all this?" As if he was responding to such sceptics, Nazarbayev recalled the finest achievement in his track record of doing the impossible:

It was during our most difficult years [he recalled] that we began and completed construction of a new national capital – Astana – at a time when nobody believed we would be able to do that. Let us now emulate that positive experience.

As a clarion call to economic modernisation, job creating, and surprising both his own countrymen and the world, leadership in building Astana has a powerful resonance, even at the worst of times in a global economic crisis. So it seems appropriate for this biography to travel, in its final chapter, to Sary Arka, the great steppe and heartland of Kazakhstan where Nazarbayev created his new and extraordinary national capital.

14

A Capital Vision

"Nursultan Nazarbayev has given this city not only his work but also his soul … truly it may be said 'Astana is his child'." These words came from Dmitri Medevev, President of Russia, during the speeches from visiting heads of state commemorating the 10th anniversary of the capital of Kazakhstan in July 2008. The celebrations, consisting of parties, ceremonies, unveilings of monuments, firework displays and cultural events, spread over seven days. They were enjoyed by the city's 750,000 residents and by many more thousands of domestic and foreign visitors, including the author. But the birthday party spirit was only one dimension of the festivities. In wider conversations, there was much discussion of what the anniversary might or might not symbolise.

Did Astana represent a visionary seat of government for a 21st century nation? The essential relocation of an overcrowded former national capital whose infrastructure was inadequate? A new strategic crossroads for Eurasia? A presidential folly of extravagant hubris? A financially overextended conglomeration of uncompleted apartment blocks? A political safety bunker designed to put Kazakhstan's power structures as far away as possible from the borders of potential invaders? A regional hub of futuristic industries and transport links? A return to the emotional roots of Kazakhstan's history and culture in the heartlands of the steppes? Some, none, or all of the above?

The arguments represented by these questions are familiar to Nazarbayev for, during the first 18 years of his Presidency, no project has engaged his emotions and his energies with greater commitment than the creation and development of Kazakhstan's new capital. It follows that a clear understanding of what Astana is, why it came into existence, how it has been built, and what it means to the country's future is essential to an understanding of Nursultan Nazarbayev.

Astana is one of the world's most unusual and idiosyncratic capitals. It is packed with surprises. If a group of strangers were blindfolded, flown to it and asked, on opening their eyes, "Where do you think you are?", their answers might begin with "fairyland" or "the set of a movie" and then move through a guessing game of countries and continents. For the exotic skyline is dominated by buildings so disparate in their shapes and sizes, contours and colours, traditions and trajectories that consistency is to be found nowhere, while unorthodoxy rules everywhere. Even more startling than the diversity of design is the discovery that there was one dominant decision-maker who instructed the planners and architects, selected the colour schemes, sketched his own drawings for many of the important buildings and conceptualised the entire city. This decision-maker was Nazarbayev.

A good place to enter the mindset of Nazarbayev in his role as creator-in-chief of Astana is Baiterek, a 97-metre tower sprouting from the heart of the central boulevard. Originally sketched out in the President's own hand, it is a modernistic representation of the tree of life, Baiterek, at whose apex stands a glass sphere and a gold ball portraying the Kazakh national myth of a golden egg laid by the legendary bird, Samruk. From the viewing platform within the golden ball of Baiterek can be seen the layout of the city, which is bisected by the Ishym River into left-bank and right-bank sectors. The right bank is the so-called old city, although precious little in the way of antiquity has been left standing apart from a handful of institutional edifices from the Tsarist and Communist eras. The left bank is where Nazarbayev's vision for the new capital takes wing, since almost every building has been erected since the new capital was inaugurated in 1998.

One of the more conservative of the contemporary creations in Astana is the Presidential Palace, Al Akorda, an approximate reproduction of America's White House. Much larger in size than its original inspiration in Washington DC, it is topped by a bright blue dome and a needle-like spire. If Nazarbayev looks across the river from his office in Al Akorda, he sees a 100-metre high pyramid designed by Norman Foster called the Palace of Peace and Reconciliation. This last word is impossible to apply to the architecture on the left bank since both the styles and the substance of the most prominent skyscrapers are irreconcilable. They include: A matching pair of circular towers known to locals as "the golden ice-cream cones"; a national archives building in the shape of a grey-green egg; a mustard-coloured international business centre; a gargantuan 5,000-residence Soviet-style colossus in the clouds which is an exact replica of Moscow's State University; a bronze glass multi-storey building with a hinge on top which locals call "the cigarette lighter"; a UFO-style spaceship which plays host to circuses and festivals; a boat-shaped 3,000-seat concert hall; an Arabian mosque; massive ministerial offices with gold window panes; the upper and lower houses of Parliament and, as far as the eye can see, more and more high-rise buildings in every imaginable tradition and fashion, from the banal to the bizarre.

The mind and the eye soon start reeling on a tour of Astana. The layout of the city is conventional, but the mixture of colours and building styles resembles a mosaic of eccentricity. Jumbled up together without planning rhyme or reason are Manhattan apartment blocks, Muscovite onion domes, Dutch windmills, French chateaux, Byzantine cupolas, Middle Eastern minarets, Chinese pagodas, Turkish bazaars, Tuscan villas, Japanese restaurants, Corinthian columns, Scandinavian convention hotels, Hong Kong high rises, Russian orthodox churches, Spanish haciendas, Korean supermarkets, Mexican wave glass skyscrapers, Stalinist office blocks in the monolithic manner of 1930s Moscow and American shopping malls which could have been plucked straight from 21st century California.

Although there are jarring juxtapositions aplenty in this extraordinary metropolis, the cumulative effect of all these contrasts and experiments is that Astana feels alive. It is a young, energetic city whose inhabitants have an average age of 32. If, in summer, a traveller strolls through the parks or visits the massive statues dedicated to such themes as "victims of totalitarianism" or "warriors of the Junghar invasions", the multiplicity of languages spoken around them brings to mind the Tower of Babel. The same phenomenon prevails in shops and supermarkets, where the variety of the international produce is as exotic as the variety of the local architecture. But Astana is a confluence not a clash of cultures. For the peoples that have flocked to come and live in the new capital are drawn from a kaleidoscope of nationalities. Only 60 per cent of Kazakhstanis are Kazakhs. The remainder come from over 100 identifiable ethnic groups of which the most prominent are Russians, Ukrainians, Uzbeks, Koreans, Germans, Uighurs, Chechens, Poles, Crimeans, Turks, Greeks, Persians, Kyrgyz, Turkmen and Chinese. The novelty of Astana has helped them all to feel at home.

But where is this home? Astana is the most isolated national capital in the continents of Europe and Asia. It is near nowhere. If you fly south-east, eventually you reach Almaty after 1,200 kilometres. If you fly west, the first city of any size is Atyrau, centre of the Caspian oil industry, some 1,600 kilometres away. Travelling due north, there is a vast expanse of emptiness punctuated only by endless wheat fields, occasional farming villages and two small provincial towns. To the north-east lies Siberia. A north-west course takes you to Moscow, a three and a half hour flight away. In between these points of the compass lies Sary Arka, the Great Steppe, a colossal wilderness of both flat and mountainous grassland traditionally regarded as the ancestral home of the Kazakh nomads. Creating a national capital in such a remote and inhospitable region would have been widely regarded as mission impossible at the time when Kazakhstan became a nation, nearly 20 years ago. Why did Nazarbayev attempt it?

* * *

The idea of creating a new national capital first floated into Nazarbayev's mind in romantic circumstances. A few months after independence he made an official visit to the northern city of Akmola. This drab provincial centre, an administrative hub in Soviet times for agriculture and rail transport, is situated at the heart of the steppes on the banks of the River Ishym. As his presidential tour took him across the town's nondescript bridge, Nazarbayev paused to stare at the twisting bends of the stream and its swirling current. Gazing into the waters of the Ishym, which Kazakhs call the Yesil, his mind began roaming towards international capitals built on rivers which gave them life, colour and vitality. He thought of Moscow on the Moskva; St Petersburg on the Neva; London on the Thames and Paris on the Seine. Coming closer to home, he conjured up the sights of Atyrau on the Ural; Kyzylorda on the Syrdara; Kostanai on the Tobol; and Pavlodar on the Irtysh. As this scenic tour of cities and their riverbanks progressed in his imagination, Nazarbayev started daydreaming of a shining new capital for the people of the steppes rising at Akmola on the Ishym.

As a romantic vision it was exciting, but as a practical proposition it was too preposterous to be mentioned to anyone else. This reticence was wise. For in 1992 Kazakhstan was in economic turmoil. Its people were struggling to cope with personal financial crises ranging from the non-payment of their wages to the provision of soup kitchens for pensioners who had lost their life savings. If, in those days of hardship, Nazarbayev had publicly floated his idea of relocating the established state capital of Almaty to an obscure outpost on the steppes, he would have been ridiculed. He acknowledged the unpropitious timing of his vision, later recalling: "I did not dare breathe a word about it, because at that time our economy was unable to carry the planning through." Nevertheless, the dreaming and the planning continued, at least in the privacy of the President's conversations with his inner circle of advisers.

The starting point of Nazarbayev's brainstorming was the realisation that Almaty had insurmountable disadvantages as the capital of an independent nation state. Emotionally and personally the President was attached to the city. He loved its beauty, its cosmopolitan culture, its vibrant life style and its jewel-like setting on the edge of the Alatau Mountains. But those mountains were a barrier to the expansion of Almaty. Already an overcrowded city of more than 1.5 million inhabitants, it had no space for future growth. Its horrendous traffic congestion made the conurbation a notorious smog trap whose air pollution problems were the worst in Central Asia. The airport was too close to the centre and too often fog-bound. Perhaps there could have been upward expansion as in Manhattan or Hong Kong, but because of the region's record of earthquakes, building skyscrapers in Almaty would have involved prohibitively expensive construction costs. In any event, the shortage of land available for development meant that there was little or no room for the new public edifices Nazarbayev envisaged.

As a sovereign state, we now needed new types of administrative buildings there had previously been no need for [he said]. For example, a Parliament, a Supreme Court, A Ministry of Defence, a Ministry of Foreign Affairs and other institutions such as the embassies of foreign states.

In addition to these environmental and ecological objections to Almaty, there were other unspoken problems. It was in style and substance a city with a Russian, indeed a Soviet, atmosphere to it. Many Kazakhs felt uncomfortable there. There was also a strategic anxiety over creating a capital in the south-east corner of the country just 100 miles from the border with China. Taking all these factors into account, Nazarbayev put aside his personal preference for Almaty, and favoured a relocation of the centre of government to some other part of Kazakhstan. But where?

*   *   *

The debate about the best site for a new national capital ranged far and wide. Nazarbayev told his advisers that 32 criteria must be taken into account in the selection process. They included social and economic indicators, climate, landscape, seismic conditions, environment, transport links, development prospects, building conditions and human resources. As he pondered on the long-term prospects for his country, Nazarbayev saw the attractions of using the project for correcting the population imbalance away from the relatively well-developed south towards the vast open spaces of the north. "There were economic and social advantages in redirecting the migratory flows to other regions of Kazakhstan", he said.

This futuristic urge towards modern social engineering was offset by a retrospective consideration of Kazakhstan's history and culture. A capital with no such roots seemed to Nazarbayev an artificial creation. For this reason, serious consideration was given to Ulytau (in Kazakh – the Great Peaks), in the centre of the country where the mountains rose out of the middle of the steppes. "In bygone days, Kazakh tribes from all over the country, from west, south, north and east used to gather in Ulytau. It was here that the Kazakh nation became, as it were, cemented", said the President.

The historic meeting place of the Kazakh nomads appealed to Nazarbayev's romantic instincts, but Ulytau soon dropped out of the running to become the national capital, because virtually nothing was left of it. The only traces of the ancient khanate headquarters were earth ramparts encircling the ruins of tribal camps. Many camels and horses had once travelled along these tracks, but no modern transport infrastructure, such as roads or railways, had ever been put in their place.

After Ulytau, Karaganda was seriously considered. Its central location appealed to Nazarbayev. So did his personal connections with the city, which in his youth he considered to be "the centre of the universe". He had married in Karaganda, brought up his children there, been employed in its steelworks and risen through the ranks of the local Communist Party as a young Komsomol official. But these nostalgic links soon faded in importance when it emerged that the city had serious water-supply and land-subsidence problems, caused by the nearby coalmines. These difficulties ruled out Karaganda as a national capital.

Seventy miles north of Karaganda stood a town which at various times in Kazakhstan's history had been called Akzhol, Akmolinsk, Tselinograd and Akmola. As early as the 10th century, the site of Akzhol was a centre of Islamic artists and craftsmen. Archaeological excavations had unearthed brick kilns of that period, along with carved tablets, tombstones and mosque decorations of ornate design.

In 1830, a unit of Siberian Cossacks founded a military fortress near Akzhol on the Ishym river, later calling it Akmolinsk. In Josef Stalin's time, soldiers from this base were deployed to guard camps holding many thousands of prisoners in the network of incarceration that became known as the Gulag archipelago. One of the most notorious of these prison camps was located just outside Akmolinsk. It was called ALZHIR, a Russian acronym for the Akmolinski Camp for Wives of Traitors of the Motherland, and was reserved for the wives of men considered "enemies of the people" by Stalin.

Nazarbayev was aware of this grim history. He also remembered the political announcements he had heard as a teenager in the mid-1950s, declaring that the Akmola province surrounding Akmolinsk would become the centre of a new Soviet agricultural project known as the Virgin Lands Scheme. This was the brainchild of Nikita Khrushchev, who ordered 100 million acres of steppe land to be turned into collective farms and settled by over 300,000 workers drafted in from Ukraine, Belarussia, Russia and other parts of the USSR. As the massive project began to develop, the city at the heart of the agricultural administration was renamed Tselinograd after the Russian words for virgin lands, *Tselinni Krai*. Like many a grandiose Soviet investment of that era, the scheme failed. But not before Moscow's planners had erected a number of imposing public buildings in Tselinograd, including a Communist Party headquarters, government offices, a palace of culture and a palace of youth. Khrushchev was so pleased with these developments that he considered making the city the capital of the Soviet Republic of Kazakhstan and renaming it Khrushchevograd. After the Kremlin coup ousting Khrushchev in 1964, nothing ever came of this proposal. For the next quarter of a century, Tselinograd stagnated. Almost the only new buildings were log cabins, giving the city a shanty town appearance. But after Kazakhstan's independence in 1991, it was renamed Akmola (which infelicitously translates as "The White Tombstone") and started to revive as a northern centre of around 100,000 people. There were occasional tensions between the various components in the population in which ethnic Russians, Ukrainians and other Slavic nationalities outnumbered Kazakhs.

The calming of ethnic tensions was high on Nazarbayev's political agenda in the early 1990s. Encouraging migration of people from the densely populated south to the vast expanses of the agro-industrial north and centre of the country was also important for the young nation. Besides, Nazarbayev felt it significant to detach the centre of the country from the culture of the old Soviet bureaucracy and to move the capital to areas which mixed Kazakhs with the predominant Russian-speaking population. So, for the second time in the 20th century, Akmola began to be considered for the status of a capital city.

* * *

Rumours about Akmola's future began to spread in the second half of 1993. This was because Nazarbayev made at least seven unannounced visits to the city. Local residents got used to seeing their President walking through their streets, gazing up at their buildings, striding along the banks of the River Ishym and holding impromptu meetings with leading citizens. Nazarbayev particularly enjoyed talking to younger businessmen who were striking out into the brave new world of free markets and free enterprise, which had been introduced into Kazakhstan after the break up of the Soviet Union. One of these entrepreneurs was Adilbek Jaxybekov, who had started up a general trading and construction company – the Tsesna group.

It was the first time I met Nursultan Nazarbayev [recalled Jaxybekov, who was later to take up a political career and become Mayor of Astana]. He was full of curiosity about Akmola, asking many questions about our business, and how the commercial life of the city was going. He also went round shops and supply companies. Before he left, I asked him if he would sign our visitors book, which he did with this inscription: "Tsesna was born by the new times, the times of reforms and the sovereign policy of the Republic of Kazakhstan. The activities of the corporation demonstrate that our course towards democratisation, privatisation, different forms of ownership and a market economy is right. I wish you success."

(Signed) President N. Nazarbayev

19/08/1993

A few moments after writing these words, the President was asked by a local journalist what Akmola's business community should be doing to make his reforms move more quickly. "They must join government and parliament", replied Nazarbayev, "and help me get the reforms going."

The date of this comment, just 20 months after independence, and its unexpected exhortation "to join government and parliament" were an intriguing indication of how the President's mind was moving. The businessmen of Akmola could hardly have been more remote from Kazakhstan's seat of government in both practical and geographical terms. Almaty, 1,600 kilometres away, was another world from the steppes if measured in political, cultural and economic advantages. What Nazarbayev did not say was that he was on a mission to bring these worlds together. His curiosity about life in Akmola was all part of his reconnaissance. He was making his own assessment of the city as a potential future capital. He liked the feedback he was getting from the new breed of younger businessmen in the north. Many of the questions he asked Jaxybekov and others were about the local and regional transport links. These were good. Thanks to Khrushchev's grandiose virgin lands scheme, Akmola had been turned into a rail and road crossroads, with connecting routes to cities all over Central Asia. These advantageous communications were probably the decisive practical factor in swinging the final decision in favour of Akmola. But the choice was even more heavily influenced by the strategic considerations that weighed on Nazarbayev's mind.

"We needed to strengthen Kazakhstan in geopolitical terms", explained Nazarbayev, "with a capital that would stand at the centre of the Eurasian continent having a synthesis of European and Asian traditions." This was a vision far beyond the horizons of his contemporaries. In the early 1990s, the number of Kazakhstani citizens who thought as geopolitically as their President, or used the term "the Eurasian continent", was negligible. Akmola itself was an isolated and introspective provincial community. Its residents were battling for survival against daily hardships, not dreaming of geopolitics or of synthesising other people's cultures. They would have been equally unmoved by Nazarbayev's second strategic argument for locating the capital on the steppes. This was based on security considerations. "Ideally, an independent state's capital should be located some distance away from external borders and situated in the middle of the country", he said. In theory, this presidential view was valid, but in reality the implied notion that Akmola could be defended against some powerful foreign invader would not have had much credibility with local public opinion in the early 1990s.

Nazarbayev's third strategic argument was expressed in terms of development potential, for he believed that a new national capital would kick-start Kazakhstan's beleaguered economy. This view undoubtedly appealed to banks and construction companies in Akmola, but it is easy to see why the business community of Almaty were underwhelmed by a huge northern development project, which would drain resources away from their part of the country.

These likely sources of scepticism about moving the seat of government to Akmola must have been obvious to Nazarbayev. A more cautious political leader might have paused because of them. But hesitation, once his mind was made up, was not one of the President's characteristics. So, on 6th July 1994, his 54th birthday, Nazarbayev formally announced in Parliament that the capital of the nation would be relocated from Almaty to Akmola.

"Stunned" is the word most often used by eyewitnesses to describe the reaction of Kazakhstan's Members of Parliament as they listened to the President's speech. Sitting in silence in the amphitheatre-shaped hall of the Supreme Council buildings in Almaty, many of the legislators could hardly believe their ears. The minority who supported the move of the capital were amazed at the boldness of the decision. The majority were appalled by it, and said so with unexpected vehemence.

They dug their heels in, declaring that given the deteriorating social and economic situation, spending vast sums on the capital's transfer was simply absurd [recalled Nazarbayev]. The debates were stormy, and the deputies were mostly against me.

To overcome the opposition to his proposal, Nazarbayev made what he later called "a cunning ploy". He gave his adversaries the impression that his concept of moving the capital was more of a theory to be studied in the future than an action plan to be implemented immediately. As he put forward a resolution for the Parliament to adopt, he deliberately obfuscated the timetable for decision-making that lay ahead. As Nazarbayev somewhat disingenuously emphasised in an interview with *Kazakhstan Pravda* on 2nd September 1994:

The date of the transfer is not indicated in the resolution. It merely states that the government has to produce all the documents required for it. It is perfectly clear this issue is not on the immediate agenda or even that of the near future, but some time after that.

After creating the illusion that the new capital was a timeless project whose horizons stretched way into the 21st century, Nazarbayev neutralised those critics who attacked him on economic grounds by declaring that "the plan to transfer the capital is to be implemented on non-budgetary funds whose sources are being looked for". This improbable proposition, which some observers compared to a fairy story that gold can be found at the end of the rainbow, apparently convinced enough Members of Parliament to support the resolution, which was titled *On the Transfer of the Capital of the Republic of Kazakhstan*. As Nazarbayev dryly noted: "Having decided that the new capital was not likely to happen for 20 or 30 years, the deputies ended up voting for it. The motion was passed by a small majority."

*   *   *

Having narrowly obtained Parliamentary authority to move the capital, even though he had used political smoke and mirrors to secure the votes, Nazarbayev acted quickly to get the fast-track results he wanted. He ordered his Cabinet Ministers to produce, by the end of 1994, a feasibility study on Akmola, together with a target date for transferring the government there. On 15th September 1995, he issued a Presidential Decree, *On the Capital of the Republic of Kazakhstan*, which set up a State Commission to organise the relocation of the principal departments of the central government to Akmola. It was perhaps fortunate that this decree was published just two weeks after Nazarbayev had received a massive vote of confidence from the Kazakhstani electorate, when they approved his new constitution by a 91 per cent majority. After such a demonstration of support, it would have been difficult to mount a well-organised opposition to almost any Nazarbayev policy. This was just as well for him, because in many parts of the country public criticism of the move of the capital was increasing.

In Almaty, opinion polls showed that 62 per cent of that city's population opposed the plan to transfer the government to Akmola. Many of those in the "No" camp were state employees who would have to be redeployed to the new northern capital. They feared that their quality of life would be downgraded when they uprooted from sophisticated Almaty to primitive Akmola. They also had concerns that the intellectual standards, as well as the living standards, of the civil service would fall because the professional qualification arrangements for government departments in Akmola were bound to be lower than in Almaty.

These worries of the public service were amplified by a spate of rumours. They ranged from gossip suggesting that only Kazakhs would be allowed to fill the top jobs in the new capital (in fact, 64 nationalities now administer the government departments there), to the "hen-pecked husband" speculation that Sara Nazarbayeva had pushed her spouse into moving to Akmola because her family originated from the same region. The tallest tale of all was that the relocation had been inspired by an astrologer telling a credulous Nazarbayev that an earthquake would flatten Almaty in 1997.

What such tittle-tattle showed was that the opposition was becoming personal. Nazarbayev was accused of getting his priorities wrong and suffering from *folie de grandeur*. It was suggested that he was seeking to emulate Peter the Great in the building of St Petersburg, or George Washington with Washington DC, or Mustafa Kemal Atatürk with Ankara. A common theme of the President's critics was that he had not provided an adequate explanation of his autocratic decision to move the capital. In this vein, the Almaty newspaper *Karavan* published an unusually hostile editorial headlined: "President Nazarbayev's personal capital", which said:

Only in conditions where there is no democracy can epoch-making projects emerge that nobody understands. No strategic considerations can justify the diversion of vast funds from the payment of wages and pensions and solution of the country's other social problems.

There were many observers both inside and outside Kazakhstan who did not believe that the relocation of the capital would ever happen. International sceptics were proportionately more numerous and more scathing about the plan than their domestic equivalents. To counter their incredulity, Nazarbayev instructed the Kazakh Foreign Ministry to organise a VIP tour of Akmola for ambassadors and other diplomatic representatives. It was not a success.

The tour began on a cold December morning in 1995. After a bumpy landing at Akmola's ramshackle airport, the dignitaries were driven to the downtown area. Their local guides did not seem to have got the message that a new era was dawning for the city, as the first hours of the visit were spent admiring Soviet monuments including a statue of Lenin, portraits of socialist labour heroes, and a plinth with a tractor on it in memory of the pioneers of the virgin lands scheme.

As they were escorted around Akmola's crumbling streets and dilapidated buildings, the diplomats seemed unimpressed. Their lack of enthusiasm for Nazarbayev's grandiose vision was increased by their lack of clothing to protect them from the arctic winds howling in from the steppes. Several of them were shivering, particularly the representatives of hot climate countries. The Iranian ambassador almost collapsed with hypothermia, as he had not thought it necessary to wear a hat. Headgear problems also affected the US ambassador, Elizabeth Jones. When the party arrived at the Ishym, her fur bonnet blew off. Out of gallantry, or perhaps to stimulate their frozen circulations, most of the diplomatic corps chased after it along the river bank, turning the sightseeing into slapstick comedy.

The serious conclusion reached by most of the VIPs was that Nazarbayev's dreams for Akmola would not come true. "None of the Ambassadors believed that the plans to transfer the capital would be implemented any time soon", recalled the Foreign Minister escorting the foreign dignitaries, Kassym-Jomart Tokayev. "My assurances were received with sceptical smiles and a cold response that the town in terms of infrastructure and climate was inadequate." One of the diplomats was undiplomatic enough to comment in a newspaper interview that Kazakhstan could not afford the costs of building a new capital. The only enthusiast for Akmola on that December day was the Mongolian ambassador, who said the city's weather and buildings reminded him of his native Ulan Bator. It was not the ringing endorsement Nazarbayev had been hoping for from the first delegation of foreign visitors to his chosen new capital.

If Nazarbayev was bothered by domestic or international criticism of his plans to relocate the capital, he never showed it. His attitude was "full steam ahead". The accusation of "Akmola autocracy", as one Almaty newspaper called his policy, was a charge he was willing to live with in the interests of getting the job done. As he put it,

I had to ignore the allegations that were distorting the true reasons for the transfer, and deliver the reality of developing Akmola as the capital. There were quite a few advisers on both sides, but it was up to me to make the decisions and take responsibility for them.

Nazarbayev took responsibility for the new capital by acting as if he were its proprietor as well as its President. Although he set up a high-powered State Commission for developing the city and relocating the government to it, each member of that body soon came to realise that they were directly accountable to Nazarbayev, and that he would personally supervise every project in detail. From the first days, his vigilance startled not only the administrative bosses but also the on-site managers and workers. When one early seven-storey building seemed to be making much slower progress than expected in the laying of its foundations, Nazarbayev made a nocturnal visit to the site accompanied only by his security detail. In the middle of the night he personally measured the excavation hole that had been dug for the foundations. He was furious to discover that these earthworks covered a significantly smaller area than the written accounts from the mayor's office had reported. Nazarbayev summoned all the officials and managers of the site to his office the following morning, and gave them a ferocious tongue lashing. After that, there were no more delays and no more internal disputes over the specifications. Despite continuing weather difficulties, the building was completed on time.

The numerous contractors engaged on the first wave of construction worried a lot about the weather conditions in Akmola. The city could be hot and windy in summer, while the winters were as arctic as Moscow's, made worse by notorious snowstorms known *buran*. Soon after New Year in 1996, Nazarbayev made a tour of the principal building sites, when the temperature was below 30° centigrade and a severe gale was blowing. He would not listen to grumbles, grievances or excuses about the climatic conditions. "This is normal weather for this place", he asserted. "It is the weather of our native land and of our forefathers. There cannot be anything bad about it! It is up to us to face these problems and to deliver these projects on time."

Asking the impossible of his team became standard practice for Nazarbayev, although he backed up his key executives with practical help as they struggled to meet the apparently unattainable targets he had set for them. The timetable was fixed by a Presidential decree, *On Declaring the City of Akmola the Capital of the Republic of Kazakhstan*. This announced that the legal starting point for the new capital would be 10th December 1997, and that its official inauguration would be 10th June 1998. Both dates seemed unrealistic, even to the President's most loyal officials. One of them, Farid Galymov, who at the time was Deputy Chairman of the Commission for Relocating the capital has recalled:

Lots of people were saying that the Germans took 10 years to move their capital from Bonn to Berlin, and that they were doing it the right way round in the sense that they relocated their government from a provincial town to a big city. We were doing it the wrong way round, going from a large city to a small town. Yet our President insisted that we must make the move in less than two years. But his willpower overcame all objections and obstacles. As a result, no capital city in the world has ever been relocated in such a short time.

Financial ingenuity was needed as much as political will. Nazarbayev solicited gifts and soft loans from foreign governments – notably Saudi Arabia, the UAE, Qatar, Turkey, Italy and Japan. He also extracted donations in cash or in kind from foreign companies. The US oil company Chevron was not best pleased to be asked to donate a new sports hall, but in the end it delivered. The strongest arm twisting went on inside the Kazakhstan Ministry of Finance. Farid Galymov has recalled an episode in September 1996 when he and Vladimir Ni, Nazarbayev's personal representative on the Relocation Commission, realised that work would have to stop on one of the largest apartment complexes in the new capital because funds had run out.

This was disastrous. We needed at least $10 million urgently. With the winter setting in, we knew that if we did not solve the cashflow crisis immediately we would have to close down the site until the spring. So Mr Ni flew down on the last plane to Almaty and saw the President at about midnight. In the small hours of the morning, the president called the Prime Minister, the Finance Minister and goodness knows who else. By the afternoon of the next day, $20 million was transferred into the Commission's bank account. So we kept the site open and finished the outside of the building before the winter closed in on us.

This was worse than hand to mouth financing. It was mouth to mouth resuscitation with government funds. Even when these emergency money arrangements worked, the city's power supplies did not. Breakdowns in the heating, lighting and telephone systems became endemic. Financing of the utilities was extremely difficult. The new capital was desperately short of new capital funding.

Nazarbayev was so ingenious in finding solutions to these problems that local businessmen began joking that if he ever lost his job as President he could easily find another one as an international project finance manager. For example, when Akmola's power supply capacity became a crisis, the only way to sort it out was to build a huge new in-feed substation with its own generating plant. Unfortunately, there was no money in the budget for such a project. Nazarbayev suggested forming a capital heat and power supply company which could build the substation after taking out a $150 million loan from Eximbank, repaying it over a number of years from its charges to customers. This was exactly the scheme that was swiftly implemented.

A rather similar innovation was introduced to solve the shortage of telephone lines. The national telephone company, Kaztelecom, still hidebound by monopolistic practices inherited from the Soviet era, could not move fast enough to meet the demand. Nazarbayev suggested bringing in competitive bidders. In no time a market-orientated international telecoms company offered to invest in a new system. Within less than a year Akmola had the best telephone system in the country.

These achievements may not look particularly startling to those whose culture and experience has long been rooted in free-market economics and competitive capitalism. But those were still revolutionary concepts in sleepy Akmola, which was only just emerging from the cocoon of communism that had prevailed in the Tselinograd of the Khrushchev/Brezhnev eras. Nazarbayev had to struggle to persuade the business and political leaders of the new capital to implement the best competitive practices. As he has recalled:

Turning a still Soviet-style provincial town into a modern capital was not the easiest of tasks. It was impossible to get rid of the old post-Soviet legacy overnight. We had to tackle the shoddy, inconveniently planned housing, the underdeveloped infrastructure and the obsolescent industry. But at the same time we had to plan well, taking into account international know-how while also honouring national traditions and giving fair opportunities to national companies.

The airport was a good example of blending together these differing factors. It was built ahead of schedule when, with Nazarbayev's encouragement, competition was introduced with the result that the number of asphalt plants in Akmola expanded from 3 to 18, within three months. These plants produced between 4,000 and 5,000 tons of asphalt per day in 1996–1997, which had been Akmola's rate of asphalt output per month in the early 1990s. With airport contractors working 18 hours a day, the runways, built to accommodate the largest of long-range Boeing Jumbos and stretched Airbuses, were completed at record speed. In this period one of the most frequent users of the airport was Nazarbayev's presidential 757. A story highlighting Nazarbayev's determination to monitor progress in his new capital is told about his aircraft's attempt to land in Akmola on a stormy night in November 1996. The winds and snow blizzards were so harsh that visibility fell below the safety limit. The air traffic controllers closed the airport. The reception committee waiting for Nazarbayev on the ground went home. However, in the air, the pilots of the presidential jet were doing extra circuits around Akmola's airspace in the hope that they might find a window of improved visibility during a break in the storm. Their patience was rewarded. After an hour or more of "stacking", the weather conditions lightened and the aircraft was able to make a safe landing. The complete absence of meeters and greeters amused Nazarbayev, who chided them later for their "lack of faith" in his zeal to come and inspect what progress had been made.

*   *   *

Faith was a necessary ingredient as Akmola went through the winter of 1997–1998, for there was a noticeable gulf between the ceremonial façade and the practical reality of progress. On 8th November 1997, Nazarbayev formally inaugurated the city as the nation's capital. Braving a bitingly cold wind, he gave the order for the national flag to be hoisted above the blue dome of the presidential residence, and delivered an idealistic address in which he declared: "Akmola has become the focus for our national spiritual richness, sanctity and tradition. Its missions may be compared to the ascent towards a high summit which calls for fortitude and endurance."

The last two words were appropriate to describe the qualities of stoicism required by the spectators as the inaugural ceremonies progressed. From the military there was a march past and a 21-gun salute. The local schoolchildren performed a pageant, "Hi Capital!" Nazarbayev went through the ancient Kazakh ritual of *alastau*, a fire cleansing ceremony culminating in a walk along an *akzhol* or lucky white carpet. The crowd watching these activities needed plenty of fortitude and endurance as the temperature dropped and the wind velocity increased. Exceptional heroism was displayed by the President's wife, Sara, who had forgotten to bring her headscarf. Her defiance of the elements seemed symbolic of the spirit of her native region, which pretended to be impervious to its mounting difficulties and discomforts. But once the flag wavings and the trumpet fanfares were over, Akmola came back to reality with a chilly shock. A few days after the inauguration, the city's major power-generating plant once again broke down, plunging Akmola into darkness and cutting off all heat.

The cause of the failure was said to be strong winds [said one influential local businessman] but there was more to it than that. In fact, the city's many minor and major shortcomings from systematic failures to systematic disruptions had passed the critical point.

Nazarbayev responded to this crisis by making Akmola an administrative and territorial entity on its own, no longer subordinate to the regional government, which had become a bottleneck. He also appointed a new Akim or Mayor of the capital. This was the same energetic entrepreneur, Adilbek Jaxybekov, who had impressed the President four years earlier on his reconnaissance visits to the city. The words which Nazarbayev spoke to his appointee were revealing:

Market economy approaches are desperately needed for developing the capital at the moment [he said]. High standards, fast rates of delivery and efficiency are the priorities.... You know how I look on Akmola. I beg you not to betray me. We shall work in full confidence, but I shall call you strictly to account for everything.

Important strategic decisions had to be taken if Akmola was going to be transformed from a sleepy provincial backwater into an international capital. One symbolic move was a name change. There was media comment that the literal meaning of its nomenclature, which translated as White Tomb or Deadly Winter, was inappropriate, or perhaps all too appropriate. In some people's minds, Akmola was associated not only with a harsh climate but also with prison camps, banishment, troublesome mosquitoes, economic failure and other negative connotations. Nazarbayev was sensitive towards the need to make a clean break with the past. There were suggestions that the city should be called Sary Arka (the heart of the steppes), Ishym (after the river) or even Nursultan. Nazarbayev himself came up with Astana. The word in Kazakh is a subtle one, implying the flight of an eagle, or a winged journey into the future. However, Nazarbayev selected it for unsubtle reasons. For the name literally means "capital". There were wags in Almaty who said that in the same spirit of originality it might as well be called "railway junction", or "city". But Nazarbayev staunchly defended his choice as "the perfect name for the capital – distinct, easy to pronounce, understandable in all languages". A few weeks later, by presidential decree, the capital of the Republic of Kazakhstan was officially renamed Astana.

On the ground, the biggest strategic issue to be resolved was the question of river banks. Former Tselinograd and former Akmola were built on the right or northern bank of the river Ishym. The left or southern bank had only a handful of residents, a park and a few roads, which acted as a buffer for the open steppe to the south. The general consensus was that the rede-velopment of the city should give priority to the rebuilding of the right bank, where an infrastructure and a solid network of homes, offices and public edifices already existed.

Nazarbayev did not agree with the consensus view. Although the Ishym seemed to most people a minor and unimpressive river, whose left bank marshlands were unsuitable for development, the President had a different vision. He saw beauty in the Ishym and potential for its neglected left bank. The first clear expression of his dream came on a cold March morning in 1998, when Nazarbayev was making one of his many tours of Astana with the Akim, Adilbek Jaxybekov, who has described the moment of decision:

We went to see the Samal residential district and then walked down to the Ishym. The Pres-ident strode ahead of his bodyguards, advisors and architects with his mackintosh flying in the wind. Then he said that any river was worth admiring, that not every capital was lucky enough to be situated on a river bank, and that it would be unwise of us not to take full advantage of this river view. He then suggested that we should construct a beautiful embank-ment, with wide promenades interspersed with beautiful rotundas. "This could be a great ornament to the city", he said. There were some moments of silence as we all pondered on this idea. Then President Nazarbayev spoke decisively as he declared "We will have this embankment. It must be finished by Presentation Day."

Presentation Day was an impossibly short three months away. But by this time there were 80 major construction companies in the city, employing more than 15,000 workers. They were set the challenge of building the em-bankment, which on Nazarbayev's orders was designed to be six metres wide. It was a project that required more than 15 square kilometres of stone blocks, to be laid down on the banks of the Ishym. Round-the-clock working was imperative, the supplies of material were chaotic and the pressure was almost unbearable. Because of the magnitude and late starting date of this project, it seemed unlikely to be finished on time.

It was not just the government's contractors who were in overdrive as Presentation Day, 10th June 1998, loomed closer and closer on the calendar. Private developers were exhorted to execute their projects by this deadline. So a host of large and small construction contracts were also racing towards completion in the spring of 1998. These ranged from gas stations, bowling alleys and car showrooms to hotels, shopping malls and apartment blocks. The result of all this frenetic building activity by both the public and private sectors was that Astana became one giant construction camp at full throttle for 24 hours a day. The clatter of pile drivers and pneumatic drills, the roar of compressors and power generators, and the revving engines of over 2,000 heavy vehicles, bulldozers and earthmovers combined into a raucous cacophony of high-volume noise, at levels that had never before been heard on the great and hitherto silent steppe.

To the overpowering *son* of Astana in the throes of construction was added unusual *lumière*. Not only was the whole city brightly illuminated by contractors' floodlighting, the dazzling blaze of arc-welding equipment in the hands of several hundred nocturnal welders created an optical phenomenon which was called "the white nights of Astana". From hundreds of miles away across the steppes, the night sky seemed to be lit up rather like the great northern lights of the Arctic Circle in summertime. It was a signal that something extraordinary was happening in the new national capital.

*   *   *

Despite all this frenetic activity, rumours circulated that Presentation Day would have to be put off. Many of the contractors were in favour of a postponement on the grounds that they needed more time to complete their assignments. Nazarbayev would not hear of it. But he did intensify the frequency of his own daily visits to each and every site in April and May 1998 – delivering on-the-spot speeches to workers and managers, urging them to get their tasks finished on time.

He made a tremendous personal impact with these visits [recalled Vladimir Ni, who often accompanied Nazarbayev on his tours]. People really felt that their President was appealing for superhuman efforts as their patriotic duty to the nation – and they responded by giving everything they had.

Nazarbayev held twice-weekly briefing meetings with all the key managers and directors in Astana in the run-up period to Presentation Day. Often these briefings resulted in big changes and new initiatives. One was the last-minute expansion of the city's football stadium, where the closing ceremonies on the big day were scheduled to take place. On a visit to this stadium in early April, Nazarbayev decided it was too shabby and too small to be a suitable venue for the grand finale he was planning. He walked round every nook and cranny of the spectators' accommodation. Then he gave an order that the two main grandstands must be completely renovated and that a third, brand-new southern grandstand would be built. The Chairman of the Committee for Tourism and Sports, T. M. Dosmukhambetov, who was standing beside Nazarbayev on the football pitch when these instructions were given, "looked as if he was going to die of a heart attack" according to one eyewitness of this scene. But remarkably, after bringing in over 1,200 new construction workers on 24/7 shift work, the stadium reconstruction was completed 10 days ahead of its two-month schedule.

Another Nazarbayev initiative was bringing in thousands of volunteers for a "greening of the city" crash programme. He appealed to Astana citizens to take part in a mass-planting of flowers, trees and bushes, as well as a clean-up campaign of the streets. After several media broadcasts there was an astonishing response, particularly from schoolchildren, students and pensioners. In less than four weeks, over 120,000 new trees, shrubs, lawns and flower beds were in place. Many streets and squares were swept immaculately clean. The initiative may have been a throwback in the President's mind to the successful Subbotnik scheme of street cleaning and tree planting, which the young Komsomol leader Nazarbayev had started 35 years earlier in Temirtau. In those days his fellow steelworkers had been reluctant to give up their spare time for such tasks, but in the swelling mood of civic and national pride in 1997, the citizens of Astana were enthusiastic volunteers. So the capital was greened and beautified in good time. 72 hours before the Presentation Day ceremonies were due to begin, Nazarbayev made his final Presidential inspection of the key sites and buildings. Not all of them were ready. The embankment was in trouble, so an extra 800 workers were put to work at hammering in the stone blocks on the river banks. They finally got the job done by the evening of 9th June.

An even closer call was the completion of the Intercontinental Hotel. On 7th June, it was a long way from being finished. The hotel was supposed to be accommodating over 200 VIP visitors, headed by the President of Turkey, Suleiman Demirel, who, with President Nazarbayev, was scheduled to cut the inaugural tape at the entrance on the evening of 8th June. At the time of the President's final inspection on 7th June, the site was in such chaos that the chances of this opening ceremony taking place looked low. But in the final 24 hours more than 3,000 workers were drafted in to the Intercontinental, and between them they performed a miracle. Apart from a strong smell of fresh paint, President Demirel's suite was in perfect condition when he arrived, as were most of the other rooms in the hotel.

Of all the behind-the-scenes dramas in the hours before Presentation Day dawned on 10th June, the most spectacular achievement was changing the weather. Although normally in the domain of God, on this occasion the business of altering the climate was handled by the President of Kazakhstan. Having learned from his meteorological experts that a front of storm clouds

was heading for Astana and would be likely to drench the inaugural ceremonies in heavy rain, Nazarbayev enlisted the help of a Russian weather control agency. Their aircraft flew sorties into the storm, seeding the clouds with
a special and ecologically safe mixture of silver iodine and dry nitrogen. The
technique worked. The weather front broke up many miles away from Astana,
depositing most of its rain on the wheat fields of grateful farmers.

Meanwhile, on the dry ground of the capital, parades, cavalcades, speeches,
dances, ceremonies and many other festivities were in full swing. One of the
highlights was a "telebridge" link from outer space. This enabled the Kazakh
astronaut Talgat Musabayev to speak on a video link from the Mir space
station (launched from Baikonur) to President Nazarbayev, congratulating
him on the inauguration of Astana.

The finale of Presentation Day was a spectacular pop concert. It featured
many famous singers from all over the world. But the trio who stole the show
were not professional artistes but the Presidents of Ukraine, Kyrgyzstan
and Kazakhstan. Their act began when Leonid Kuchma, Askar Akayev and
Nursultan Nazarbayev suddenly came on stage to give an impromptu render-
ing of a well-known Ukrainian folk song, "You've Been Unfaithful to Me".
Because of recent political turbulence in their countries involving allegations of betrayals and backstabbing by some of these leaders, the performance was hilariously topical. Nazarbayev, who had learned "You've Been
Unfaithful to Me" during his student days in Dneprodzerzhinsk, appeared
to be word-perfect in the Ukrainian lyrics. This was more than could be said
of the President of Ukraine, for Leonid Kuchma, to the great amusement of
the crowd, had evidently forgotten the lines of his country's most famous
ballad. One way and another, the three singing Presidents added great mer-
riment to an already joyful evening.

Before the concert ended, a light shower sprinkled the crowds. This had
probably not been organised by the weather-control experts in their aircraft
but, if they were responsible, they could not have performed their duties
better. For there is an old Kazakh saying: "A short summer rain is a sign of
good luck." This rural folklore was repeated over and over again by the
crowds thronging the streets of the capital on the evening of Presentation
Day. They were convinced that the gentle shower was an omen of fortune for
the future prosperity of Astana.

* * *

The sign from the rain clouds on Presentation Day proved to be an accurate
portent of success. Astana became a boom town in the decade of 1998–2008.
Under Nazarbayev's leadership, the left bank of the Ishym was transformed

from marshland to metropolis. Included in the construction programme were substantial social projects such as six new hospitals, known as the Hospital Cluster, providing state-of-the-art healthcare in the fields of cardiology; maternity; emergency and trauma services; neurosurgery; paediatrics; and general teaching medicine. Creating the equivalent of a Mayo Clinic on the Steppes has been a costly undertaking, but Nazarbayev's vision has been the creation of a centre of medical excellence that will attract patients from all over Central Asia and the former Soviet Union.

Conspicuously absent from the building programme were industrial factories. This was because Nazarbayev decided that the capital should be an environmentally friendly and white-collar city. However, all other forms of commerce and business were high on the Astana agenda, so much so that half of the development was paid for by the private sector. Investors, companies and banks fell over each other to compete in the race to make Astana the Eldorado of the steppes, as new skyscrapers of increasingly ambitious and avant-garde architecture shot up by the month.

Nazarbayev presided over this expansion with enthusiasm. Maintaining the momentum seemed to be his highest priority. The fact that the designs of the buildings ranged across a huge spectrum of taste, from Disneyworld kitsch to Wagnerian Valhalla, did not seem to bother him. But he did care about the overall master plan, which he entrusted to the Japanese architect, Kisho Kurokawa. This renowned planner gave the capital a thematic atmosphere of exciting innovation. It became a city of moods that changed with the seasons. Expectant and restless in spring. Hot and pulsating in summer. Tranquil and beautiful from November to March when the snow, the skaters on the Ishym, and the cold starry nights give Astana a winter wonderland feel of being the setting for a 21st century fairy tale by Hans Christian Andersen.

The harsh climate became less of a problem. This was because Nazarbayev managed to alter the ecology of the city by planting trees on a heroic scale in a 45,000-hectare circuit around its outer perimeter. This green belt acted as a wind break and as a softening protection against the blizzards howling across the steppes.

The President chose the types of trees personally from forests and woodlands he visited all around the world [recalled one of Astana's principal contractors, Shamil Bekbolatov]. He was totally dedicated to the mission of improving the environment for all its citizens.

Not everyone agreed with the President's determination to create an ever-greater national capital. "It is just unethical to bolster one city at the expense of everywhere else", said Bulat Abilov, chairman of the opposition party, Azat. However, there were clearly many other Kazakhstanis willing to vote with their feet, since over 500,000 new residents moved into the capital during the past 10 years, and more than 2,000 companies set up offices there. Love it or loathe it, Nazarbayev's Astana has become established as a prominent and prosperous Asian population centre.

The prosperity was dented by the global banking crisis of 2008. Initially, it came as a surprise to Nazarbayev that loan defaults on sub-prime mortgages in Florida could stop apartment building in Kazakhstan. But that is what happened, as local bank interest rates rose to 14 per cent, inflation soared and the country's rate of economic growth halved to 5 per cent. The construction boom in Astana sputtered to a halt under these pressures. At least 50 high-rise building sites were frozen in a state of abandoned half-completion. Parts of the city took on the air of a ghost town, as cranes were immobilised, pile drivers fell silent and thousands of workers were laid off. This was no small embarrassment to Nazarbayev as the 10th anniversary of Astana's inauguration drew near. He had planned a grand repeat performance of the 1998 Presentation Day ceremonies, but some observers thought this would look foolish against the backdrop of a slump in the construction industry. The government's nervousness was increased by a noisy demonstration outside the Prime Minister's office by several hundred redundant building workers. The impact of this unprecedented action was somewhat diminished by the discovery that many of the demonstrators had been paid to make their protest by local banks. Even so, the problem was real. Nazarbayev eased the growing tensions by announcing that the government would provide financial assistance worth approximately $250 million to enable work on unfinished construction sites to be restarted. This was not the President's finest hour as a champion of free-market forces, but his announcement did restore confidence. It also allowed the 10th anniversary show to go on in a more economically positive atmosphere.

Astana, in the first week of July 2008, was a mixture of a chaotic carnival and a carefully choreographed ceremonial. The first part of these celebrations consisted of many thousands of young people partying in the streets, dancing to amplified music on the embankment, drinking in the open-air cafés and blowing horns in their cars. The exuberant atmosphere seemed spontaneous and genuine, its enjoyment visibly increased by the huge numbers of children milling around the various events in colourful costumes. Astana certainly felt like a happy and hedonistic capital for the general populace on the main anniversary weekend of 5th–7th July.

6th July was Nazarbayev's 68th birthday; so inevitably many of the ceremonies were focused on him and his historical record as the creator of Astana. There were speechmaking sessions by visiting heads of state in the great

Pyramid. At the unveiling of a new 100-foot monument, a pageant was enacted of mediaeval Kazakh warriors defeating Jungar invaders. The national orchestra played ancient folk songs with talented soloists accompanying their performances on the dombra. Other big set pieces included a firework display, a sports festival, and a spectacular pop concert. To these circuses was added bread and other basic foods at half price – a weekend birthday present to the public from the big supermarket chains. Nazarbayev was present at all the major events, giving addresses at many of them.

The most politically fulsome and, at the same time, the most emotionally intimate of these orations came on the last evening, when the Akim, or Mayor of Astana, staged a dinner for what was called "The President's Family". This meant not only his blood relatives (including great granddaughters), but also his oldest personal friends and his staunchest political allies.

"You warriors on the invisible front, who stood with me in times of trial and in times of hope", was how he addressed the audience. After regaling them with low jokes about the early hardship years when toilets were frozen and electricity supplies failed, Nazarbayev struck high notes of vision about Astana, describing it as: "one of the youngest capitals of the world, built on these ancient steppes … the geopolitical centre of the country … the heart of global inter-confessional dialogue … the crossroads of Eurasia." Then he changed gear into a tribute to his own family and to the wider family of friends and colleagues who had helped him to create the capital. This was Nazarbayev with the bark off – humorous yet passionate about his adored Astana. Although it was a powerful political speech, his words self-evidently flowed from the heart, for they created a warm intimacy in their rapport with his inner circle. Then came an unscripted finale as Nazarbayev took to the dance floor and "worked the room", as American politicians would call it. But at this penultimate party of the anniversary celebrations, it would be more accurate to say that the room worked the President. Protocol evaporated, as individual after individual, and small group after small group came up to exchange hugs and handshakes with their head of state. It was a moving scene. Inevitably, Nazarbayev was playing to his home crowd, but everyone in the room knew that the bonds of emotion were real. So was the historic achievement of Astana they were celebrating.

After the dinner, Nazarbayev set off to his final engagement of the night, a spectacular extravaganza of a concert set between those two golden ice-cream cone towers on the left bank. High classical culture (*Swan Lake* ballet, and the National Symphony Orchestra playing Strauss) was followed by Kazakh tradition (Jungar war dances and virtuoso dombra artists), and western hit songs (*Phantom of the Opera* and Whitney Houston). But about two-thirds of the way through these performances, the President slipped quietly away. His unscheduled exit was a complete surprise, not least to his official entourage. Unencumbered by his usual escort of protocol aides and security guards, Nazarbayev strolled out onto the piazza. Enjoying the warmth of the midnight air and the auspicious sight of the 6th July new moon glowing delicately above the capital's skyscrapers, he talked and joked in the street with passers-by, most of them students. After a few minutes of this impromptu conversational banter, he called for his car and drove off. To still more surprise, he spontaneously ordered it to take him outside the city. Where Nazarbayev wanted to be in the early hours of the morning at the end of the 10th anniversary celebrations of Astana was on the Great Steppe, Sary Arka, the heartland of his people and his ancestors.

Epilogue

The view from the Great Steppe, or Sary Arka, is cloudy in economic outlook these days as the world struggles with recession and the credit crunch.
But by the time Nazarbayev celebrates his 70th birthday (6th July, 2010) and
Kazakhstan reaches the 20th anniversary of its independence (16th December, 2011), it is likely that the worst effects of the global crisis will be easing.
Certainly, the country's vast natural resources of oil, gas and minerals together
with its best human resources of increasingly well-educated young people are
national assets which will not diminish in value. And Nazarbayev himself
shows no signs of diminishing in energy or in determination to lead Kazakhstan into a new epoch of political and economic development.

In the last of the 23 hours of interviews he gave me for this biography, we
were discussing his legacy. I quoted the words of Sophocles: "Sometimes one
has to wait until the evening to see how glorious the day has been." To which
Nazarbayev riposted: "What makes you think I have reached the evening?"
It was perhaps a hint that, health and circumstances permitting, he may well
decide to run for a third term as President in 2012. With or without that
extension of his leadership, he has been governing Kazakhstan through so
many eras, from Communism through chaos under Soviet domination to
success and stability as a young nation state, that he is widely described as
"Father of his country". Given that accolade, it is timely to ask: What has
been Nursultan Nazarbayev's footprint on the path of history? What is his
legacy to his people, his region and the international community?

Looking at the futuristic skyline of 21st century Astana, it is easy to forget
the poverty and primitivism of Kazakhstan's 20th century past. Its brutal
subjugation as a humiliated colony in the Russian-ruled Soviet empire has
been replaced by a bitterness-free liberation to multi-ethnic statehood. It is
underpinned by political stability and national self-confidence. Jeffersonian
democracy may be some way off, yet personal and economic freedoms are
growing. Nazarbayev runs his government under tight control, but his
centralised Presidency is a benevolent form of autocracy, responsive to the
pressures of private criticism and public opinion.

In a region of the world which is used to, and apparently likes to have, a dominant leader in charge, Nazarbayev is genuinely popular – in part because of his willingness to engage and explain. He is often prepared to admit the mistakes and excesses of his administration, which is still over-weighted with "old guard" figures for whom the President has a personal loyalty that can last too long. Such ministers and officials do not always serve the country well. There are grumbles to be heard in Kazakhstan about some public servants' open-handedness when taking bribes, and their heavy-handedness when conducting police or security service investigations. Yet, on the credit side, there are no political or religious prisoners in Kazakhstan, and few institutionalised infringements of human rights. They can happen – as the unpleasant Aliyev saga demonstrates – but Nazarbayev has learned lessons from past outrages against opponents. He is well aware that his country's riches have brought international responsibilities. In other unsatisfactory areas of Kazakh life he knows that sooner or later he needs to clean up the widespread corruption in local, regional and national government. He also needs to make visible further progress towards transparently fair elections. But at this stage of a former Soviet republic's advance towards the ideals of a free and democratic society, Kazakhstan's glass deserves to be described as half full rather than half empty.

On the domestic front, Nazarbayev's governance as an economic President has established a solid record of achievement. In the last 15 years, per capita GDP has grown from $400 to $8,400. Living standards have more than quadrupled in the last five years. A property-owning middle class has emerged, even though it is still overshadowed by a small élite of inner-circle entrepreneurs. They have neither the wealth nor the status of the Russian oligarchs, but their importance to the economy is undeniable and their influence is at times undesirable. Perhaps the emergence of these mega-rich millionaires is inevitable when a country leaps from the poverty of Soviet communism to the wealth of a Caspian-led natural resources boom within less than two decades. But Kazakhstan is not an "anything goes" Klondyke. It is a capably if at times over-bureaucratically governed nation state, whose mixed economy is rooted and growing from free-market foundations.

Building an economically successful country which did not exist on the world's political map until the collapse of the Soviet Union has been a remarkable historical achievement. It would not have been done without Nazarbayev's leadership. His personal and diplomatic dexterity with the rulers of Russia and China delivered secure borders to Kazakhstan. This was an unexpected result, because the newly independent state started out with only slim prospects of establishing legally agreed frontiers in a region notorious for anarchic aggression over territorial claims.

Peaceful coexistence with powerful neighbours has been matched by wider acceptance of Kazakhstan as a respected member state in the international community. Nazarbayev's first and greatest test in this arena was his handling of the negotiations over the world's fourth largest arsenal of nuclear missiles. Kazakhstan inherited them from the Soviet military, and bargained responsibly with Washington and Moscow for their disarmament. The kudos he gained in Western capitals for his cooperation on nuclear issues, and the undeniable progress in economic and political development of the nation helped him to secure the election of Kazakhstan to chair the 56-nation Organisation for Security and Cooperation in Europe (OSCE) as from 2010.

The OSCE is a creation of the West, and its drive to reproduce the Western ideals of free and democratically elected governments in all its member states will take time to implement. It would be optimistic to expect the full realisation of these ideals in Kazakhstan during Nazarbayev's political lifetime. This is not because he is anti-democracy, but because he favours a steadily evolving democracy. He is respectful of his own country's traditions and wary of repeating some of the mistakes made by neighbouring leaders, most notably Boris Yeltsin's dash to democracy which deteriorated into an ungovernable Russia. But Nazarbayev's caution should not be interpreted as obstruction. He knows, as every Kazakh knows, that there is an inevitability of gradualness about the coming of full democracy for his country. The process is moving forward now. Whether it takes a decade or a generation; a shorter period or a longer period to become fully established will be a matter for both grass-roots and well-educated levels of Kazakh society to decide. Nazarbayev's political intuition will play a large part in the decision-making process. But so will the mood of the rising generation of Kazakhstan, which is developing a mind and a momentum of its own.

In his youth, Nazarbayev had the nomad's skill of listening to the wind on the Steppes. Today he has the political skill of listening to the winds of change which are blowing through the multi-ethnic communities, the multi-coloured skyscrapers, and the ambitious middle classes that now characterise the hopes and dreams of contemporary Kazakhstan.

Nazarbayev is an attentive listener and an eager learner. He absorbs facts, opinions and fresh ideas with the enthusiasm of a much younger politician. These skills have served him well. He would have climbed to the top, or near to the top, of the greasy pole of politics in many international societies. "Never forget that Nazarbayev is a man of two cultures", said Mikhail Gorbachev in an interview for this biography. "He is both Russian and Asian in his roots and outlook." It might be added that he possesses several of the talents that would have propelled his political career upwards if he had been born in the West. He is a shrewd tactician, a charming conversationalist, a persuasive speaker and a charismatic leader of vision and courage, particularly when facing difficult situations.

Some of those strengths came from his sturdy upbringing in a traditional nomad family. Others were acquired from his Russian education, his workaholic industry and his continuous curiosity both intellectual and international. He has always been an outward-looking President. His enthusiasm for free markets and privatisation started because he listened to Margaret Thatcher. His creation of the Samruk group of industries grew out of the Singapore blueprint designed by its chief mentor, Lee Kuan Yew. His establishment of Kazakhstan's national oil fund (a vital lifeline in the global credit crunch) was an idea derived from his studies of comparable funds in Norway and the Gulf States. Nazarbayev, always an ardent listener and note taker on foreign visits, has imported many international good practices into Kazakhstan.

It has been said that the difference between a politician and a statesman is that the former is focused on the next election, while the latter plans for the next generation. Nazarbayev does both, but the certainties of Kazakhstani politics have given him the leeway to concentrate on the longer-term outlook. He is good at identifying and promoting young talent. He has visionary plans (delayed but not derailed by the global crisis), for Kazakhstan in 2030. His ambition is that his society's education and innovation will be so well developed in the coming decades that the country will avoid an overdependency on its natural resources. This may be a temptation if the Caspian is pumping over 5 million barrels of oil a day, but even as a future Eldorado, Kazakhstan will need free thinkers and free markets as well as freeloaders. So Nazarbayev's vision of a multi-ethnic nation with its doors open to both talent and tolerance could turn out to be one of the success stories of Asia in the 21st century.

There is an old Kazakh proverb: "When you drink from a well, always remember the man who built it." Nazarbayev has been the builder of modern Kazakhstan. This achievement has secured his place in history. And, as the political and economic wells of Kazakhstan are a long way from running dry, Nursultan Nazarbayev's most interesting years of power may yet lie ahead of him.

Source Notes

Abbreviations used in source notes:

ACTI   Aitken Collection of Transcripts and Interviews (2007–2009).

CD   Nazarbayev, Nursultan, *The Critical Decade* (London, First Books, 2003).

Conradi   Nazarbayev, Nursultan, *My Life, My Times and the Future* (translated and edited by Peter Conradi) (Pilkington Press, 1998).

EP   Nazarbayev, Nursultan, *Epicenter of Peace* (Puritan Press, 2001).

KW   Nazarbayev, Nursultan, *The Kazakhstan Way* (translated by Jan Butler) (Stacey International, 2008).

NRNL   Nazarbayev, Nursultan, *No Rightists Nor Leftists: Answers to Questions of the Day.*

Brummell Brummell, Paul, *Kazakhstan* (Bradt Travel Guides, 2008).

Kunanbay Kunanbay, Alma, *The Soul of Kazakhstan* (Easton Press, 2001).

LeVine   LeVine, Steve, *The Oil and the Glory – The Pursuit of Empire and Fortune on the Caspian Sea* (Random House, 2007).

Robbins   Robbins, Christopher, *In Search of Kazakhstan: the Land that Disappeared* (Profile Books, 2007).

Schreiber Schreiber, Dagmar, and Tredinvick, Jeremy, *Kazakhstan, Nomadic Routes from Caspian to Altai* (Odyssey Books, 2008).

Tokayev   Tokayev, Kassym-Jomart, *Meeting the Challenge* (New York, Global Scholarly Publications, 2004).

Source notes – Chapter 1

Author's interviews: Nursultan Nazarbayev, Kydyrgalgi Baybek, Kenes Bekaidarov, Narjamal Ibirayqizi, Seitkhan Issayev, Yedigae Junisbekov, Saylaubek Kydiraliyev, Abdilda Medenov, Bolat Nazarbayev, Esimbay Saduakas, Jomart Seksenbayev (ACTI 2007).

Source material: *How the Steel Was Forged* (Moscow, 1933); Conradi, pp. 11–16; *NRNL*, pp. 9–19.

Source notes – Chapter 2

Author's interviews: Nursultan Nazarbayev, Satybaldy Ibragimov, Toktarkhan Iskakov, Arguen Junasov, Vladimir Kolbasa, Nikolay Litoshko, Maksut Navikbayev, Bolat Nazarbayev, Dariga Nazarbayeva, Kuanish Omashev, Kabidulla Sarekenov, Toletau Suleymenov, Sabit Zhadanov (ACTI 2007).

Source material: *How the Steel Was Forged* (Moscow, 1933); Brummell, pp. 194–195; Conradi, pp. 21–28; *NRNL*, pp. 30–39.

Source notes – Chapter 3

Author's interviews: Nursultan Nazarbayev, Manura Akhmetova, Bayken Ashimov, Satybaldy Ibragimov, Tokhtarkhan Iskakov, Seitkhan Issayev, Maksut Narikbayev, Bolat Nazarbayev, Dariga Nazarbayeva, Kuanish Omashev, Kabidulla Sarekenov, Toletau Suleymenov, Sabit Zhadanov (ACTI 2007).

Source material: Conradi, pp. 26–28; *Kazakhstankaya Pravda*, 3rd September 1960; *NRNL*, pp. 43–49; inscription on back of Nazarbayev photograph in a tuxedo – The Presidential Archives, Astana.

Source notes – Chapter 4

Author's interviews: Nursultan Nazarbayev, Manura Akhmetova, Bayken Ashimov, Sultan Dzhiyenbaev, Zheksembek Erkimbekov, Sagidulla Kubashev, Dariga Nazarbayeva, Zhanibek Shangerey, Kanat Saudabayev, Ibragim Yedilbayev (ACTI 2007).

Source material: Conradi, pp. 43–48; *NRNL*, pp. 44–55, 58–72, 74–76; *Pravda*, 8th June 1973.

Source notes – Chapter 5

Author's interviews: Nursultan Nazarbayev, Nurtai Abikayev, Manura Akhmetova, Bayken Ashimov, Shamil Bekbolotov, Mikhail Gorbachev, Erik Gukasov, Dariga Nazarbayeva, Vladimir Ni, I. B. Yedilbayev, Sabit Zhadanov (ACTI 2008).

Source material: Conradi, pp. 45–48; *NRNL*, pp. 90–97.

Source notes – Chapter 6

Author's interviews: Nursultan Nazarbayev, Nurtai Abikayev, Manura Akhmetova, Mikhail Gorbachev, Erik Gukasov, Kupzhasar Naribayev, Dariga Nazarbayeva, Nurtai Sabilyanov (ACTI 2007).

Source material: Conradi, pp. 49–52; *NRNL*, pp. 102–106.

Source notes – Chapter 7

Author's interviews: Nursultan Nazarbayev, Mikhail Gorbachev, Igor Romanov, Nikolai Ryzkhov, Kanat Saudabayev, Margaret Thatcher (ACTI 2008).

Source material: Conradi, pp. 61–83; *NRNL*, pp. 144–166.

Source notes – Chapter 8

Author's interviews: Nursultan Nazarbayev, Serik Akhanov, Baurzhan Mukhamedjanov, Erlan Idrissov, Nurlan Kapparov, Vladimir Kim, Igor Romanov, Nikolai Ryzkhov, Kanat Saudabayev, Daulet Sembayev, Umirzak Shukeyev, Sergei Tereschenko, Kassym-Jomart Tokayev (ACTI 2008).

Source material: Conradi, pp. 87–101; *KW*, pp. 1–15; Abai, *Collected Sayings* (Almaty, 1906); Alexandr Solzhenitsyn, *Russia's True Borders*, *Pravda*, 3rd June 1992; Tokayev, pp. 137–147; Khodza Akhmet Yassaui, *Collected Poems of Central Asia* (Moscow, 1964); Vladimir Zhironovsky, "Kazakhstan will crawl back to Russia", *Nezavisimya Gazeta*, 21st May 1994.

Source notes – Chapter 9

Author's interviews: Nursultan Nazarbayev, Mikhail Gorbachev, Dariga Nazarbayeva, Nikolai Ryzkhov, Kanat Saudabayev, Vladimir Shkalnik, Kassym-Jomart Tokayev (ACTI 2008).

Source material: Conradi, pp. 87–101; *EP*, pp xiii–xvii, 9–48, 59–71; Joint Statement from the White House by Presidents George H. W. Bush and President Nursultan Nazarbayev, 21st December 2001; Robbins, pp. 191–212; Tokayev, pp. 132–135; *Los Angeles Times*, 15th September 1993, 15th February 1994, and 30th July 2000; *New York Times*, 19th October 1993 and 15th February 1994; *Washington Post*, 15th February 1994 and 2nd December 1994; Letter from President William Clinton to President Nazarbayev (White House Archives), 25th February 1994; *Washington Times*, 18th December 2003.

Source notes – Chapter 10

Author's interviews: Nursultan Nazarbayev, Nurtai Abikayev, Serik Akhanov, Galym Bainazarov, Zagipa Balieva, Erlan Idrissov, Vladimir Kim, Grigory Marchenko, Baurzhan Mukhamedjanov, Igor Romanov, Kanat Saudabayev, Daulet Sembayev, Umirak Shukeyev, Sergei Tereschenko (ACTI 2008).

Source material: Conradi, pp. 99–109; *KW*, pp. 37–87, 125–159; *NRNL*, pp. 117–125.

Source notes – Chapter 11

Author's interviews: Nursultan Nazarbayev, Nurtai Abikayev, Nurlan Balgimbayev, Mikhail Gorbachev, Erlan Idrissov, Nurlan Kapparov, Igor Romanov, Nikolai Ryzkhov, Kanat Saudabayev, Kassym-Jomart Tokayev, Kuanish Zhadanov (ACTI 2008).

Source material: Conradi, pp. 162–175; *KW*, pp. 88–125; *NRNL*, pp. 4, 160; Le Vine, pp. 94–98; 99–101, 109–127, 137–143, 252–262, 276–288, 342–367; Brummell, pp. 303–307; Robbins, pp. 151–155; Tokayev, pp. 138–177; *New York Times*, 16th October 1989 and 30th July 1990; *Washington Post*, 30th July 1990.

Source notes – Chapter 12

Author's interviews: Nursultan Nazarbayev, Alikhan Baimenov, Nurlan Balgimbayev, Danik Beshymbaev, Dariga Nazarbayeva, Kassym-Jomart Tokayev (ACTI 2008).

Source material: Amnesty International (Concerns in Europe) Report, 1st July 2002; OSCE/ODIHR Report on Kazakhstan Parliamentary Elections, 15th February 2004; OSCE/ODIHR Report on Kazakhstan Parliamentary Elections, 19th September 2004; *The Economist*, 6th August 2005; OSCE/ODIHR Report on Kazakhstan Presidential Elections, 28th September 2005; *The Economist*, 8th December 2005 and 16th February 2006; OSCE/ODIHR Report on Kazakhstan Presidential Elections, 21st February 2006; *The Economist*, 2nd March 2006; *Roberts Report*, 23rd August 2006; *New York Times*, 14th November 2006; *Roberts Report*, 16th February 2007; *Financial Times*, 18th May 2007, 27th May 2007, 28th May 2007, 30th May 2007 and 27th June 2007; *New York Times*, 6th July 2007; *Washington Post*, 18th July 2007; *The Economist*, 24th July 2007; OSCE/ODIHR Report on Kazakhstan Parliamentary Elections, 18th August 2007; *International Herald Tribune*, 19th August 2007; *The Economist*, 21st August 2007 and 23rd

August 2007; *Huffington Post*, 6th October 2007; OSCE/ODIHR Report on Kazakhstan Parliamentary Elections, 30th October 2007; *Independent*, 1st November 2007; *Financial Times*, 26th March 2008 and 27th March 2008; *New York Times*, 27th March 2008; *Wall Street Journal*, 13th May 2008.

Source notes – Chapter 13

Author's interviews: Nursultan Nazarbayev, Nurlan Balgimbayev, Sir Richard Evans, Erlan Idrissov, Vladimir Ni, Karim Massimov, Dariga Nazarbayeva, Lord Renwick, Kassym-Jomart Tokayev.

Source material: CBC Arts, 21st April 2006; *Daily Mail*, 12th September 2006 and 22nd September 2006; *New York Times*, 28th September 2006; *Harpers Magazine*, 29th September 2006; *Daily Mail*, 29th September 2006; *Forbes Magazine*, 12th October 2006; *Independent*, 22nd October 2006; *Daily Mail*, 25th October 2006; *US Today*, 31st October 2006; *Independent*, 1st November 2006; *Roberts Report*, 3rd November 2006; *Daily Mail*, 20th November 2006; *The Times*, 22nd November 2006; *Daily Mail*, 2nd December 2006; *Kazakhstan Embassy News*; *Bulletin Report*, 3rd March 2009; *Kazakhstan Embassy News*; *Bulletin Report*, 10th March 2009; *Kazakhstan Embassy News*; *Bulletin Report*, 21st March 2009.

Source notes – Chapter 14

Author's interviews: Nursultan Nazarbayev, Alikhan Baimenov, Shamil Bekbolatov, Sir Richard Evans, Farid Galymov, Erlan Idrissov, Adilbek Jaxybekov, Vladimir Ni, Igor Romanov, Kassym-Jomart Tokayev (ACTI 2009).

Source material: *KW*, pp. 296–320; Adilbek R. Jaxybekov, *Shining Like a Star – The Mayor of Astana Remembers*; Brummell, pp. 67–93; Budapest, 2001; *Karavan Journal*, 20th October 1995; Schreiber, pp. 333–337, 346–351; Summer Coish and Lucy Kelaart, *A Hedonist's Guide to Almaty and Astana* (Filmer Ltd, 2007).

Select Bibliography

Nazarbayev, Nursultan, *No Rightists Nor Leftists: Answers to Questions of the Day* (Noy Publications, 1992).

——, *Kazakhstan – 2030: Prosperity, Security and Ever-Growing Welfare of All the Kazakhstanis* (The Embassy of the Republic of Kazakhstan, 1998).

——, *My Life, My Times and the Future* (translated and edited by Peter Conradi) (Pilkington Press, 1998).

——, *Epicenter of Peace* (Puritan Press, 2001).

——, *The Critical Decade* (London, First Books, 2003).

——, *The Kazakhstan Way* (translated by Jan Butler) (Stacey International, 2008).

Akiner, Shirin, *The Formation of Kazakh Identity: From Tribe to Nation State* (London, Royal Institute of International Affairs, 1995).

Baker, III, James A., and Defrank, Thomas M., *The Politics of Diplomacy: Revolution, War and Peace* (New York, G. P. Putnam's Sons, 1995).

——, and Fiffer, Steve, *Work Hard, Study ... and Keep Out of Politics!* (New York, G. P. Putnam's Sons, 2006).

Benson, Linda, and Svanberg, Ingvar, *China's Last Nomads: The History and Culture of China's Kazakhs* (New York, Armonk, 1998).

Brown, Archie, *The Gorbachev Factor* (Oxford, Oxford University Press, 1996).

Brummell, Paul, *Kazakhstan* (Bradt Travel Guides, 2008).

Colton, Timothy J., *Yeltsin: a Life* (New York, Basic Books, 2008).

Fergus, Michael, and Jandosova, Janar, *Kazakhstan: Coming of Age* (Stacey International, 2003).

First Congress of Leaders of World and Traditional Religions: Astana, 23–24 September 2003. Collected Materials, Speeches and Letters of Greeting (Edelweiss Printing House LLP, 2003).

Gorbachev, Mikhail, *Memoirs* (London, Transworld, 1995).

Kazakhstan: The Crown Jewel of Central Asia (Kazinvest Advisor for the Centre of Foreign Policy & Analysis, 2003).

Kazakhstan 2006 (Randevu Publishing House, 2006).

Kunanbay, Alma, *The Soul of Kazakhstan* (Easton Press, 2001).

LeVine, Steve, *The Oil and the Glory – The Pursuit of Empire and Fortune on the Caspian Sea* (Random House, 2007).

Ministry of Industry and Trade of the Republic of Kazakhstan, *Investor's Guide 2003* (Publishing Centre OKO of Zholdas A Ltd).

Olcott, Martha Brill, *The Kazakhs* (Hoover Institution Press, Stanford University, 1995).

Robbins, Christopher, *In Search of Kazakhstan: the Land that Disappeared* (London, Profile Books, 2007).

Saudabayev, Ambassador Kanat, and Nunn, Senator Sam (Foreword), *Kazakhstan Nuclear Disarmament: a Global Model for a Safer World* (Embassy of the Republic of Kazakhstan, USA, and Nuclear Threat Initiative, 2006).

Schreiber, Dagmar, and Tredinvick, Jeremy, *Kazakhstan, Nomadic Routes from Caspian to Altai* (Odyssey Books, 2008).

Shayakhmetov, Mukhamet, *The Silent Steppe: The Story of a Kazakh Nomad under Stalin* (translated by Jan Butler) (Stacey International, 2006).

Tokayev, Kassym-Jomart, *Meeting the Challenge* (New York, Global Scholarly Publications, 2004).

Yeltsin, Boris, *The View from the Kremlin* (London, HarperCollins Publishers, 1994).

Yesenberlin, Ilyas, *The Nomads* (The Ilyas Yesenberlin Foundation, 2000).

Index

255